'Written by the internationally renowned Dr Robert Leahy, *The Worry Cure* provides readers with a rich insight into the causes of worry and how to help oneself reduce it. Based on Dr Leahy's extensive knowledge and clinical experience the reader will find a wealth of fascinating cases that often mirror our own experiences with clear guidance on how to change our thinking and approach to worry. You should only worry if you don't have this book.' **Paul Gilbert, Professor of Clinical Psychology and author of** *Overcoming Depression*

'If you are prone to worry, then read this book. In it Dr Leahy describes what we know about worrying and why worrying is so self-perpetuating. Central to the book is a self-help programme based on the latest evidence-based form of treatment. I strongly recommend the book and its treatment programme.' **Christopher Fairburn, Professor of Psychiatry, Oxford University**

'*The Worry Cure* is engaging and accessible, yet up-to-date and highly informative about the latest psychological understanding and treatment of the common but important problem of worry. It will have appeal to both worriers and professionals alike, committed to the common goal of understanding and managing the daily mind.' **Philip Tata, Scientific Chair, The British Association of Behavioural and Cognitive Psychotherapies**

'Engagingly and persuasively Leahy coaxes self-tormentors to have mercy on themselves ... and gives pointers on how they can realistically deal with their concerns.' *New York Times*

'*The Worry Cure* is destined to be in the elite group of cognitive therapy classics that will have enormous impact on the general public. [It is] remarkable for its engaging writing style and clarity, its clinical acumen, and its accessibility to general readers.' *Cognitive Behavioral Therapy Book Reviews*

ALSO BY DR ROBERT L. LEAHY

The
Worry
Cure

STOP WORRYING

AND

START LIVING

Dr Robert L. Leahy

PIATKUS

PIATKUS

First published in Great Britain in 2006 by Piatkus Books
This paperback edition published in 2006 by Piatkus Books
First published in the US in 2005 by Harmony Books
A division of Random House Inc., New York

Reprinted 2008

A CIP catalogue record for this book
is available from the British Library

ISBN 978-0-7499-2724-0

Printed and bound in Great Britain by
Clays Ltd, St Ives plc

Piatkus Books
An imprint of
Little, Brown Book Group
100 Victoria Embankment
London EC4Y 0DY

An Hachette Livre UK Company

www.piatkus.co.uk

To Helen

ACKNOWLEDGMENTS

This book owes a great deal to many people.

I would like to thank my agent, Bob Diforio, who has been wonderfully supportive and effective throughout the entire project. I look forward to our working together on other projects in the future. I want to thank my editor, Julia Pastore, of Harmony Books, who has been everything that you would want in an editor. Julia helped me sharpen the message, clarify my thinking, and understand better what this is all about.

None of this would have been possible without the work of so many dedicated researchers in psychology scattered throughout the world. I wish to thank the following people whose work I have found most helpful: David Barlow, Thomas Borkovec, David A. Clark, David M. Clark, Michel Dugas, Paul Gilbert, Leslie Greenberg, Steven Hayes, Richard Heimberg, John Kabat-Zinn, Robert Ladouceur, Marsha Linehan, Douglas Mennin, Susan Nolen-Hoeksema, Costas Papageorgiou, Christine Purdon, Jack Rachman, Steven Reiss, John Riskind, Paul Salkovskis, Steven Taylor, and Adrian Wells. Special thanks goes to Aaron T.

Beck, the founder of cognitive therapy, who has been mentor, colleague, and friend for the past twenty-two years.

I also wish to thank my colleagues at the American Institute for Cognitive Therapy who allowed me to test out these ideas for the past several years. Thanks to Danielle Kaplan, Elisa Lefkowitz, Lisa Napolitano, Laura Oliff, and Dennis Tirch. My editorial and research assistant, David Fazzari, from Columbia University, has been a constant source of support throughout this project.

I also want to thank my friends Frank Datillio, Steve Holland, Bill Talmadge, Philip Tata, and David Wolf, and my brother, Jim Leahy, for their support and insight.

And, most of all, I want to thank my wife, Helen, whose understanding ear and whose companionship on weekly hikes along the Appalachian Trail has put everything in perspective.

CONTENTS

PART 3

SPECIAL WORRIES AND HOW TO CHALLENGE THEM

THE
WORRY
CURE

INTRODUCTION

The Seven Rules of Highly Worried People

WORRYING IS SECOND NATURE to you, but imagine that someone who has been raised in the jungle and knows nothing about conventional modern life approached you and asked, "How do I go about learning how to worry?" Of course, you've been worrying spontaneously for years, but how would you teach someone to worry? How would you come up with a rule book for worry?

First, you'd have to come up with some good reasons why you *need* to worry. What could they be? How about "Worry motivates me" or "Worry helps me solve my problems" or "Worry keeps me from being surprised"? Those sound like excellent reasons to worry.

Then you can come up with some ideas about when to start worrying. What is going to trigger this experience for you? You might say, "When something bad happens," but that's not really the case, because you worry about bad things that haven't happened *yet*. Or you might say, "When something bad is *about* to happen." But how would you know if it's *about to happen*? It hasn't happened yet, and almost everything that you worry about happening never has happened. You could say, "Worry about things that you can *imagine* happening that are really bad." You can now imagine a million bad things that never *have to happen*. It's an unlimited supply of worries.

Now that you have some potential material to work with, you will have to focus on your worries. There are so many other things to distract you: work, friends, family, hobbies, aches and pains, even sleep. How will you keep your mind on your worries?

That's easy. Tell yourself some stories about all the bad things that could happen. Embellish them with details. Start each sentence, where possible, with "what if" and then come up with every possible horrible outcome. Keep telling yourself these bad stories, each time trying to figure out if you left out something important. You can't trust your memory. Come up with all of the possibilities—and then *dwell on them.* Remember, if it's possible, it's probable.

And don't forget, keep thinking that *if something bad could happen—if you can simply imagine it—then it's your responsibility to worry about it.* That's the first rule of worry.

But if something bad could happen, what does it have to do with you? Well, the second rule is, *don't accept any uncertainty— you need to know for sure.*

So solve every problem that you can think of right now. You'll feel better. You'll finally be able to relax once you've eliminated uncertainty from your life. If you had absolute certainty, you wouldn't be worried, would you? You have to go out and get that perfection, that certainty.

Now, let's start with your health. You can't be completely *certain* that this discoloration isn't cancer. You just saw the doctor— but haven't doctors been wrong before? Moving along, you can't be sure that all of your money won't run out. Or that you won't lose your job. If you did lose your job, you can't be absolutely, 100 percent sure that you would get another job. Or that people who respect you now won't lose all of their respect if you don't keep things going at the highest level possible.

Let's face it—is there anything that you are really certain of?

Maybe you can get some certainty by getting other people to reassure you. Maybe someone else is a better judge than you are. Go to the doctor as many times as you can afford to and ask her if she can tell you *absolutely for sure* that there is nothing wrong with you, or if she can tell you that you will never get sick and die. Ask your friends if they think you still look as good as you did last year. Maybe you can catch things before they slide too far. Maybe, before you completely fall apart—get sick and lose your money, job, friends, and your looks—you can catch it all and reverse it in a heroic effort of self-help. Maybe it's not too late. That's the great thing about demanding certainty. You will eliminate any oversights. You won't be naive. You won't be caught by surprise.

But simply being motivated and not accepting uncertainty is not enough to be a worrier. You need evidence that things can go badly. So the third rule is, *treat all of your negative thoughts as if they are really true.*

If you think someone doesn't like you, it's probably true. If you think you'll get fired, count on it. If you think that someone else is upset, then it's all about you. The more you treat your thoughts as if they are reality, the more you will be able to worry.

But why should you care what people think about you or how you do on your job? Why should it matter to you?

The fourth rule solves this problem: *anything bad that could happen is a reflection of who you are as a person.*

If you don't do well on the exam, you are incompetent. If someone doesn't like you, you must be a loser. If your partner is angry, it must mean you'll end up alone and miserable. It's all about who you *really* are.

But some things are just not a big deal. Why should a loss or a failure be so important? Why worry if it's a small loss or a small failure?

Because the fifth rule of highly worried people is: *failure is unacceptable*.

You can think of everything as your responsibility, and if you fail, you think about how everyone will know and how this is entirely the final test of who you are. You can make your worries as powerful as possible by thinking, "I can never handle any failure."

Now your worries are really important.

You know they are really important because you feel how powerfully they affect you: knots in your stomach, rapid heart rate, whirring in your ears, headaches, cold sweats, sleepless nights. Now that you notice you have all of these feelings, you need to get rid of them right away. And that's rule six: *get rid of any negative feelings immediately*.

But wait. You can't get rid of them? They're not going away? That's a bad sign. You should be able to get rid of bad feelings *right now*. Who knows what they'll turn into if left to fester? Maybe the fact that you can't get rid of those bad feelings means something really awful is going to happen. Maybe there are terrible things you haven't thought of. Maybe you're losing control. And that's unacceptable. That's something that needs to be addressed as soon as possible. Therefore, the seventh rule is, *treat everything like an emergency*.

Don't kid yourself by thinking you can wait to get around to handling these things. Everything has to be solved *right now*—all of your problems, all of your worries, everything. You can lie in bed and go over every single problem that you will face tomorrow or next year and say to yourself, "I need the answers *immediately*."

So far, we are imagining bad stories and treating them like facts to motivate you to be responsible and worry. You're not going to accept any uncertainty; you'll put yourself in the center of every situation and see yourself as a failure. You realize that your emotions have to be completely controlled, and so you will treat everything like an emergency to get rid of any bad thoughts or feelings.

Now you can go back to the guy who came out of the jungle and tell him that you have the Seven Rules of Highly Worried People. Let's take a close look at them and make sure we have everything:

1. If something bad could happen—if you can simply imagine it—then it's your responsibility to worry about it.
2. Don't accept any uncertainty—you need to know for sure.
3. Treat all of your negative thoughts as if they are really true.
4. Anything bad that could happen is a reflection of who you are as a person.
5. Failure is unacceptable.
6. Get rid of any negative feelings immediately.
7. Treat everything like an emergency.

But wait. Didn't you leave out something? Isn't there something you overlooked? Can you really trust your memory? You forgot the most important thing. You forgot to *worry about worrying*. You forgot to tell him, "All of this worrying is going to drive you crazy, give you a heart attack, and ruin your life completely." How could you forget the eighth rule—the rule that says, "Now that you're worried, you've got to stop worrying completely or you'll go crazy and die"?

But maybe you didn't worry enough about the assignment. Isn't that why you worry, anyway? To be prepared? So you won't overlook anything? If you had worried about getting the assignment right, you would have seen that teaching your new friend to worry would ultimately drive him mad—or kill him.

Well, you're probably saying to yourself, "Very funny. It sounds just like me. But what does this have to do with helping me get rid of my worries?"

It's really quite simple. You worry because you follow a rule book that you think will actually help you. You think that you will catch things before they get out of hand, get rid of any unpleasant emotion immediately, and solve all your problems. You think that following these rules will make you feel more secure. But so far it hasn't worked.

In fact, your solutions are the problem. Your rule book makes you worry.

There Is Good News

For the past twenty years I have helped people suffering from depression and anxiety through cognitive therapy. Cognitive therapy addresses the *biases in your thinking* (cognitions are your thoughts) that are causing your anxiety and depression. Anxiety disorders are really *problems in the way you think*. The relevance of cognitive therapy is that it helps you understand and modify these biases to effectively diminish your anxiety.

For many years chronic worriers had to suffer without any signifi-cant hope of getting better. Occasionally they would seek out help with antianxiety medications or antidepressants, which can help reduce some of the unpleasantness. Traditional forms of psychotherapy might be helpful in about 20 percent of cases, but the other 80 percent would not improve. Fortunately, though, we now have very good news for people who are chronic worriers.

There have been significant advances in the last ten years in new approaches that expand far beyond what cognitive therapists used to do. For example, we now know:

- People are actually *less* anxious when they are worrying.
- Intolerance of uncertainty is the most important element in worry.
- Worriers fear emotions and do not process the meaning of events because they are "too much in their heads."

Worry is not simply pessimism; it's a reflection of many different parts of who you are. Once you understand why you worry and why your worry makes sense to you, you can begin to explore some things that you can do—or not do—to help yourself.

- We now have a much greater understanding of how worry works.
- We can use this new understanding to reverse these troublesome worries.
- Three-quarters of people with this problem can be significantly helped with newer forms of therapy.

Based on the new research, I've developed a seven-step program to help you understand your own "theory" about worry, how your mind works, how your personality affects your worry, and the most effective techniques for defeating your worry and breaking those rules once and for all:

1. Identify productive and unproductive worry.
2. Accept reality and commit to change.
3. Challenge your worried thinking.
4. Focus on the deeper threat.
5. Turn "failure" into opportunity.
6. Use your emotions rather than worry about them.
7. Take control of time.

Let's briefly examine each step.

1. *Identify productive and unproductive worry.* Most worriers are of two minds: "My worry is driving me crazy" and "I need to worry to be prepared." Thus, you may be worried about giving up your worry, since you think it prepares and protects you. You

will learn that you have mixed feelings about giving up on your worry, which is why you persist even when it makes you miserable. *Your worry is a strategy that you think helps you.* Until you give up this belief, you will continue to worry. You will learn how to get the motivation you need to stop and challenge your worries rather than think of your worries as a sign of how responsible and conscientious you are. Without the motivation to change your worry, all the advice in the world will be useless.

You will learn how to use *productive worry* by identifying problems that you can address immediately, such as getting a road map for your trip from New York to Boston. Unproductive worry involves imaginary what-ifs, such as "What if I get there and no one wants to talk with me?" Once you make this distinction you will learn how to use effective problem-solving strategies for real problems.

2. *Accept reality and commit to change.* You are unwilling to accept certain realities or possibilities that you might not like. Your worry is like *a protest against reality.* Acceptance of something doesn't mean that you like it or that you think it's fair. Acceptance doesn't mean that you can't do anything to change certain things. But before you can change anything you will have to learn to accept that real problems exist. You will also learn to accept your limitations. Your worries are always about something that *you should be doing*—you should make more money, make sure you don't get sick, help someone else who hasn't asked you for help. Worry puts you in the middle of the universe. In this step, you will learn that you can become more of an observer of reality and less of the determining force of the universe.

3. *Challenge your worried thinking.* You are constantly making predictions about the future ("I might fail"), reading people's minds ("He thinks I'm a loser"), or thinking negative thoughts ("It would be awful if I didn't get what I want"). I will give you

ten ways to defeat these irrational and extreme thoughts so that your life can be more balanced. In this step, you will also learn how to identify what triggers your worry, common themes of your worry, and several techniques, such as how to practice worrying, in order to reduce your anxiety level.

4. *Focus on the deeper threat.* You worry about some things but not others. Why? Your core belief is the source of the worry. It may be your concern about being imperfect, being abandoned, feeling helpless, looking like a fool, or acting irresponsibly. Here you'll find out how to identify and challenge these core beliefs about yourself that are causing you so much stress.

5. *Turn "failure" into opportunity.* Your worries are attempts to prepare for, prevent, and anticipate failure. Failure to you may seem like a catastrophic eventuality—something that can happen any minute unless you keep your guard up and worry. I will give you twenty things to say to yourself to overcome your fear of failure. Once you know how to handle failure, what would you have to worry about?

6. *Use your emotions rather than worry about them.* Worry is actually a strategy for avoiding unpleasant emotions. You are afraid of your feelings because you think you should be rational, in control, never upset, always clear in how you feel, and on top of things. Even though you recognize that you're a nervous wreck, your fear of your feelings drives you into more worry. Rather than trying to worry your emotions away, you will learn to experience them and use them to your advantage.

7. *Take control of time.* You feel controlled by a constant sense of urgency, the need to know everything right now. Here you will learn how to turn the urgency off and improve on the present moment so that you can get more out of life right now.

Part 3, "Special Worries and How to Challenge Them," addresses the five most common areas of worry—approval, relationships, health, finances, and work—and uses the seven-step approach to deal with them. Although each area of worry draws on the seven-step program, we will also examine specific issues involved in each area. For example, when we describe relationship worries, we will look at how your childhood experiences affected your view of relationships. When we discuss your health worries, we will evaluate your perfectionistic ideas about appearance and physical functioning. And when we evaluate your money worries, we will also examine specific distortions in thinking that lead you to become obsessed with losing money.

Now, let's begin by looking at why you worry—and why you keep worrying.

PART I

THE
HOW AND WHY
OF WORRY

1

Understanding Worry

WORRY IS EVERYWHERE. All of us worry, including me. You are not alone. In fact, 38 percent of people worry every day. And many people describe themselves as chronic worriers—they say, "I've been a worrier all my life." But that's only a modest indication of how worry has come to impact every aspect of our lives, limiting our enjoyment and satisfaction. Worry is the central component of all the anxiety disorders and depression. Research shows that worry *precedes* the onset of depression—you literally worry yourself into depression. Fifty percent of the people in the United States have had serious problems with depression, anxiety, or substance abuse at some time.[1] Depression, anxiety, and substance abuse have increased during the past fifty years.[2]

The problem of worry is one that urgently needs a solution. To find one, we first need to understand it.

The Different Kinds of Worry

Let's consider three people who worry.

- Jane is thirty-two years old and single. She and Roger just broke up after a two-year relationship. They had been talking about getting married, but Roger got cold feet, and Jane got fed up with him. She felt she didn't want to wait forever for Roger to get his act together, so she broke it off. She knows she did the right thing, but now she worries: "Will I ever find a guy who can make a commitment?" and "Will I ever be able to have kids?" She sits in her apartment at night eating cookies and watching sitcoms.

- Brian is forty-five. He hasn't filed his taxes for two years. He is sitting at home alone—just like Jane—thinking that he's a loser for being so stupid not to file his taxes. He imagines the feds coming to his home and taking him away in handcuffs. Brian knows, in his rational mind, that he hasn't committed a crime—his employer withheld the taxes, and he's only late in filing. The worst case would probably be some kind of fine. But every time he sits down to start his taxes, his stomach clenches, his mind races, and he's overcome by an overwhelming sense of dread. To avoid this feeling, he turns on ESPN and thinks, "I'll wait for a better time."

- Diane turns forty next month. She just had a complete medical exam two weeks ago, and everything is fine. But she feels a slight irregularity in her breast and begins to think, "Is this cancer?" Even though the doctor assured her she is healthy, Diane knows you can never be too careful. Just six months ago she thought she had Lou Gehrig's disease. Diane was relieved to learn she didn't have a serious neurological problem—only a bad case of nerves. Diane knows her fears are real—even though everyone else tells her to see a therapist.

I could fill several volumes with stories about people who worry. One of the volumes could probably be written by you! We worry about everything—getting rejected, ending up alone, doing badly on an exam, not looking that good, what someone thinks of us, getting sick, falling off cliffs, crashing in airplanes, losing our money, being late, going crazy, having weird thoughts and feelings, being humiliated.

You find yourself puzzled with thoughts like these:

- I know that I keep predicting the worst, but I can't help myself.
- Even when people tell me it's going to be OK, I still can't stop worrying.
- I try to put these thoughts out of my mind, but they just keep coming back.
- I know it's not likely to happen, but what if I'm *the one*?
- Why can't I get control of my thoughts?
- Why am I driving myself crazy with these worries?

For example, Greg worries that things at work might go badly if he doesn't get this project done on time. Even if he gets it done, he thinks it might not be up to par. The boss could get angry at him. What if he gets so angry he decides to fire him? After all, three people were laid off last month. And then what would his wife think? She'd be disappointed. Now Greg notices that he's worrying again, and he thinks, "I'm worried all the time, and I can't get any control over this worry. I'll never get any sleep tonight, and then I'll be tired, and then I won't be able to get this project done." And so on in a vicious circle.

Greg has *generalized anxiety disorder (GAD)*, or what I call the "what-if disease." A lot of what we will discuss in this book relates directly to this particular kind of worry. If you have this problem, then you worry about a number of different things— money, health, relationships, safety, or performance. And you worry you don't have control of your worries. This is one of the longest-lasting anxiety disorders. You jump from one worry to another, predicting one catastrophe after another. Plus you worry about the fact that you are worrying so much. Not only are you worried, but you also have difficulty sleeping, are irritable and tense and tired, have indigestion, sweat a lot, and just feel nervous a good deal of the time. It's hard to relax. No wonder you are often depressed or have physical problems such as irritable bowel syndrome.[3]

About 7 percent of us have GAD. Women are twice as likely as men to have this problem. This is a chronic condition, with many people saying that they have been worriers all their lives.[4] The first severe worry tends to begin during late adolescence or early adulthood. Most people with GAD never seek out psychotherapy; they generally see their doctor and complain about vague physical symptoms, such as fatigue, aches and pains, irritable bowel, and sleep problems. Those who do eventually go to therapy wait a long time before doing so—an average of ten years. In fact, worry is such a widespread problem that it may not even seem like a problem. That's because you think, "Oh, I'm just a worrier" and believe that there's nothing you can do about it. You think, "I've always been a worrier—and I always will be."

Worry is not limited to GAD. In addition to this general what-if disease, others confront more specific types of worry—a fear of a specific situation, for example. These more targeted worries are part of every anxiety disorder and a central component of depression. This is important for two reasons. First, if you have GAD—or if you are a chronic worrier—then you probably have some problems with another anxiety disorder or depression. Second, if we cure your worry, your anxiety and depression should dramatically improve.

Look at the different kinds of worries and anxiety disorders in the table below and see if any of them fit you at times. You probably have some of the worries listed in this table.

TABLE 1.1

Worry	Examples	What You Avoid or Do	Anxiety Disorder
Being evaluated by others Humiliation Rejection	They'll see I'm nervous. My hands will tremble. My mind will go blank.	*What you avoid* Speaking in public Meeting new people	Social anxiety disorder
Fear of a specific situation or thing	I'll fall over the edge. I'll drown. I'll get trapped. The plane will crash. It's dangerous.	*What you avoid* Heights Water Insects, snakes, rats Closed spaces Flying	Specific phobia
Leaving something undone, being contaminated, making mistakes, having thoughts and feelings that you fear	I didn't lock the door. I have germs on my hands. If I have a violent thought, I might act on it.	*What you do* Repeat actions over and over Check repeatedly Won't touch certain things Avoid situations or people that trigger your unwanted thoughts and feelings	Obsessive-compulsive disorder
Feeling that your physical sensations will go out of control and cause you to cause or get sick	My heart is beating rapidly— I will have a heart attack. I'm so dizzy I will fall. I'll get so anxious, I'll start to scream.	*What you avoid* Being in places— theaters, restaurants, airplanes—where your exit is blocked Open spaces— streets, malls, fields	Panic disorder

Worry	Examples	What You Avoid or Do	Anxiety Disorder
Believing that intrusive images and thoughts mean that something terrible is going to happen to you	I had another image of a disaster—I have to get out of here. I had a nightmare—it's dangerous.	*What you avoid* Situations associated with your initial trauma—people, places, movies, stories	Post-traumatic stress disorder
Thinking that the future is hopeless and bleak Having repetitive thoughts and feelings about your own suffering	Nothing will work out. I'll end up a failure. What's wrong with me? Why do I have so many problems?	*What you avoid* Doing things to help yourself—meeting people, taking on new challenges, establishing goals, and solving your problems	Depression

If you have social anxiety, then you worry that people will see you as weak, vulnerable, and anxious. You are shy, intimidated, afraid to speak in public, and worried that people will see that you are anxious. If you have post-traumatic stress disorder, then you worry that the intrusive images and frightening nightmares will never go away and that something terrible will happen. If you have specific fears, such as a fear of flying, then you worry that you will be injured or killed. And if you have obsessive-compulsive disorder, you worry you may have left something undone, or that you are contaminated, or that your thoughts will lead to dangerous impulses.

Now that you have evaluated the different kinds of worries you have for these different anxiety problems, let's take a closer look at why your worry persists—no matter how many times things turn out OK.

Why You Keep Worrying

You have mixed feelings about your worries. On one hand, your worries are bothering you—you can't sleep, and you can't get these pessimistic thoughts out of your head. But there is a way that these worries make sense to you. For example, you think:

- Maybe I'll find a solution.
- I don't want to overlook anything.
- If I keep thinking a little longer, maybe I'll figure it out.
- I don't want to be surprised.
- I want to be responsible.

You have a hard time giving up on your worries because, in a sense, your worries have been working for you.

Your Parents Taught You to Worry

Where did all of this worry come from?

It's interesting that worriers don't generally describe terrible things happening in their recent lives. In fact, nothing unusual seems to be happening in their lives. No big traumas, few big losses—*at least not now.*

- *Trauma.* Chronic worriers had a higher level of trauma— especially physical threat of harm—when they were kids. But as adults, chronic worriers were *least likely* to worry about physical threat![5] One reason is that they may avoid thinking about things that are upsetting. College students who worried a lot said that they worry about certain things because they don't want to think about *other* things that might be more frightening.[6] This is important because—as you will see later—a lot of worry is an attempt to avoid your emotions.

- *Worried and overprotective parents.* Adults who worry had parents who worried. The children may very well have imitated this style of worried thinking. The mothers of worriers were overprotective and tried to protect their kids from what they saw as a dangerous world.[7] "Don't stay out too late—it's dangerous" and "Don't forget to wear your gloves" and "Be sure that you watch and look both ways when you cross the street." The message was that you've got to always keep your guard up, and you've got to control your environment.

Many of these mothers combined this overprotection with a lack of warmth. These mothers were controlling and intrusive but showed very little affection. The child learned, "Not only is the world unsafe and I am not competent (because my mother has to tell me what to do), but there's no safe and comfortable place for me to go for support."

- *Reversed parenting.* These mothers often made the child take on the role of acting as the parent to the mother. The mother shared her problems with the kid and hoped the child would soothe her. This rever-sal of roles contributes to the tendency to worry later—especially to worry about what other people think and feel. One worrier told me that her mother's reversal of roles made her feel that there was no one to protect *her*. So she worried.

An offshoot of this is that the most common worry for chronic worriers is concern about relationships. Worriers are most concerned they are not nurturing and caring enough toward other people. They worry about letting other people down, that other people are upset with them, and that other people are unhappy. In fact, worriers tend to be better than nonworriers in anticipating the feelings of other people.[8]

- *Parents dismissed emotion.* Worriers had parents who treated the child's emotions as if they were an annoyance or as if the child was self-indulgent for having painful or unpleasant feelings. Thus, these kids grow up thinking that they can't have emotions and that no one will be supportive of them.

- *Insecure attachments.* Adults who worry are more likely to have had a parent who died before the child was sixteen. The loss of a parent may make the child more worried about other interpersonal losses such as relationships breaking up, people being upset with them, or any conflicts and arguments that might arise. They often had very insecure attachments with their parents. This means that they were not always sure that their parents would be there for them, couldn't count on their parents paying attention to them, or feared that the parents might leave or die.

A woman who worried about her relationship ending told me that her mother used to threaten suicide when she was a kid. She now felt that any relationship could end at any time unless she was vigilant.[9] Another woman worried about her finances and being left alone, although she was independently wealthy and had numerous friends. She explained that when she was a girl her mother would complain about pains in her chest and would tell her that there were all kinds of danger out there. She feared that her mother would die if she went out and played for too long. In fact, she told me that she felt that she couldn't do things on her own because she thought it could kill her mother. As irrational as this might sound, this continued to be a fear for her as an adult.

- *Shame.* Mothers of people who are shy were very focused on shame as a way to control their kids. They say things like "What will people think?" or "I am really disappointed in you" or "Don't let anyone know that you did that." Shame makes you feel that who you are and what you are needs to be hidden. Kids who grow up with parents like this are ashamed that people will see them as flawed or nervous.

It Makes Sense to You

I don't believe that people want to be anxious or want to suffer. In fact, worry is a way that people think they can avoid having *worse* things happen. Worry is your strategy to adapt to a reality that you view as uncertain, out of control, dangerous, and filled with problems. You view worry as a way to act responsibly, prevent your worst fears from happening, motivate yourself to get things done, and avoid the unpleasant feelings that you believe are right below the surface. Until you recognize why worry makes sense and why your theories about worry may be wrong, you may be reluctant to give up on worry. Let's look at these ideas more closely.

1. *You believe that worry helps you solve problems.* People worry and ruminate because they think that they will find an answer to their problems. They believe that worry will prepare them, protect them, and prevent bad things from happening. When researchers ask people what they hope to gain from worrying about bad things, they say, "Maybe I'll figure out a way to solve my problems" or "Maybe I'll figure out what's wrong."[10]

2. *You believe the world is dangerous and that you are unable to cope.* You believe that terrible things are likely to happen, so you worry in order to prevent these things from happening. Worriers attend to threatening information (for example, signs of rejection) and interpret ambiguous information as threatening.[11] Ambiguous information could be something like "I'm not sure how

Carol really feels, but I bet she is not talking to me because she doesn't like me." Worriers have their antenna out looking for threat. They see danger even when it isn't there. They have the radar up and running because it always seems like it's wartime.

In one study, worriers were asked to write down their worries over a two-week period and predict what would happen. In fact, 85 percent of the actual outcomes were *positive*. Things almost always turn out better than you think. Also, 79 percent of the time worriers coped with different negative outcomes better than they expected they would.[12]

Worriers assume that the world is filled with opportunities for rejection and failure and that their predictions are accurate. One woman, after the disastrous events of September 11 in New York City, thought the chances that she would be killed in the future by a terrorist attack were 100 percent. Other worriers believe that it is likely that they will have a serious illness, go bankrupt, or fail in their relationships. They are guided by pervasive pessimism.

3. *Worry helps you avoid thinking about the worst possible outcome.* You focus on things that you can catch early that will prevent some feared future disaster from occurring.[13] Although I just said in the section above that you might worry about the worst possible outcome, what you actually do is worry about all the bad outcomes that happen *before* the worst outcome could occur. The rationale behind this is "If I can notice all the smaller things that happen before the catastrophe, I can catch it early and avoid thinking or imagining that catastrophe."

For example, a dentist worried that his practice would shrink. He was anxious whenever a patient canceled or whenever he had an empty hour: "Gee, I have empty slots in my schedule. My income is dropping. I wonder if there's a downturn in my practice. I wonder if Dr. Smith is not referring to me because the last patient didn't work out. I wonder if I might be losing my contacts with referral sources. I wonder if I should call up Dr. Smith and have lunch with him."

He did not allow himself to go to the most feared thought: "My practice will completely collapse and I will be bankrupt." He avoided this thought by focusing on the immediate events in front of him—a patient canceling—and then tried to figure out how they could be avoided in the future.

When I ask chronic worriers to try to think through the string of events that could lead to the worst possible outcome, they actually *take longer* to get to the worst outcome. They keep coming up with less than the worst outcome, or all the things that happen before the worst outcome. This is important: since chronic worriers focus on little things to be caught and changed (if possible), they seldom face their worst fears—the fears of a terrible catastrophe. As a result, they don't have the opportunity to *reject* that fear.

4. *Your worry keeps you from feeling powerful emotions.* People have probably said to you, "You think too much." There's some truth to this. Worry is a way that you avoid feelings by "overthinking." As a worrier, you are thinking more than feeling. You try to think about problems rather than feel your emotions. Worry is your way of "keeping it in your head" and not feeling the emotional impact.

5. *You are not anxious when you are worried.* While you are worrying, your anxiety level does not increase. Worriers and nonworriers respond very differently to threat. When nonworriers look at a threatening image, they feel afraid and their heart rates go up. With repeated exposure to the threatening image, their anxiety goes down. But for worriers, the process is very different. Worriers tend to be at higher levels of tension at most

times, so when a threatening image is presented, the chronic worrier shows no increase. It's as if he is experiencing it as a "normal threat."

The worrier shows no decrease with repeated exposure to the threatening image.[14] This is very important, because with almost all other things that we fear, we find ourselves less afraid the longer we stay in the situation. Thus, if I am afraid of taking an elevator but I take it a thousand times, I become much less afraid. But this does not happen with worriers. Worriers take a much longer time to become less anxious when they view a threat. *It's as if they are not feeling the threat.* This is because worriers are always on guard—in a state of tension. Your worry suppresses your anxiety because you actually think you are doing something constructive when you are worrying. However, when you stop worrying, your anxiety level goes up.[15] It's as if your anxiety incubates when you worry. That's why worriers are actually more anxious in general, even though they are less anxious when they are actually worrying!

6. *Worry gives you the illusion of control.* If you are a worrier, someone has probably called you a "control freak." When you are anxious, you believe that things will go out of control. You try to control what will happen by thinking about all the worst possibilities and then finding solutions. You're saying to yourself, "I've got to find out how things can go wrong and then make sure it doesn't happen." You're trying to solve a problem before it becomes a bigger problem—before it becomes a *catastrophe*.

Because you feel that things or events are out of your control, you turn to worry to gain control. You keep thinking, "What can go wrong?" and "How can I control it?" When we anticipate danger or threat, we attempt to gain some control. For example, if you have a fear of dogs, you manifest control by avoiding dogs when you see them on the sidewalk. If you have an obsessive concern about contamination, you manifest control by washing your hands thirty times. If you worry about making a fool of yourself in front of strangers, you might hold on to the side of a table to make yourself feel steady. You search for some way to control things. We call these "safety behaviors" because they make you feel safe. You are actually using your worry as a way of gaining control. Since you worry before the bad thing *might* happen, and it does not happen, you begin to think that the worry prevented a bad outcome.

So if I am worried about bad things happening—failing the test, getting run over by a bus, getting rejected by every woman I talk to—but these things do not actually happen, why don't I just immediately abandon all of my worries and become the happy guy I was meant to be? Because my primitive brain is saying something like this: "Bob, let's put two and two together. You've been worrying about the test, the bus, and all these women. You didn't fail the test, you haven't been hit by a bus, and not *all* the women reject you. So nothing terrible has happened. Doesn't that *prove* that the worry is working? You worried. Bad things didn't happen. It worked. Case closed. Stop bothering me. I'm busy worrying."[16]

This is what psychologists call "illusory correlation." Two things are correlated when they seem to occur together in time. So when the light turns green, the cars move forward. The two things occur around the same time. But correlation does not prove that one is a *cause* of the other. Let's imagine that Penny gets out of bed every morning and fifteen minutes later the sun rises. Did she cause the sun to rise?

7. *You feel that worry means you are responsible.* You may believe that you have a responsibility to think of all the bad outcomes that could happen, then come up with ways of preventing these things from occurring. You think, "I wonder if this mole is

cancer. Now that I think it might be, I would be irresponsible and negligent not to do everything I can to figure out what it really is."

People worry because they think worrying is a sign of being a careful, responsible and conscientious person.[17] Take Lisa. Her thirty-two-year-old son, Chuck, wasn't married but was living with a woman he really cared about. He had a good job and just got his MBA from a top business school. But Lisa worried that Chuck would never get married, might not be successful in his career, and, of course, wasn't taking care of himself. Lisa's worry was driving Chuck crazy. But Lisa thought that worrying about Chuck was a sign that she cared and was a good mother.

8. *Worry is a way to reduce uncertainty.* You can't stand not knowing something for sure. You keep saying things like, "I don't really know" or "It could happen" or "It's always possible" or "I don't feel sure yet." You feel you can't tolerate not having certainty.

Worriers are intolerant of uncertainty.[18] In fact, worriers would rather know a negative outcome for sure than face the possibility of an uncertain outcome that could be positive. You believe that you can consider all of the possible ways that something can go wrong and reduce the uncertainty by collecting information and considering every alternative. This, of course, increases the sense that things are out of control. So you worry even more.

You believe that you will finally be able to figure things out, or come up with new information that will make things entirely clear, or arrive at the perfect solution. These attempts to eliminate uncertainty only make you more frustrated, since it is impossible to eliminate uncertainty.

If you are a chronic worrier, then the following will seem familiar to you.

- You believe that gaining certainty will reduce your risk of harm.
- You seek reassurance to gain more confidence.
- You demand more information.
- You wait indefinitely to take action.
- You feel you need to know for sure.
- If you don't know it for sure, then you conclude it's going to turn out badly.
- Even when you seem to have a solution in hand, you ask if it will absolutely, definitely solve everything. If it doesn't, you reject it.
- You keep worrying in order to find the absolutely perfect answer that will eliminate uncertainty.
- Uncertainty is equated with threat, lack of control, mistakes, and regret.

But if you think about it rationally, uncertainty is actually *neutral*. If I say that I am uncertain about the weather next month (as I am), then it does not follow that the weather will be bad. I simply don't know.

You scour the health encyclopedia for any symptoms of illness. Since you are jumping to conclusions about the worst possible outcome, you think, "If I have a headache, it *could* be a brain tumor." Consequently, you seek out an enormous amount of information about brain tumors and various neurological disorders, visit doctors unnecessarily, and demand reassurance from everyone around you. You want certainty.

Information is power, but information should be balanced. What you collect is information that is biased toward the negative. This makes sense to you because it makes you feel that you will catch something early and reverse the danger. What you don't realize is that—because you are biased—you are using information that is not accurate. So you can easily end up making the wrong decision.

You might come up with reasonable solutions to problems but then reject these solutions because you are not completely certain or the solutions are not perfect. This is poor problem solving, since not only are you looking for a solution, you are looking for the *perfect solution*. It doesn't exist, so you worry even more until you can find one.

Some worriers worry so much that they *avoid* information. This is because you can view getting certain information as telling you for sure that you really do have a catastrophic problem. Your reasoning is, "If I know for sure that I have a terrible problem, it will be devastating to me and I'll just worry about it all the time."

A forty-eight-year-old woman did not have a gynecological exam for over twenty years. She was too worried that the exam would make her worry about cancer. Another worrier refused to look at his stock portfolio because he felt it made him too anxious; he was afraid that he had lost too much money. A woman who worried about her looks avoided any mirrors lest they remind her that she was turning into a "hag." In fact, she was quite healthy and attractive, but she might be the last to know.

The intolerance of uncertainty is shown in Figure 1.1, below. As you examine this figure, think about your worries when you are uncertain about something. For example, you think, "Maybe my boss is angry at me" (something bad could happen). You then think, "I can't stand not knowing for sure. If I knew for sure, perhaps I could fix the problem" or "I don't want to be surprised." You then decide that you need to collect more information, so you start looking for any signs—past, present, or future—that she is angry with you. You begin contemplating all the bad things that could happen—getting criticized, humiliated, and fired, and never getting another job in this field. You start coming up with solutions:

flattering your boss, working harder, getting back on track. You also turn to your coworkers and ask for reassurance that things will be OK. You get reassurance, but you reject it, and you reject all the solutions that you thought of because you can't be certain that they will make you absolutely *sure* that your boss isn't angry and won't eventually fire you. So you continue to worry.

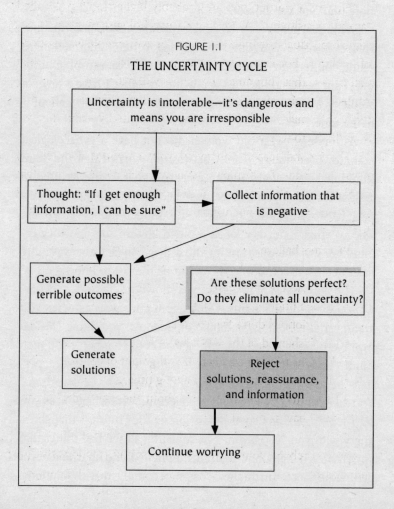

FIGURE 1.1

THE UNCERTAINTY CYCLE

Uncertainty is intolerable—it's dangerous and means you are irresponsible

Thought: "If I get enough information, I can be sure"

Collect information that is negative

Generate possible terrible outcomes

Are these solutions perfect? Do they eliminate all uncertainty?

Generate solutions

Reject solutions, reassurance, and information

Continue worrying

9. *You worry to control your thoughts and feelings.* You may overemphasize rationality at the expense of experiencing or processing your emotions. You have a negative view of your emotions and are intolerant of your feelings. You believe your emotions will spin out of control and last too long, and your feelings just don't make sense to you.

Why would you be so intolerant of your emotions?

First, as a worrier, you are probably higher in what is called "anxiety sensitivity." According to psychologist Stephen Reiss, some individuals are highly sensitive or averse to their sensations of anxiety.[19] For example, if you have anxiety sensitivity, then you believe that your anxiety or stress will make you sick or lose control. You are *afraid of your own sensations*. Females are more likely than males to be high in anxiety sensitivity—and they are more likely to worry.[20]

The second reason you avoid your emotions and rely on worry instead is that you have *negative beliefs about your emotions* in general. In our research we found that worriers believe that other people would not validate or understand how bad they felt.[21]

Worriers believe:

- I can't accept my feelings.
- No one understands how I feel.
- My emotions don't make sense.
- I feel ashamed of the way I feel.
- If I have a strong emotion, it will go out of control.
- My strong feelings will last a long time.
- I have to be absolutely sure about the way I feel—I can't stand having mixed feelings.

So you rely on your worry to suppress any emotions that are unpleasant.

Third, you are afraid your worry is going to spin out of control and overwhelm you emotionally. When you are worrying you might also think, "This worrying is going to drive me nuts. I've got to stop this right now." So you try to keep from getting too emotional—you look for solutions, you anticipate problems, you avoid situations that are uncomfortable. Because you believe your worry is spinning out of control, you start paying more and more attention to your worries, which makes you even more frightened that you are losing control of your thoughts. You begin to watch your thoughts—what we call "thought monitoring"—to see if you are worrying. This makes you worry more.

Since you cannot control your thoughts and feelings all the time, you might worry about your lack of control. You then worry about how you can get more control—making you feel even less in control.

10. *Worry motivates you.* You think that your worry will motivate you to get things done. One of the most common explanations for worry among college students is that worry will motivate them to work hard: "I need to worry to get myself to study." People worry about exams, and they think this will get them to study. You worry about relationships, and you think this will make you work harder at a relationship. You worry about your health and appearance, and you think it will make you go to the doctor, work out, and diet.

Some people say, "If I didn't worry, I'd get lazy" or "I wouldn't get anything done." Now, it is true that a certain amount of anxiety and discomfort can be motivating. Why bother studying for an exam or working on a project that is unpleasant? You think, "Maybe worrying a little can help motivate me. Will worrying a lot more really fire me up and get me to do things?"

There are two very different strategies that people use. One strategy is called "defensive pessimism." People who are defensive pessimists are concerned about their performance, and as a result, they worry that they won't be motivated to work hard enough—they don't want to let their guard down.[22] Defensive pessimists will lower their expectations for themselves; they tell people they are worried that they are not prepared enough. However, these defensive pessimists actually do work harder, and in the long run they do well. When defensive pessimists are prevented (through distraction) from worrying, they actually do worse on the test.

In contrast to defensive pessimists, in depressed and overly anxious people worry leads to difficulty concentrating, avoidance, procrastination, and difficulty recalling information. Intense anxiety often impairs performance, leading to intrusive thoughts, doubts, and feelings of panic.[23] If you are a worrier and you are not a defensive pessimist, your worry probably interferes with your performance on tests and adds to your conflicts in relationships.

Summing Up

You believe that worry will protect you, prepare you, and keep you safe in a world that you see as dangerous and unpredictable. You think worry will motivate you to solve your problems and allow you to collect all the information you need to make sure everything turns out your way. You believe that you are being responsible when you worry, because you are taking things *seriously*. You believe you will avoid regret and mistakes, and keep from sliding down a slippery slope. You will keep your emotions in check, live abstractly in your head, and postpone dealing with the emotions that bother you.

But is it really working?

You may be collecting the wrong information, focusing on the wrong things, and assuming that everything is dangerous before you test the waters. In fact, you may worry so much that you will not test the waters. Rather than being motivated, you are stuck in your tracks, procrastinating on the important things.

In fact, your worry may be a "solution" that is really a problem. Rather than making the world more certain, it only makes you more uncertain about the world. Rather than helping you cope with your emotions, worry makes you afraid and confused about your emotions. Rather than solving your problems, worry generates more problems to solve.

Of course, you have been trying to cope with your worry for years. You have gotten all the best advice you could, and none of it has worked. Let's turn now to why this bad advice not only does not work but actually adds to your worry.

2

The Worst Ways to Handle Worry

DO THESE COMMENTS SOUND FAMILIAR?

- Try to be more positive.
- You have nothing to worry about.
- Everything will turn out OK.
- You need to believe in yourself.
- I believe in you.
- Try to get your mind off it.
- Just stop worrying!

Most worriers have heard this advice from well-meaning friends or even well-meaning therapists. You might—if you are really lucky—feel better for about ten minutes.

Trying to be more positive is a good idea at times, but as a worrier, *you are actually afraid of being more positive*. Telling you to "think positively" is like telling someone who has a fear of heights, "trust me, you won't fall. You can climb that mountain." The chance that this advice would work is zero.

What about saying to you, "You need to believe in yourself"? It sounds nice, but if you are a worrier, how do you make that happen? Imagine that someone says, "Gee, I see you have all these doubts about yourself and your relationship. I want you to just start believing in yourself right now—this very minute." How likely is that to be helpful for you?

Again, zero.

The fact that your friend believes in you is wonderful, but how does it help you believe in yourself if you are a worrier? In fact, not only does your friend's confidence in you seem to have absolutely no relevance to your confidence in yourself, but you might conclude, "She doesn't know the real me." If you are a worrier, you probably harbor a "private self" that is the core of your self-doubt, the "neurotic me" that no one knows. So when your friend says she believes in you, it may simply demonstrate that she doesn't really know you as well as you know yourself.

Sound familiar?

Or what if your friend says, "Try to get your mind off it" and urges you to distract yourself with something else, like taking a walk? As you are walking you will probably think, "I wonder if Pete is trying to call me and can't get through." And when the walk is over, you return home and go right back to your worry. And then you ask yourself, "What does she think I should do, spend my *entire life* taking a nice long walk?" Since you don't view yourself as the Forrest Gump marathon walker, you believe that this well-meaning advice—to get your mind off it—is not going to do the trick.

Perhaps your therapist says to you, "This thought that Pete will break up with you sounds like an obsession." Since the therapist is an "expert," you believe that what will come out of his mouth next will be incredibly valuable words of wisdom. He is about to provide you with an insight that will make everything crystal clear and will free you forever of these terrible worries. As you lean forward in your chair, your heart beating rapidly, ears straining to catch every important syllable he is about to utter, he says, "Just stop worrying."

Your eyes blink in disbelief. Surely you have missed something. "But how do I just stop worrying?" you ask.

He smiles, looking down confidently at your perplexed face, and says, "Whenever you worry, just yell 'Stop!' at yourself."

This simple solution had escaped you over the past ten years of your reoccurring worry. You could have solved it all by simply telling yourself to stop. How simple it is. You can use this thought-stopping technique.

Then the therapist reaches into his desk drawer and pulls out a rubber band.

"Here. Put this on your wrist. Whenever you worry, just snap the rubber band and say to yourself, 'Stop!' "

Even more perplexed, but with a faint feeling of hope, you go home and start snapping. You snap all week. You keep telling yourself to stop those thoughts. A few times, when no one is looking, you yell out loud, *"Stop!"* That distracts you for a bit—but then your worries come right back.

You return the next week to your therapist, now worried that your last chance to cure your worry hasn't worked, and tell him, "Doctor, it worked the first few times. I was distracted by the pain. But I'm still worrying just as much as before."

The doctor looks at you, thinking you might be a long-term case, and says, "You are just going to have to tell yourself to stop worrying."

"I don't know if that's enough," you respond.

"Well, you're going to have to believe in yourself."

If you are like the millions of people who worry, then you have probably heard some, if not all, of this bad advice. If anything, it makes you feel even more depressed. You don't feel understood, and you even think that your situation must be really hopeless because all these well-meaning people and highly trained experts can't seem to help you. The truth is, they can't help you because they are trying to get rid of your worries.

You are probably saying, "Isn't this what this book is about?"

It is. But your worries persist because of the *ways* that you try to get rid of them. You use techniques that make things worse.

It's like an alcoholic trying to get rid of his alcoholism by having another drink. It'll take his mind off the problem for an hour, but the problem is still there, and worse than before.

The reason you persist in doing many of these self-defeating things to help with your worry is that they all work in the short run. Each of these strategies you use will make you less anxious for a few minutes or a few hours. You might ask, "Well, isn't that an advantage for me? After all, if I can feel better for a few minutes or even a few hours, then what is wrong with a little bit of relief from my worries?" These techniques are self-defeating because they maintain your belief that you need to worry in order to reduce threat, they convince you that you cannot live with uncertainty, and they keep you from facing and conquering your worst fears. In this chapter we will review twelve common failing strategies that not only will fail to reduce your worries over the long term but will actually make things worse for you. By highlighting these strategies, you can begin to understand why you need to relinquish the "solutions" that you have been trying. In fact, unless you abandon your failing solutions and strategies, you will continue to worry.

Let's take a closer look at the "dirty dozen."

The "Dirty Dozen": Twelve Strategies That Don't Work

1. You Seek Reassurance

You are worried that you don't look as good as you wish you did (who does?), so you turn to your partner and say, "Do you think I look OK?" Or you think that a small discoloration is a sign of cancer, so you go to doctors over and over to find out if you'll live. Or you are worried about the guy you met at a party who yawned while you were talking with him, and you ask your friends, "Is he bored with me?"

But, of course, you don't seek reassurance just once. You keep going back, again and again. In fact, you may have read other books about worry that actually encourage you to get reassurance from people that you are OK, or to keep telling yourself that things will work out.

Seeking reassurance does not work because you *can always doubt the reassurance later*. Maybe your friend is trying to bolster your ego by telling you that you look fine, but she really believes that you are looking worse than ever. Or maybe the doctor cannot really tell if it is cancer without doing extensive tests. As we will see throughout this book, the main problem with seeking reassurance is that it tries to eliminate uncertainty. Relying on reassurance will keep you from learning to live with uncertainty—an essential element in reducing your worry. Consequently, seeking reassurance is a strategy that will fail. What is worse, it will make you go back over and over to try to get more reassurance, since it will reduce your anxiety (and uncertainty) for a few minutes. Seeking reassurance is like a compulsion to check if you locked the door. If you check the door forty times, then chances are that the next time you leave the house you'll check it forty-one times. The real trick is to be able to walk through the door.

2. You Try to Stop Your Thoughts

Perhaps you took a course in psychology once and heard about "thought stopping," a therapy that involves getting rid of negative or unwanted thoughts by suppressing them. Thus, whenever you have the worry that you will lose all your money in the stock market, you are encouraged to force yourself to stop having these thoughts by snapping a rubber band on your wrist (to distract you) or just yelling to yourself, "Stop!" This is supposed to reduce your worries. Unfortunately, not only does thought stopping not work, but it actually leads to "thought rebounding" and makes things worse in the long term.

Let's try thought stopping. Close your eyes and relax. I'd like you to get a very clear image in your head of a white bear—a cute furry white bear. Now that you have this thought of a white bear clearly in your mind, I want you to stop thinking of white bears for the next ten minutes. Whatever you do, don't think of any white bears. Psychologist David Wegner found that attempts to suppress thoughts of white bears actually led to an *increase* in these thoughts after the suppression.[1] Thus if you suppress for ten minutes, you will have a substantial *increase* after the ten minutes is over.

Thought stopping is based on the idea that you cannot stand having a certain kind of thought—say, an obsession or a worry.

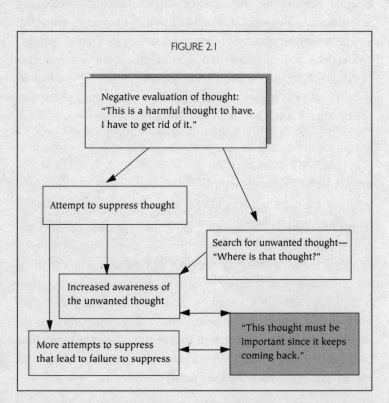

FIGURE 2.1

Negative evaluation of thought:
"This is a harmful thought to have.
I have to get rid of it."

Attempt to suppress thought

Search for unwanted thought—
"Where is that thought?"

Increased awareness of
the unwanted thought

More attempts to suppress
that lead to failure to suppress

"This thought must be
important since it keeps
coming back."

It confirms your idea that these thoughts are harmful or will lead to your losing control. Thought rebounding occurs because you cannot eliminate thoughts that are in your mind—you cannot erase your memory. Not only is it impossible to erase your memory, but by actively engaging in suppressing a thought, you must pay attention to that thought—you must actually look for the thought that you are trying to suppress! To make things even worse, you are saying to yourself that this thought that you are trying to suppress may actually be a dangerous (that is, important) thought. Therefore, when you have the thought again, you should really pay attention to it.

Figure 2.1 shows this process of labeling a thought as "unwanted" or "bad" and how attempts to suppress it will lead to thought rebounding. We will see how intentionally practicing your worries through "thought flooding" is better than the useless thought stopping.

3. You Collect Information

When you worry about something, you might go out and collect as much information as you can. You might say, "Isn't information power? Isn't information just getting the facts?" The information that you are getting might be a set of facts (and it might not). But even if it is a set of facts, it might be a *biased selection of facts*. They may be facts that are not only useless but misleading. This is because you look for information to confirm your negative beliefs, you see trends that don't exist, you overestimate risk, and you use information that is irrelevant.

YOU TRY TO CONFIRM ONLY NEGATIVE THOUGHTS

When you worry, you try to find out if a negative prediction could come true—"Could I have cancer?" As a result of this, you are driven by what's called "confirmation bias." If you are worried about having cancer, then you will seek out information that suggests you do have cancer.

YOU SEE TRENDS THAT DON'T EXIST

Let's take the screen watcher who owns stocks. He sits in front of his monitor tracking all his stocks for hours every day. His thought is, "I'll catch a trend before everyone else."

In a fascinating book, *Fooled by Randomness,* investor and statistician Nassim Taleb points out that individual stocks will vary *randomly* daily and that real trends might not show up for months or years.[2] The investor sitting there watching his monitor is looking at noise but interprets it as useful information. Watching the screen every hour of every day leads you to see patterns that are not really there. According to Taleb, it is very difficult for us to accept that there are random events (such as daily stock fluctuations). As a result, when we look at the variations of price in a stock on an hourly basis, we believe that there are trends emerging, when we are actually watching random fluctuations in prices.

When we collect information about our worries, our information selection and interpretation are driven by confirmation bias. Thus, if you are worried that someone is annoyed with you, you are biased toward all the negative information about how that person acts toward you. You interpret neutral behavior as indicative of something really negative. Research shows that chronic worriers interpret neutral or ambiguous information as threatening. Thus, people who are shy interpret ambiguous faces as angry faces.

YOU OVERESTIMATE RISK

In collecting information about a threat, you are really trying to evaluate risk: "How likely is it that something bad will happen?" But we now know that we almost always overestimate risk when we are anxious.

Psychologists Paul Slovic and Gerd Gigerenzer show in their research that calculating risk is a complicated process.[3] Let's imagine that we are trying to calculate the risk of airplanes crashing. Ideally, in order to calculate future risk we should do the following: (1) collect all of the information about how many times airplanes have crashed in the past; (2) collect information about the amount of exposure to this risk (that is, the number of times people have flown); (3) estimate whether there are new conditions that increase or decrease this risk (for example, technological improvements decrease the risk, and terrorism increases the risk); (4) evaluate how accurate these estimates are (that is, how do you really know how technology or terrorism affects the risk); and (5) estimate how negative the outcome will be (in this case, getting killed is a highly negative outcome).

Unfortunately, when you estimate risk, you almost never use these rational thought processes. You do not collect all of the information about past accidents, you do not know how many people flew in airplanes last year, you have no accurate information about how technology or terrorism could affect future risk, and you only focus on the downside (getting killed). In fact, psychologist Paul Slovic found that you are likely to estimate risk by relying on several irrational rules of thumb, outlined in the following table:[4]

TABLE 2.1

HOW YOU MISUSE INFORMATION TO OVERESTIMATE HOW RISKY SOMETHING IS

- Accessibility: If I can recall the information easily, it must be very relevant.
- Recency: If there is recent information, it must be more likely.
- Powerful images: If I have a strong image of this, it must be more likely.
- Personal relevance: If it's relevant to my plans, it's more likely.
- Emotional thinking: If I am anxious, it's more likely.
- Severity of outcome: If it could be really awful, then it is more likely.

We are more likely to overestimate risk if we can easily recall examples of negative outcomes (for example, we can recall images of planes crashing), these negative events occurred recently (a plane crashed at a local airport last week), the image that we have is quite powerful (we saw an image of the plane burning), it is relevant to our plans (we are planning on flying tomorrow), we were upset thinking about it (our emotion "tells" us that it is more likely to happen), and we imagine the outcome as awful (we imagine that we die in the crash). We are also more likely to overestimate risk if we think that the cause of the negative event is invisible and difficult to block. For example, we are likely to overestimate risk when we think of terrorism or contagious diseases, such as SARS or AIDS, since the cause is invisible and may seem difficult to block.

Thus, when we search for information we are seldom objective. In fact, not only are we driven by these irrational rules of thumb, but we almost never look for the most important information—*how often does the predicted outcome not occur?* Thus, if you have a fear of flying, how often do you collect information about planes landing safely? Or if you have a fear of getting fired, how many days are you not getting fired?

YOUR INFORMATION ISN'T RELEVANT

As you surf the Net for information about rare infectious diseases or hard-to-detect cancers, you think that symptoms such as shortness of breath or a pain somewhere in your body are sure signs of the dreaded disease that two people in three hundred million get. Information can be misleading. The question is whether the information is *representative*. "Does this information represent what is generally true, or does it accurately reflect your circumstances?[5]

Let's take headaches. You notice that you have a headache. You go to the Web and start reading about neurological disorders and other serious maladies. Maybe you are having a stroke, aneurysm, brain tumor. By the time you are finished looking up "headaches," you are convinced that you have to review your will and arrange for someone to adopt your cat.

Information is useful only if it is *relevant*. For example, relevant information about the headache is whether a painkiller will help. Another piece of information might be, "What percentage of people have headaches at one time or another?" Is it . . . let's see . . . 100 percent? When you go to the Web and check out all of the diseases associated with headaches, you are driven by the rules of thumb that I outlined above. The information about dreaded diseases on the Web is highly accessible, very salient (it is powerful in that you can see the dreaded diseases listed here), recent (you are looking at it right now), and personally relevant (it is your headache). Plus you are anxious (which increases your estimates of risk), and the outcome is a dreaded event (disability or death). The more times you look at this biased information, the higher the risk seems to you and the more likely you are to worry and seek out reassurance.

4. You Check—Over and Over

You try to reduce your anxiety by checking to make sure that everything is OK. You think, "I may have forgotten something," "I may have failed to notice something," "If I can catch something early, I can prevent worse things from happening," and "I have a responsibility to check these things, since maybe I can do something about them." The key elements of checking are the following:

- If I check, I can reduce uncertainty.
- I cannot tolerate uncertainty.
- If I catch it early, I can prevent worse things from happening.
- I can't rely entirely on my memory.

- I can never be too careful.
- It's my responsibility.

Let's consider two people who are anxious, worried checkers.

Brenda worried that she was looking old and unattractive. Every time she thought this, she thought she should look in the mirror to make sure her makeup was right and that her face hadn't fallen. She would inspect her face in a high-magnification mirror and notice a wrinkle or notice a broken capillary in her eye. This led to more worries about her looks fading. Brenda said, "I check the mirror to make sure I can catch something and do something about it." The "do something about it" involved retouching the makeup, hiding in the shadows of a room, or even refusing to go to social events. Brenda believed that hiding in the shadows kept people from seeing how old and unattractive she was and that avoiding parties when she didn't feel just right kept her from facing people at her worst.

Brenda's checking led to three things: fixing her makeup, further checking, and avoiding parties or sitting in the light. In each case, the checking actually reduced her anxiety, since fixing her makeup made her feel better, and avoiding parties (or the light) made her feel safer. Consequently, Brenda could not learn that going to parties without double-checking could actually help her overcome her worries. How could she ever find out that she was wrong about these beliefs unless she gave up the double-checking and the hiding?

Debbie was worried that her boyfriend hadn't called, so she checked her answering machine every thirty minutes. When she didn't receive a call in the first two hours, she called her machine to leave a message and then checked the message, to see if the answering machine was working. Her thought was, "If I check, I might find out he called, and then I'll stop worrying." But what was really bothering her was this thought: "If he doesn't call right when I want him to, then it means he's dumping me."

Debbie's checking was driven by the thought that she could feel reassured by getting his message immediately. When she took action and checked her answering machine, this led her to believe that she was taking control by finding out what was really going on. Debbie told me that she needed to know whether he was dumping her. Because she was so driven by her need to know for sure, she actually provoked her boyfriend into fights just to get things finalized: "I guess I thought that if I could just end it, I wouldn't have to worry anymore about it ending."

Checking is a *compulsion,* a behavior that you use to decrease your anxiety. It is driven by an obsessive thought or a worry.[6] The worry might be "Maybe there's something wrong with the airplane," so you check for sights and sounds of mechanical malfunction. Or the checking might involve examining your breasts or your skin daily for any signs of cancer developing. Each time you check it is driven by the thought "I should make sure I don't have cancer." You check, find you don't have a lump, and feel relieved. Or you check, find a lump, run to the doctor and ask for a biopsy, and the doctor reassures you it's nothing. You feel better for *one hour*. And then you wonder where this doctor went to medical school and whether she is as smart as you used to think she was.

Checking can never address your fundamental concern: "I can't stand uncertainty." The costs are that you are nervous, you spend a lot of time and energy checking, and you reinforce your belief that you need to check to be safe. What are the benefits? You feel better for an hour, but then you check again.

5. You Avoid Discomfort

A very common strategy to deal with your worries is to avoid or procrastinate about things that make you anxious or worried. If you are worried about your taxes, then you avoid filing. If you are worried that you are not the prettiest woman in the world, then you avoid parties. If you see a man who looks attractive but worry that he'll reject you, then you avoid eye contact. If you are worried that you might have a disease, then you don't go to doctors.

Avoiding things that make you worry works immediately.[7] However, it reinforces the belief that you are not competent to handle these problems, and this makes you even more worried about them in the future. Furthermore, you do not have the opportunity to find out that you can handle things on your own. *You have no chance to disconfirm your negative beliefs.*

6. You Numb Yourself with Alcohol, Drugs, or Food

Every anxiety disorder and depression is associated with an increase in the abuse of alcohol, drugs, and food. If you are worried that you will lose your job, you overeat and drink excessively to calm yourself. If you worry about being ignored at a party, you have several drinks or smoke marijuana to "take the edge off." Numbing yourself with drugs, alcohol, or food tells you that you cannot handle your worries or your feelings. You never think these things through and examine how irrational your thinking really is.

The great appeal of numbing and escape is that it works immediately and it's easily available. And the costs can be put off—at least for a few hours. You won't get sick until later, your hangover is tomorrow, and you can enjoy the pot and avoid thinking about life in the real world because your motivation or ambition will be reduced. You can put off the costs until later— very much like your American Express bill, at 20 percent interest.

You can run away from your feelings—numbing yourself, getting high, or stuffing down food. Perhaps it seems less threatening to do these things. But the problem is that you won't be able to really find out what is bothering you and solve the problems that you have.[8] As a result, you'll have two problems—the anxiety and the self-defeating behavior.

7. You Overprepare

You worry that you have to give a talk next week. Although you know that you are very competent and that you have considerable expertise on this topic, you begin to worry, "What if my mind goes blank? What if someone asks me a question that I can't answer?" You are aware that you are fairly bright, and you have worked on this material and read what needs to be read . . . but *you don't know everything.* You're not perfect. So you think that the thing to do is prepare your talk right down to the last word so that you can read it from your paper. You get up there and read it to the group and . . . well, you're really boring.

You were worried that being even a little spontaneous would leave you vulnerable to forgetting and getting sidetracked. You didn't forget—but you sounded mechanical. You think, "I need to be completely prepared so that I will never lose my train of thought." You think that everything has to be totally predictable and in your control or else things will unravel. So next time you overprepare even more and rehearse in front of a video camera—thirty times. And you are still boring.

Being overprepared feeds right back into the belief that you have to be totally in control of your worries or everything will fall apart. It also feeds into your worry that if you are not perfect you will sound like an idiot. And, of course, you equate sounding like an idiot—or pausing, or going off track for one minute, or feeling not completely sure—with not knowing *everything.* Ironically, researchers found that speakers who were rated higher in quality actually prepared very little right before the talk. They just felt they knew the material. The speakers the audience liked least were the ones who prepared the most right before the talk.[9]

Overpreparing doesn't work because it is never possible to be completely prepared—there are always unknowns. Most importantly, it reinforces your belief that you have to be perfect and know everything in order to feel safe.

8. You Use Safety Behaviors

When we feel worried or anxious, we use "safety behaviors." These are things we do that make us feel momentarily safe and secure. For example, if you have to give a speech but are afraid that you will sound nervous, you will overprepare and read your talk as I described above, but you will also tense up, avoid looking at the audience, not drink from the water glass because you don't want anyone to see your hands shaking, keep asking yourself if you forgot something, keep checking your notes, pray, sigh, and take deep breaths because you think this will calm you.

Safety behaviors are very common, and we often don't realize we're engaging in them until someone points them out. For example, a man with a fear of driving across bridges had the following safety behaviors: drive really slowly, plan way ahead so as to anticipate every possible bridge, avoid looking over the edge, drive on the inside lane, not look in the rearview mirror, clutch the steering wheel, breathe deeply, and pump the brakes. He thought each one of these safety behaviors gave him more of a sense of control. Of course, the reality was that engaging in these safety behaviors reinforced his belief that he had no real control while he was driving across bridges.

Safety behaviors are important in *maintaining* fear and worry.[10] Continued use of these safety behaviors only reconfirms that you cannot handle the situation on your own and that it will remain dangerous or problematic unless you "protect" yourself with these cautionary safety behaviors. Once you relinquish them and expose yourself to the things that you are afraid of, you will realize that you really are OK without these safety behaviors.

Look at Table 2.2 and see if any of these examples of safety behaviors sound familiar.

TABLE 2.2	
EXAMPLES OF SAFETY BEHAVIORS	
Worry	*Safety behaviors*
I'll make a fool of myself speaking to that group.	Overprepare, read notes, rehearse over and over, avoid looking at the audience, scan the audience for signs of rejection, don't pick up water glass because of fear of hands shaking.
I'll get rejected by that attractive person at the party.	Wait for the person to talk to me, avoid eye contact, smile stupidly so I'll look friendly, lower my voice so I don't call attention to myself, answer in short statements, leave as soon as the conversation drags.
I'll lose control of my car and go over the side of the bridge.	Avoid bridges, have someone accompany me, turn off the radio because it distracts me, pump brakes, slow down, avoid looking over the side.
My anxiety will make me breathe so fast I'll suffocate.	Avoid vigorous exercise, take deep breaths, yawn, watch my breathing, look for exits.
When I'm anxious I'll get dizzy and fall.	Look for places to sit down, walk slowly, tense my body, take deep breaths, avoid walking too far, check my pulse, ask someone to accompany me.

9. You Always Try to Make a Great Impression

You might worry about how you look, whether you will have anything interesting to say, whether anyone will even initiate a conversation with you, and whether you will say something stupid and awkward. You worry about whether people will see your anxiety, insecurity, and awkwardness, and then judge you severely.

Your thought is, "If I don't make a really good impression in everything that I do, then people will think less of me." Then you carry it a bit further: "They'll think I'm a loser and word will spread." As I noted in the section on why worry makes sense to you, worriers were brought up with insecure attachment to their parents, emphasis on what other people think and feel, a responsibility to soothe other people's feelings, and lack of warmth. As a consequence of these problematic experiences during childhood, you feel insecure about being liked or maintaining relationships, you focus too intently on making everyone feel good about you, and you are hypervigilant about mind reading—"What are they thinking?" If you believe that you always have to really impress people, you will anticipate being judged by the harshest critics—and worry accordingly.

10. You Ruminate, Chewing It Over and Over

When you ruminate, you chew things over and over, like a cow chews its cud. Rumination is a little different from worry. Worry involves predictions about what will happen in the *future,* while rumination involves a review of what is going on now or what happened before. People who ruminate are far more likely to be depressed and anxious, and they are more likely to have reoccurrences of depression and anxiety.[11] Moreover, women are more likely to ruminate than men are.

If you ruminate, you believe that if you keep thinking about your problem you will find a solution, stop feeling bad, and stop ruminating. This belief in the utility of rumination is completely false. Rumination increases your awareness of how bad you feel—you become internally focused on your bad feelings. It reduces your awareness of positive feelings or alternatives, and it reduces the likelihood that you will seek out positive behaviors or rewards. Ruminators are often looking for a simple explanation for everything, and they can't stand having mixed feelings.[12] Furthermore, you reject potential solutions because they are imperfect, and you continue to ruminate until you can decide on a perfect solution—which is never forthcoming. You're chewing things over because *there is some reality you can't swallow*.

11. You Demand Certainty

You may think that achieving certainty—and achieving it *now*—will make you feel less anxious, but searching for certainty actually makes you more worried. *There is no certainty in an uncertain world*. You keep thinking, "I've got to be sure," and you keep worrying until you can feel sure. Once you have the feeling of being sure, you examine whether you have the perfect solution—one with no possibility of a flaw. As you examine your solution you realize that it is not perfect—there's still some uncertainty—and so you worry some more.

Because anything is possible, looking for certainty will guarantee only one thing—more worry. Living with uncertainty is living in the real world.

12. You Refuse to Accept the Fact That You Have "Crazy" Thoughts

Many people worry over thoughts that seem out of character.[13] Almost everyone reports having "crazy" thoughts about things that are disgusting, illegal, or violent.[14] Three things go on that make people worry about these thoughts. First, you interpret them as a sign of losing control and going crazy. Second, you feel ashamed and guilty about these thoughts. Third, you think you have to get rid of these thoughts immediately.

Worriers of all kinds believe that their thoughts or impulses are signs that something really bad is about to happen. For example, people with panic disorder worry that their thoughts that they could have a panic attack predict a panic attack; people with obsessive-compulsive disorder believe that their thoughts about losing control predict they will act violently or inappropriately; people with social anxiety disorder believe that thinking their mind will go blank predicts losing control of all thought processes in front of other people. Worriers also tend to believe that their thoughts will lead to action (thought-action fusion) and consequently fear their "crazy" thoughts.[15]

It is quite useful to ask yourself, "How many times have I had these 'crazy' thoughts?" and "How many times have these predictions actually come true?" Research on people with obsessive-compulsive disorder indicates that almost 30 percent of these people have pure obsessions—unwanted thoughts—*without* any associated behavioral rituals or compulsions. Thinking about something is not the same as doing it or proof that you will do it.

Many people believe that having certain thoughts means that they are immoral, disgusting, or uniquely messed up.[16] These thoughts are presumed to reveal something central about your character or sanity. Character and sanity, however, are not determined by your thoughts—they are determined by what you actually do. For example, if you have violent thoughts and images, the real question is whether you are *acting* on them. If you are not, these thoughts say nothing about your character.

Fighting to get rid of these thoughts, rather than acknowledging that they are normal, only increases your worry.

Summing Up

Like many people who worry, you have been relying on strategies, techniques, and advice that you thought would help. You may have been surprised that some of these things not only don't help but may even make matters worse. The "dirty dozen" don't work because they convince you that you cannot face your fears, you should not think about the worst outcome, you should avoid things that upset you, you need someone else to tell you that you will be OK, you cannot face uncertainty, and you need to get rid of negative emotion. These useless techniques keep you from disconfirming your negative beliefs about worry. Knowing that you should avoid these strategies will help you in overcoming your worries. You will have to learn how to break these bad habits—which you may have thought of as "solutions."

I have summarized these useless strategies in the table below. Keep this table as a list of things not to do.

TABLE 2.3

THE WORST WAYS TO HANDLE WORRY

1. Seeking reassurance
2. Trying to stop your thoughts
3. Collecting information
4. Checking over and over
5. Avoiding discomfort
6. Numbing yourself with alcohol, drugs, and food
7. Overpreparing
8. Using safety behaviors
9. Always trying to make a great impression
10. Ruminating—chewing it over and over
11. Demanding certainty
12. Refusing to accept the fact that you have crazy thoughts

Now that you know what you should *not* do to handle your worry, it's time to find out more about your personal style of worrying. Not all worriers are alike. Let's look at your worry profile. Once you understand what particular issues you worry about—and how this is related to your style of worry and your personality—you will be better able to target your worries and change them.

3

Take Your Worry Profile

You don't worry about everything. Some of us worry about relationships, others worry about money, and still others worry about our health. We have already established that you are someone worried about your worry, but we haven't figured out yet the specific areas that you worry about. In this chapter, we will develop your personal worry profile. This will involve the following dimensions of your worry:

- Do you worry too much?
- What areas of your life do you worry about?
- How do you think about your worry?
- Can you tolerate uncertainty?
- How is your worry related to your personality?

Each of us has a different profile for how and why we worry. Included in this chapter are five questionnaires that can help you discover your worry profile. These results will help you focus on the techniques in this book that will be the most helpful to you.

Do You Worry Too Much?
The Penn State Worry Questionnaire

Tom Borkovec and his colleagues at Pennsylvania State University have developed a rather straightforward measure called the Penn State Worry Questionnaire (PSWQ), which can be used to determine if you worry more than most people.[1] The PSWQ really consists of one general factor—*worry*.[2] Scores on the PSWQ are related to overall anxiety level and are also related to problematic coping styles, such as blaming yourself, dreading, wishful thinking, and avoiding problems.[3]

TABLE 3.1

PENN STATE WORRY QUESTIONNAIRE

Enter the number that best describes how typical or characteristic each item is of you, putting the number next to the item.

1	2	3	4	5
Not at all typical		Somewhat typical		Very typical

_____ 1. If I don't have enough time to do everything, I don't worry about it. (R)

_____ 2. My worries overwhelm me.

_____ 3. I do not tend to worry about things. (R)

_____ 4. Many situations make me worry.

_____ 5. I know I shouldn't worry about things, but I just cannot help it.

_____ 6. When I am under pressure I worry a lot.

_____ 7. I am always worrying about something.

_____ 8. I find it easy to dismiss worrisome thoughts. (R)

_____ 9. As soon as I finish one task, I start to worry about everything else I have to do.

_____ 10. I never worry about anything. (R)

_____ 11. When there is nothing more I can do about a concern, I don't worry about it anymore. (R)

_____   12. I've been a worrier all my life.

_____   13. I notice that I have been worrying about things.

_____   14. Once I start worrying, I can't stop.

_____   15. I worry all the time.

_____   16. I worry about projects until they are done.

Your Total Score: _____

(R) indicates a reverse score. To reverse score your question, if you give an answer of 1 ("not at all typical"), score it as a 5. If you answer 2, score it as a 4. If you answer 4, score it as a 2. If you answer 5, score it as a 1. A score of 3 remains unchanged.

Add up your scores on the test—and be sure to note which items are reverse scored (see above for how to reverse score your responses). People with some problems with worry score on average above 52, and really chronic worriers score above 65. Nonanxious people average around 30.[4] It is also quite possible to score below the clinical range (somewhere between 30 and 52) but still feel that your worries are bothering you. If your scores are elevated on the Penn State Worry Test, you might want to examine which areas in your life are the main sources of your worries. Let's look at that now.

What Areas of Your Life Do You Worry About? The Worry Domains Questionnaire

The second test assesses the different areas in your life that you worry about. For example, are you more likely to worry about money and work, or are you more likely to worry about your future and relationships? Or do you worry about everything? I have found that some people who worry about relationships might not worry about work; another person who worries about work does not worry about her health. College students worry most about interpersonal relationships and academic performance and least about physical harm.[5] Higher scores on the Worry Domains Questionnaire (WDQ) are related to maladaptive behaviors that include smoking, drinking and eating, and depression.[6] Let's now look at these different areas of your life and see what tends to get to you.[7]

TABLE 3.2
WORRY DOMAINS QUESTIONNAIRE

Please check the appropriate box to indicate how much you worry about the following:

I worry . . .	Not at all	A little	Moderately	Quite a bit	Extremely
	0	1	2	3	4
1. That my money will run out	☐	☐	☐	☐	☐
2. That I cannot be assertive or express my opinions	☐	☐	☐	☐	☐
3. That my future job prospects are not good	☐	☐	☐	☐	☐
4. That my family will be angry with me or disapprove of something that I do	☐	☐	☐	☐	☐
5. That I'll never achieve my ambitions	☐	☐	☐	☐	☐
6. That I will not keep my workload up to date	☐	☐	☐	☐	☐
7. That financial problems will restrict holidays and travel	☐	☐	☐	☐	☐
8. That I have no concentration	☐	☐	☐	☐	☐
9. That I am not able to afford things	☐	☐	☐	☐	☐
10. That I feel insecure	☐	☐	☐	☐	☐

I worry . . .	Not at all	A little	Moderately	Quite a bit	Extremely
	0	1	2	3	4
11. That I can't afford to pay bills	☐	☐	☐	☐	☐
12. That my living conditions are inadequate	☐	☐	☐	☐	☐
13. That life may have no purpose	☐	☐	☐	☐	☐
14. That I don't work hard enough	☐	☐	☐	☐	☐
15. That others will not approve of me	☐	☐	☐	☐	☐
16. That I find it difficult to maintain a stable relationship	☐	☐	☐	☐	☐
17. That I leave work unfinished	☐	☐	☐	☐	☐
18. That I lack confidence	☐	☐	☐	☐	☐
19. That I am unattractive	☐	☐	☐	☐	☐
20. That I might make myself look stupid	☐	☐	☐	☐	☐
21. That I will lose close friends	☐	☐	☐	☐	☐
22. That I haven't achieved much	☐	☐	☐	☐	☐
23. That I am not loved	☐	☐	☐	☐	☐
24. That I will be late for an appointment	☐	☐	☐	☐	☐
25. That I make mistakes at work	☐	☐	☐	☐	☐

The Worry Domains Questionnaire breaks down into five general areas of worry: relationships, lack of confidence, aimless future, work, and finances.[8] You can find your score for each of these areas by adding up your scores for the questions indicated in the table below. An answer of "not at all" is scored as 0 and a score of "extremely" is scored as 4, with the intervening answers corresponding to the numbers near the top of Table 3.3. In the table below you can find your score for each of the worry domains by adding up your scores on the items indicated. Then, in the right column, write out your total score on that domain.

TABLE 3.3	
Your Worry Domain	*Your Score*
Relationships Add items 4, 16, 19, 21, 23	
Lack of confidence Add items 2, 10, 15, 18, 20	
Aimless future Add items 3, 5, 8, 13, 22	
Work Add items 6, 14, 17, 24, 25	
Finances Add items 1, 7, 9, 11, 12	
Your total score (Add all scores in the right column)	

On average, chronic worriers (people with generalized anxiety disorder) score 5.7 for relationships, 10.2 for lack of confidence, 9.5 for aimless future, 7.7 for work, and 7.1 for financial issues. People with GAD have an average overall score of 40 on the WDQ.[9] Even if your overall score is not in the range for someone with GAD, you can see if your worry in certain areas decreases as you use the techniques in this book.

Let's look at how two different people responded to the Worry Domains Questionnaire. Paul is working for a major investment company. He has very high standards for himself when it comes to making money. He gets to the office before anyone else, he reads all the financial magazines and newspapers, and he tries to do research on different companies that he might evaluate for his firm. Although he seems to be doing well at work, he complains that he is worried about things getting out of control—losing his edge. On the WDQ he indicates that he worries "I'll never achieve my ambitions" and "I will not keep my workload up to date." He also says, "I have no concentration," "I leave work unfinished," and "I make mistakes at work." Paul's worries are focused on his demanding standards at work—he wants to be number one.

Contrast this with Lenore. She is also very smart, and she has a good job. She works hard, and her work is often difficult and challenging. But she doesn't seem to worry about it. On the WDQ Lenore worries about the following: "my family will be angry with me or disapprove of something that I do," "I feel insecure," "I lack confidence," "I am unattractive," "I might make myself look stupid," and "I am not loved." Lenore's worries are about relationships and lacking confidence—being loved and approved of, and letting other people down.

How You Think About Your Worry: The Metacognitions Questionnaire

One of the most intriguing areas of work in recent years is the research and theory conducted by psychologist Adrian Wells. According to Wells, when we worry we have conflicting thoughts about our mental activity. This is called a "metacognitive" model—where *meta-* means "standing above" and *cognitive* means "having to do with thoughts." Thus, his model attempts to account for how we stand back and think about our thoughts—especially when we are worrying. Wells developed a questionnaire that taps the various theories or thoughts that we have about our worry. The Metacognitions Questionnaire (MCQ) consists of thirty questions.[10]

TABLE 3.4

METACOGNITIONS QUESTIONNAIRE 30

This questionnaire is concerned with beliefs people have about their thinking. Listed below are a number of beliefs that people have expressed. Please read each item and say how much you *generally* agree with it by circling the appropriate number. Please respond to all the items; there are no right or wrong answers.

	Do not agree	Agree slightly	Agree moderately	Agree very much
1. Worrying helps me to avoid problems in the future	1	2	3	4
2. My worrying is dangerous for me	1	2	3	4
3. I think a lot about my thoughts	1	2	3	4
4. I could make myself sick with worrying	1	2	3	4
5. I am aware of the way my mind works when I am thinking through a problem	1	2	3	4
6. If I did not control a worrying thought, and then it happened, it would be my fault	1	2	3	4
7. I need to worry in order to remain organized	1	2	3	4
8. I have little confidence in my memory for words and names	1	2	3	4
9. My worrying thoughts persist, no matter how I try to stop them	1	2	3	4

	Do not agree	Agree slightly	Agree moderately	Agree very much
10. Worrying helps me to get things sorted out in my mind	1	2	3	4
11. I cannot ignore my worrying thoughts	1	2	3	4
12. I monitor my thoughts	1	2	3	4
13. I should be in control of my thoughts all of the time	1	2	3	4
14. My memory can mislead me at times	1	2	3	4
15. My worrying could make me go mad	1	2	3	4
16. I am constantly aware of my thinking	1	2	3	4
17. I have a poor memory	1	2	3	4
18. I pay close attention to the way my mind works	1	2	3	4
19. Worrying helps me cope	1	2	3	4
20. Not being able to control my thoughts is a sign of weakness	1	2	3	4
21. When I start worrying, I cannot stop	1	2	3	4
22. I will be punished for not controlling certain thoughts	1	2	3	4
23. Worrying helps me to solve problems	1	2	3	4
24. I have little confidence in my memory for places	1	2	3	4
25. It is bad to think certain thoughts	1	2	3	4
26. I do not trust my memory	1	2	3	4
27. If I could not control my thoughts, I would not be able to function	1	2	3	4
28. I need to worry, in order to work well	1	2	3	4
29. I have little confidence in my memory for actions	1	2	3	4
30. I constantly examine my thoughts	1	2	3	4

This questionnaire pinpoints the five most common ideas about worry. These include *positive worry beliefs* ("Worrying helps me to avoid problems in the future"), *beliefs about the uncontrollability and danger of worry* ("My worrying is dangerous for me"), *beliefs about your cognitive confidence or competence* ("I have difficulty knowing if I have actually done something, or just imagined it"), *the need to control your worry* ("If I did not control a worrying thought, and then it happened, it would be my fault"), and *cognitive self-consciousness* ("I think a lot about my thoughts").

These factors reflect conflicting functions that you believe worry serves. For example, you may have positive views of worry and at the same time believe that worry is uncontrollable and dangerous. You may also distrust your own memory, believing that there is something that you may overlook. This distrust in your memory may make you worry that you will neglect something. You may be scanning your mind to monitor your own thoughts, continually focusing on what you are thinking, perhaps because you believe your worry thoughts may signal impending danger. Go through the Metacognitions Questionnaire, score it using the scoring key that I have provided below, and then examine the degree to which your worries fall along these five dimensions.

In order to determine your score for each of these five factors, use the table opposite. Thus, to find your score for positive worry beliefs, add up your scores for each of the six questions listed (1, 7, 10, 19, 23, 28). Go through each of the factors this way. Then, at the end, add up your scores for all of the factors. Although there are no established norms yet for this scale, you will be able to see if you are relatively more elevated on certain factors than others.

Let's look at Carl's responses. He is worried about his finances, since his business has taken a downturn in the past year. Carl complains that he can't seem to get a handle on his worry, and he can't keep his mind on his work. He also believes that he is responsible for making sure that he covers everything to take

| TABLE 3.5 | |
Factor—Your Theory About Your Worry	Your Score
Positive worry beliefs 1, 7, 10, 19, 23, 28	
Uncontrollability and danger 2, 4, 9, 11, 15, 21	
Cognitive confidence 8, 14, 17, 24, 26, 29	
Need for control 6, 13, 20, 22, 25, 27	
Cognitive self-consciousness 3, 5, 12, 16, 18, 30	

care of his business and his family. Carl is elevated on the factors of uncontrollability and danger, cognitive competence, and general negative beliefs about worry. Carl is suffering from generalized anxiety disorder and depression and feels incapacitated by his worry. In contrast to the debilitating effects that Carl is experiencing, Bonita is worried about whether she will be able to take care of herself financially in the event of a divorce. Although a divorce seems unlikely, she is beset with worries that she is not prepared to live on her own. Bonita has elevations on the positive worry beliefs, since she believes that her worry may lead her to a solution. She is also elevated on cognitive competence, since she does not believe that she is able to process all of the financial information that she will need to examine. However, Bonita does not believe that her worry is too much out of control or dangerous, and she is not overly concerned with a sense of responsibility. What is interesting in contrasting these two individuals is that Carl is an overly conscientious, somewhat compulsive personality who believes that he must take care of everyone in his family and that he should succeed at everything he pursues. Bonita, in contrast, is a dependent and somewhat histrionic (dramatic) personality, more worried about the loss of a relationship and her potential for helplessness if she is on her own.

Are You Intolerant of Uncertainty? The Intolerance of Uncertainty Scale

All of us experience uncertainty on a regular basis, but people differ considerably in their attitude toward it. The Intolerance of Uncertainty Scale (IUS) is related to your overall anxiety and worry.[11] People with higher intolerance of uncertainty are more likely to focus on information (or words) denoting uncertainty and to interpret uncertainty as threatening. Research has shown that intolerance of uncertainty precedes worry and that changes in intolerance of uncertainty will reduce worry and generalized anxiety disorder in general.[12]

Look at the scale below and check off your responses.[13]

TABLE 3.6

INTOLERANCE OF UNCERTAINTY SCALE (IUS)

You will find below a series of statements that describe how people may react to the uncertainties of life. Please use the scale below to describe to what extent each item is characteristic of you (please write the number that describes you best in the space before each item).

1	2	3	4	5
Not at all characteristic of me	A little characteristic of me	Somewhat characteristic of me	Very characteristic of me	Entirely characteristic of me

_____ 1. Uncertainty stops me from having a firm opinion.

_____ 2. Being uncertain means that a person is disorganized.

_____ 3. Uncertainty makes life intolerable.

_____ 4. It's not fair that there are no guarantees in life.

_____ 5. My mind can't be relaxed if I don't know what will happen tomorrow.

_____ 6. Uncertainty makes me uneasy, anxious, or stressed.

_____ 7. Unforeseen events upset me greatly.

_____ 8. It frustrates me not having all the information I need.

_____ 9. Being uncertain allows me to foresee the consequences beforehand and to prepare for them.

_____ 10. One should always look ahead so as to avoid surprises.

_____ 11. A small unforeseen event can spoil everything, even with the best of planning.

_____ 12. When it's time to act, uncertainty paralyzes me.

_____ 13. Being uncertain means that I am not first-rate.

_____ 14. When I am uncertain I can't go forward.

_____ 15. When I am uncertain I can't function very well.

_____ 16. Unlike me, others always seem to know where they are going with their lives.

_____ 17. Uncertainty makes me vulnerable, unhappy, or sad.

_____ 18. I always want to know what the future has in store for me.

_____ 19. I hate being taken by surprise.

_____ 20. The smallest doubt stops me from acting.

_____ 21. I should be able to organize everything in advance.

_____ 22. Being uncertain means that I lack confidence.

_____ 23. I think it's unfair that other people seem sure about their future.

_____ 24. Uncertainty stops me from sleeping well.

_____ 25. I must get away from uncertain situations.

_____ 26. The ambiguities in life stress me.

_____ 27. I can't stand being undecided about my future.

_____   Total score (sum of your scores above)

There are five different factors on the IUS:

1. Uncertainty is unacceptable and should be avoided.
2. Uncertainty reflects badly on a person.

3. Uncertainty is frustrating.
4. Uncertainty causes stress.
5. Uncertainty prevents action.

In order to obtain your total score, simply add up your responses for each question. Overall scores below 40 reflect tolerance of some uncertainty, scores above 50 reflect problems with uncertainty, and scores above 70 suggest real problems handling uncertainty.[14] People with GAD score 87 on average on the IUS.[15] However, even if your score is below 87, your intolerance of uncertainty can be a factor in your worry and anxiety.

Take Carl, whose business problems were described above. He was highly intolerant of uncertainty, indicating to me that this was exactly his problem—the need to know for sure. Carl's score in the IUS was 108, indicating an extraordinary level of intolerance of uncertainty. Carl's assumptions were that if he did not know for sure what was going to happen with his business, then it was going to end up as a disaster. Interestingly, though, his intolerance of uncertainty was entirely focused on finances and business, not on his relationship with his wife or his health.

How Is Your Worry Related to Your Personality? The Personal Beliefs Questionnaire

Some people are concerned about being criticized, others worry about loved ones leaving, and some of us worry about not living up to our own standards. Psychologists have categorized people according to these different personality types and have linked certain beliefs to these personalities. For example, a person who has low self-esteem and who believes that he cannot assert himself in a relationship might worry that people will reject him and abandon him. If his self-esteem is low, he might worry that he cannot take care of himself on his own. Another person might think that she should be responsible and in control all the time.[16]

This kind of person, the overly conscientious type, might worry that she might make mistakes, do something that might be viewed as unethical, or lose control of things in her life.

Psychologists at the University of Pennsylvania Medical School have developed a questionnaire that taps your beliefs about different things in your life—especially how you view yourself and your relationships. It's called the Personal Beliefs Questionnaire (PBQ).[17] Go through this questionnaire and check off the answers that best fit the way you think and feel. Then we'll go back and look at the patterns that might emerge from your responses.

TABLE 3.7

PERSONALITY BELIEFS QUESTIONNAIRE—SHORT FORM

Please read the statements below and rate *how much you believe each one*. Try to judge how you feel about each statement *most of the time*. Do not leave any statements blank.

4—I believe it totally
3—I believe it very much
2—I believe it moderately
1—I believe it slightly
0—I don't believe it at all

1. Being exposed as inferior or inadequate will be intolerable.	4	3	2	1	0
2. I should avoid unpleasant situations at all costs.	4	3	2	1	0
3. If people act friendly, they may be trying to use or exploit me.	4	3	2	1	0
4. I have to resist the domination of authorities but at the same time maintain their approval and acceptance.	4	3	2	1	0
5. I cannot tolerate unpleasant feelings.	4	3	2	1	0
6. Flaws, defects, or mistakes are intolerable.	4	3	2	1	0
7. Other people are often too demanding.	4	3	2	1	0

8. I should be the center of attention.	4	3	2	1	0
9. If I don't have systems, everything will fall apart.	4	3	2	1	0
10. It's intolerable if I'm not accorded my due respect or don't get what I'm entitled to.	4	3	2	1	0
11. It is important to do a perfect job on everything.	4	3	2	1	0
12. I enjoy doing things more by myself than with other people.	4	3	2	1	0
13. Other people try to use me or manipulate me if I don't watch out.	4	3	2	1	0
14. Other people have hidden motives.	4	3	2	1	0
15. The worst possible thing would be to be abandoned.	4	3	2	1	0
16. Other people should recognize how special I am.	4	3	2	1	0
17. Other people will deliberately try to demean me.	4	3	2	1	0
18. I need others to help me make decisions or tell me what to do.	4	3	2	1	0
19. Details are extremely important.	4	3	2	1	0
20. If I regard people as too bossy, I have a right to disregard their demands.	4	3	2	1	0
21. Authority figures tend to be intrusive, demanding, interfering, and controlling.	4	3	2	1	0
22. The way to get what I want is to dazzle or amuse people.	4	3	2	1	0
23. I should do whatever I can get away with.	4	3	2	1	0
24. If other people find out things about me, they will use them against me.	4	3	2	1	0
25. Relationships are messy and interfere with freedom.	4	3	2	1	0
26. Only people as brilliant as I am understand me.	4	3	2	1	0

27. Since I am so superior, I am entitled to special treatment and privileges.	4	3	2	1	0
28. It is important for me to be free and independent of others.	4	3	2	1	0
29. In many situations, I am better off to be left alone.	4	3	2	1	0
30. It is necessary to stick to the highest standards at all times, or things will fall apart.	4	3	2	1	0
31. Unpleasant feelings will escalate and get out of control.	4	3	2	1	0
32. We live in a jungle and the strong person is the one who survives.	4	3	2	1	0
33. I should avoid situations in which I attract attention, or be as inconspicuous as possible.	4	3	2	1	0
34. If I don't keep others engaged with me, they won't like me.	4	3	2	1	0
35. If I want something, I should do whatever is necessary to get it.	4	3	2	1	0
36. It's better to be alone than to feel "stuck" with other people.	4	3	2	1	0
37. Unless I entertain or impress people, I am nothing.	4	3	2	1	0
38. People will get at me if I don't get them first.	4	3	2	1	0
39. Any signs of tension in a relationship indicate the relationship has gone bad; therefore, I should cut it off.	4	3	2	1	0
40. If I don't perform at the highest level, I will fail.	4	3	2	1	0
41. Making deadlines, complying with demands, and conforming are direct blows to my pride and self-sufficiency.	4	3	2	1	0
42. I have been unfairly treated and am entitled to get my fair share by whatever means I can.	4	3	2	1	0
43. If people get close to me, they will discover the "real" me and reject me.	4	3	2	1	0

44. I am needy and weak.	4	3	2	1	0
45. I am helpless when I'm left on my own.	4	3	2	1	0
46. Other people should satisfy my needs.	4	3	2	1	0
47. If I follow the rules the way people expect, it will inhibit my freedom of action.	4	3	2	1	0
48. People will take advantage of me if I give them the chance.	4	3	2	1	0
49. I have to be on guard at all times.	4	3	2	1	0
50. My privacy is much more important to me than closeness to people.	4	3	2	1	0
51. Rules are arbitrary and stifle me.	4	3	2	1	0
52. It is awful if people ignore me.	4	3	2	1	0
53. What other people think doesn't matter to me.	4	3	2	1	0
54. In order to be happy, I need other people to pay attention to me.	4	3	2	1	0
55. If I entertain people, they will not notice my weaknesses.	4	3	2	1	0
56. I need somebody around available at all times to help me to carry out what I need to do or in case something bad happens.	4	3	2	1	0
57. Any flaw or defect in performance may lead to a catastrophe.	4	3	2	1	0
58. Since I am so talented, people should go out of their way to promote my career.	4	3	2	1	0
59. If I don't push other people, I will get pushed around.	4	3	2	1	0
60. I don't have to be bound by the rules that apply to other people.	4	3	2	1	0
61. Force or cunning is the best way to get things done.	4	3	2	1	0
62. I must maintain access to my supporter or helper at all times.	4	3	2	1	0
63. I am basically alone—unless I can attach myself to a stronger person.	4	3	2	1	0

64. I cannot trust other people.	4	3	2	1	0
65. I can't cope as other people can.	4	3	2	1	0

In order to get your score for the different scales (or personality types) go through your responses and add up your total score for the items that correspond to each scale. For example, sum up your responses for the first scale, "avoidant," and write that number in the column labeled "raw score." You can use the table below to enter your scores.

TABLE 3.8

SCORING KEY, PERSONALITY BELIEF QUESTIONNAIRE—SHORT FORM[18]

PBQ scale	Sum items to calculate raw score	Raw score	Use formula to calculate your score	Your score
Avoidant	Sum items 1, 2, 5, 31, 33, 39, 43	____	(Raw score— 10.86)/6.46	____
Dependent	Sum items 15, 18, 44, 45, 56, 62, 63	____	(Raw score— 9.26)/6.12	____
Passive-Aggressive	Sum items 4, 7, 20, 21, 41, 47, 51	____	(Raw score— 8.09)/5.97	____
Obsessive-Compulsive	Sum items 6, 9, 11, 19, 30, 40, 57	____	(Raw score— 10.56)/7.20	____
Antisocial	Sum items 23, 32, 35, 38, 42, 59, 61	____	(Raw score— 4.25)/4.30	____
Narcissistic	Sum items 10, 16, 26, 27, 46, 58, 60	____	(Raw score— 3.42)/4.23	____
Histrionic	Sum items 8, 22, 34, 37, 52, 54, 55	____	(Raw score— 6.47)/6.09	____
Schizoid	Sum items 12, 25, 28, 29, 36, 50, 53	____	(Raw score— 8.99)/5.60	____
Paranoid	Sum items 3, 13, 14, 17, 24, 48, 49	____	(Raw score— 6.99)/6.22	____
Borderline	Sum items 31, 44, 45, 49, 56, 64, 65	____	(Raw score— 8.07)/6.05	____

Again, we do not yet have norms for each of these personality styles—but you can look at the pattern of your scores and see which styles are elevated for you. Keep in mind that we all tend to be a mix of personality styles—very rarely is anyone exclusively one style.

Columbia University psychiatrist John Oldham has developed different categories to identify your personality styles. There are both positive and negative aspects for each personality style. For example, if you have the style of being "conscientious," then you are probably a hard worker who takes things seriously—but sometimes your work gets in the way of relationships and having fun. Let's look at some of these personality styles that correspond with some of the scales on the test above.[19]

- *Avoidant—sensitive.* People with this style often have low self-esteem and are sensitive to criticism. They can form relationships with people and open up with them once they have established that they can trust them.

- *Dependent—devoted.* People with this style will often cling in relationships and do a lot to keep the relationship going. They are concerned about being abandoned and left alone. They often feel that they cannot function without someone else in their lives—often someone who they feel will take care of them. They can be very devoted and loyal.

- *Passive-aggressive—leisurely.* These people have mixed feelings about going along with things. They may say that they will do something, but they often don't follow through. They appear to have a casual attitude about deadlines and rules.

- *Compulsive—conscientious.* These people are highly devoted to work and productivity. They often make lists, keep a tight schedule, and have high standards for themselves and other people. They are often viewed as reliable and honest, but sometimes they can be seen as overly devoted to work. Some of these people hoard things because they believe that they might find some use for those items in the future.

- *Antisocial—adventurous.* These people like excitement and taking risks. They often believe that the rules do not apply to them, and they may break the rules just to get what they want. They seek out wild times and can sometimes seem charming and fun to be with. They seem not to care about the rights and needs of other people.

- *Narcissistic—self-confident.* These people believe that they are superior to other people and deserve special attention and admiration. They often can be insensitive to other people; sometimes they are unable to understand how they can offend people. Because they often have a lot of confidence, they may be able to achieve things, although their confidence may not be based on reality.

- *Histrionic—dramatic.* These people are very dramatic and try to impress people with their glamour and personality. They can seem very emotional—which can add to how interesting and exciting they may be. They have a lot of imagination and energy and often focus on their appearance. They try to be sexually attractive and seductive.

Your worries may reflect aspects of your personality, such as your need to be perfect, your fears of abandonment, your concern about approval, your belief that you should be in control of things, and your fear of being controlled by others.

Your Worry Profile

Now that you have completed the five tests in this chapter, you can go back and construct an overview of your worry profile. No two people will have exactly the same worry profile. Overleaf is a table to record your scores for each of these five tests. List your scores on the Penn State Worry Questionnaire, noting in the right column the most elevated items. On the Worry Domains Questionnaire you can list your overall score as well as the items and scores on the specific subscales corresponding to worries about relationships, lack of confidence, finances, and so on. On the Metacognitions Questionnaire, list your scores for the various factors that correspond to positive beliefs about worry, concern about uncontrollability and danger, and the other factors. Similarly, on the Intolerance of Uncertainty Scale, list your overall score and the elevated items. Finally, on the Personal Beliefs Questionnaire, list the elevated subscales that may reflect your mixture of personality styles.

For all the questionnaires, note any specific items that are of particular interest or importance to you.

TABLE 3.9

YOUR WORRY PROFILE

Questionnaire	Specific areas that are elevated or of importance
Penn State Worry Questionnaire	_____
	_____
Worry Domains Questionnaire	Relationships: _____
	Lack of confidence: _____
	Aimless future: _____
	Work: _____
	Financial: _____
	Total score: _____
Metacognitions Questionnaire	Positive worry beliefs: _____
	Uncontrollability and danger: _____
	Cognitive competence: _____
	Need to control your worry: _____
	Cognitive self-consciousness: _____

Intolerance of Uncertainty
Scale   Total score: _____

Personal Belief   Avoidant: _____

Questionnaire   Dependent: _____

                               Passive-aggressive: _____

                               Compulsive: _____

                               Antisocial: _____

                               Narcissistic: _____

                               Histrionic: _____

                               Schizoid: _____

                               Paranoid: _____

                               Borderline: _____

Overall conclusions   _____

about your personality _____

and your worries   _____

Now that you have completed these different tests of your worry and your personality style, you can begin to get a sense of the particular areas of vulnerability that you have. For example, do you seem to worry a lot? Are you more worried about health issues or finances? Do you believe that worry prepares you for the worst? Do you believe that your worry is out of control? Are you intolerant of uncertainty? Are you someone who is more concerned about being abandoned or rejected? Or do you feel you have to do a perfect job on everything because you are so overly conscientious?

Take a few minutes to reflect on your patterns. Write down some of your ideas. Understanding your worry profile will help you as you go through the seven-step program to handle your worries. This is because you can identify the specific problems associated with your worry—for example, is your worry primarily based on intolerance of uncertainty, or do you have the belief that worry protects and prepares, or is your worry related to specific aspects of your personality? By developing your worry profile, not only will you understand your own special style of worry, but you will be able to tailor your self-help to this style.

PART 2

THE SEVEN STEPS TO TAKE CONTROL OF YOUR WORRY

4

Step One: Identify Productive and Unproductive Worry

SOME WORRY IS *PRODUCTIVE*—for example, it's worth thinking about having a map and a full tank of gas before a long trip. *Productive worry* is worry that helps you get problems solved and that leads to action that you can take right now. *Unproductive worry* generates a lot of what-ifs that do not lead to any concrete practical action.[1] Unproductive worry is based on three beliefs: that (1) "If I have a worry, then it is important and I should dwell on it"; (2) "If I have a worry, then I need to identify all of the possible solutions"; and (3) "I cannot accept uncertainty."

Worry More Effectively

In contrast to the naive advice to "just stop worrying," I suggest that you *worry more effectively*. The important thing is to be able to determine when you should pay attention to a particular worry and when to dismiss it. Learning to worry more effectively involves three steps:

1. Distinguish productive worry from unproductive worry.
2. Deal with unproductive worry *without using worry*.
3. Take productive worry and turn it into problem solving as soon as possible.

Let's imagine that you are in court and you think the prosecution wants to put you behind bars for twenty years. Your lawyer says to you, "I never worry about anything. I always try to think positively." Would you want this lawyer to defend you? Absolutely not. You want your lawyer to cover all the bases, anticipate every plausible motion that the prosecutor might make, and collect evidence to support your side. In other words, you want the lawyer to worry and you want him to take action to be prepared.

What if he said, "I don't *prepare* for cases—I just *worry*"? What if he then went on to say, "The sign that I am a good lawyer is that I worry a lot. Sometimes I worry so much that I feel like throwing up"? You might think, "Maybe he ought to read this book, but I want a lawyer who is going to help me solve my problems."

What Are the Rules for Productive Worry?

How can you tell if your worry is productive or unproductive? The best way to think of productive worry is to do the following:

1. Identify a problem that is plausible or reasonable.
2. Decide it's a problem that you can do something about right now (or very soon).
3. Quickly move from worrying about the problem to finding solutions to the problem.

Let's take each step in order.

1. *Identify a problem that is plausible or reasonable.* The following are some examples of plausible or reasonable problems. You are driving from New York to Washington, D.C. Possible problems to think about are: (1) Do you have a map? (2) Are you giving yourself enough time? (3) Do you have gas in your car? These are plausible and reasonable because you generally want to know where you are going, if you have enough time, and if your car is in good condition. It is plausible and reasonable. Almost everyone would agree that you should think of these things before a long trip. Another example of a plausible and reasonable worry is to ask yourself if you have paid your rent or your mortgage on time. It's plausible and reasonable because you might easily forget to pay the bill.

An example of an implausible worry is "What if there is a sniper in Washington?" or "What if I drive to Washington and my partner betrays me while I am gone?" These are implausible because they are (generally) very unlikely to happen. A reasonable person would not worry about these things.

2. *Decide it's a problem that you can do something about right now (or very soon).* As you can see by the examples of the trip to Washington and the payment of your rent, these are worries that can be turned into action right now or very soon. These are worries that don't remain worries for very long. I can get gas for the car in ten minutes, I can get the map out right now, and I can pay my rent by taking out my checkbook. *Productive worries become productive solutions almost immediately.* I remember a couple of years ago I began to worry that I was late in writing a book (ironically, the book was on resistance). I recognized I was in this stage of unproductive worry, thinking that my publisher would be angry with me. Rather than worry, I decided to sit down and write one page. Starting some action turned my worry into the beginning of a solution to the problem.

If you think, "Is there anything I can do right now?" you will turn yourself from focusing on the distant future to focusing on the present. For example, let's say that you are worried about being overwhelmed with a lot of work. You begin to generate what-ifs about not meeting deadlines. You then feel more and more overwhelmed. You can shift your thinking to "right now" by asking yourself what actions you can engage in today. Whenever I have this feeling of being overwhelmed by lots of projects, I sit down and make a list of things that I need to do, begin outlining a project, and start writing. This shifts my thinking from worrying about the future to focusing on taking action now.

3. *Quickly move from worrying about the problem to finding solutions to the problem.* Productive worry quickly leads to action. The action is plausible and reasonable. Let's say that you are worried about your finances. What are some plausible and reasonable actions that you can take? First, you need to define the problem. For example, you might be able to define the problem as "I am spending more than I make." Now, it may be the case that you don't even know if this is true. So you might then say, "The first problem to solve is to get some information about my spending and my earnings." This immediately leads to developing a budget. After you have kept records for a while, you can analyze them and determine if there are certain areas you could cut back on. Maybe there was nothing to worry about. Maybe all you needed was information followed by a plan of action.

Let's take Brian, who was worried that he hadn't filed his taxes for two years—although his employer withheld taxes on his account. Brian would worry about how awful it would be if he filed, since he thought that he would face penalties and interest and even possibly jail. Whenever he worried about this, he procrastinated on collecting the information and filing. We decided to focus on actions that he can take immediately to deal with two problems: first, what were the laws regarding late filing, and second, what liabilities did he actually face? His immediate assignment was to contact his accountant and to collect this information. Brian found that this focus on present and immediate action reduced his worry. Fortunately, his liabilities were quite small—something that he would not have found out if he had not taken action immediately. The elements of productive worry are illustrated in Figure 4.1, below.

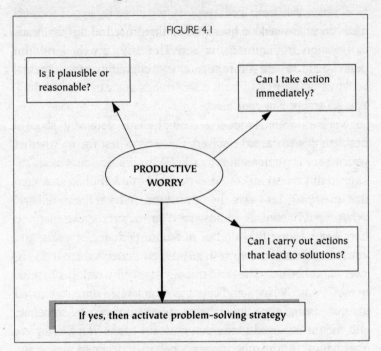

FIGURE 4.1

Is it plausible or reasonable?

Can I take action immediately?

PRODUCTIVE WORRY

Can I carry out actions that lead to solutions?

If yes, then activate problem-solving strategy

How You Get Sidetracked into Unproductive Worry

I have identified a simple set of rules to help you turn worry into a question about a problem to be solved and quickly move to solving that problem by developing a plan and taking action. You can get sidetracked from this simple formula in a number of ways.

Worrying About Unanswerable Questions

As I've noted, a typical form of worry is rumination—chewing over and over on a thought that you can't accept, such as "I can't believe that they were so unfair to me." Or you might dwell on an unanswerable question such as "Why is life so unfair?" or "Why did this happen to me?" Yale psychologist Susan Nolen-Hoeksema has described ruminative thinking as a continual focus on unanswerable questions and negative feelings that leads to isolation from productive activities and increased risk for depression.[2] When you ruminate, you engage in useless mental activity that keeps you from doing things that can be rewarding. You get trapped in your head.

None of your ruminative thoughts is a statement about a problem that needs to be solved. One way of testing out whether your worry is rumination is to ask, "What would count as an answer to this question?" or "How would I know if I had answered this question?" Let's take the rumination "Why is life so unfair?" What would count as an answer? You may recognize that you have been asking this kind of question, perhaps for years, and you have never come up with an answer. Perhaps there is no answer. Another unanswerable question is, "Why did this happen to me?" Again, what would count as an answer? I once ruminated for quite some time about being treated unfairly by someone, and then it occurred to me that even if I could find a complete explanation for the other person's behavior, I would not be any better off. So I dropped the rumination.

Ask yourself how you can turn your questions and ruminations into problems that really need to be solved. Ask yourself, "What is the problem I need to solve?" One man worried about his sales decreasing and kept ruminating, "I wonder why this is happening." Then it occurred to him that ruminating would produce nothing of any value. So the problem to solve—getting more sales—would have to be addressed by making more phone calls. As he made the phone calls, he ruminated less. Turn your rumination into *action questions:* "What action should I be taking?" If there is no immediate action to be taken, then you can categorize this as useless worry.

Worrying About a Chain Reaction of Events

Another form of sidetracking is to worry about one event leading to another, which in turn eventually leads to a catastrophe.[3] "What if my boss is angry and then she thinks she needs to get rid of me and then I lose my job and then I can't find a job?" This chain reaction multiplies your worries over and over. Since you cannot do very much about things that have never happened, and since it is unlikely your chain reaction will unravel in the frightening or catastrophic way that you predict, you might ask yourself, "What is the immediate issue here for me to address?" or "Is there an immediate problem for me to solve?"

For example, Ellen worried that her boss was angry, that she would lose her job, and that life would unravel. Rather than try to anticipate life unraveling, we focused on how to get on the good side of her boss. We came up with an immediate solution: flatter her boss and talk about the work that she was accomplishing. This worked like a charm. Her boss began to appreciate Ellen, and Ellen stopped worrying.

Unproductive worry often has this chain-reaction quality. You generate a series of negative consequences, each dependent on the previous negative consequence. Unproductive worry treats chain reactions as if they are highly probable outcomes. The real question, however, is "How likely is this chain reaction?" In most cases, it's highly implausible.

Rejecting a Solution Because It Is Not Perfect

"Is this a perfect solution? Will it absolutely give me certainty?"[4] What is a perfect solution anyway? Perhaps you think a perfect solution is one with no downside, no negatives. Thus, a perfect solution to your worry about how well you will do on an exam is for you to *know absolutely everything* before the exam. That's not possible, of course, so you may reject this as a possible solution. Or you think that a perfect solution to your fear that you have cancer is that you have taken every possible test in the world for cancer, and every doctor has signed a statement guaranteeing that you don't have the disease. Since this won't happen, you always have room for doubt. No medical test can totally exclude any possibility.

Consider the disadvantages of demanding perfect solutions: you will continue to doubt everything, nothing will satisfy you, you will end up feeling helpless and hopeless, and you will equate the lack of perfection with failure and vulnerability. Are there advantages to demanding perfection? You might think that this will motivate you to find the best solution—but does it really lead to the best solution? Rejecting all alternatives because they are not perfect does not guarantee any solution whatsoever. Or you might think that demanding perfection will reduce any chances of regret. Again, perfectionism actually leads to the opposite—if you demand perfection, then you will look back on any decisions that you make that do not lead to the best possible outcome as a reason for regret. Your regrets will be magnified by your demand for perfection. In contrast to this, if you allow yourself some room for error, then you will accept that some decisions can possibly lead to a negative outcome, and you will consider this as something that comes with the territory. Negative outcomes are inevitable if you make enough decisions.

Consider the perfectionist who invests in stocks. She will worry about any possible downside in her investment. On the other hand, if she accepts that decisions are made with imperfect knowledge and lack of complete predictability, she will conclude that decreases in value come with the territory of investing. In order to invest, you need to accept some risk.

If you demand perfection in your decision making, then you will refuse to take a risk on anything, since any decision has a potential downside and can lead to regret. However, the risk of never taking any risks is that you forfeit opportunities for growth. If you never make decisions—or if you think that you need to worry in order to find perfect solutions—your regret will be even greater, because spending your life worrying is a waste of valuable time. *Regret is inescapable*. The only issue is whether you will regret the occasional decision that you made or whether you will regret the thousands of useless worries that you have.

Rather than looking for perfect solutions, consider looking for *highly probable* or *practical* solutions. For example, rather than looking for a guarantee that you won't get fired, figure out how you can be more productive at work. Or look for some options to your current job—not perfect options, but alternatives. Every option has some disadvantages. If you can accept the disadvantages or costs of a solution, then you are in business. Otherwise you will search for perfect solutions forever.

As the artist Salvador Dalí once said, "Don't worry about perfection. You'll never find it."

Thinking You Should Worry Until You Feel Less Anxious

I often ask worriers, "How do you know when to stop worrying?" Sometimes they tell me, "When I feel less anxious." Now, this is an interesting rule, something we find in a lot of people who are anxious about a lot of different things. For example, people who are obsessive-compulsive say that they continue performing rituals and checking until they have a "feeling" they have done enough.[5]

Worriers believe they should worry until they feel they have "done enough." When they have "done enough" they say, "I can't think of anything else that I haven't already gone over," and their anxiety may decrease. Worrying is not essential to the reduction of anxiety, however. If you are distracted from your worry and thus are prevented from seeking information or reassurance, you will see a gradual decrease in your anxiety.[6] It takes time to see this reduction, however, and in fact your anxiety level may rise temporarily. This is because you believe that you are overlooking something important, thereby making you feel vulnerable. For example, people who compulsively check the stove before leaving the house become more anxious if they refrain from checking. However, once they refrain from checking long enough, their anxiety will abate. Similarly, the hypochondriac who worries about a dreaded disease may have an initial boost of anxiety when he is prevented from seeking reassurance or seeking more information, but this anxiety will decrease the longer he refrains from the worrisome search for information.

Thinking You Should Worry Until You Control Everything

Another common way of getting sidetracked into unproductive worry is to think that you need to control everything in order to be safe and comfortable. This interferes with the problem-solving approach because you may be trying to control things that cannot be controlled.[7] Problem solving involves managing the things that you *can* control and being able to distinguish these from things you *cannot* control. For example, I can control what I say when I give a lecture, but I cannot control whether someone likes what I say. You may worry about what people think of you, and so you think that the problem to be solved is to get everyone to like you. But you cannot get everyone to like you—you cannot control that. Giving up some control over the uncontrollable frees you to focus on any immediate problems to solve. Once you define the problem in terms of what you *cannot* control, however, you have a problem that cannot be solved.

As the old saying goes, "Know the things that you can control and the things that you cannot control. And know the difference between the two." If you make the problem "things I cannot control" (for example, what a stranger thinks of you), then you have a problem that cannot be solved.

Summing Up

Now that you have examined how worry can be useful—and also how much of worry is useless—you can decide which things are worth worrying about and doing something about, and which are unproductive worries. The signs of unproductive and productive worry are shown in Table 4.1. In the next chapter we will examine how you can learn to accept reality and commit yourself to making meaningful changes.

TABLE 4.1
The Signs of Unproductive Worry
• You worry about unanswerable questions.
• You worry about a chain reaction of events.
• You reject a solution because it is not perfect.
• You think you should worry until you feel less anxious.
• You think you should worry until you control everything.
The Signs of Productive Worry
• There is a question that has an answer.
• You are focused on a single event—not a chain reaction.
• You are willing to accept imperfect solutions.
• You do not use your anxiety as a guide.
• You recognize what you can control and what you cannot control.

5

Step Two: Accept Reality and Commit to Change

WE HAVE SEEN that a lot of your worry is motivated by your belief that worry protects, prepares, and motivates you. You may think that your worries are realistic and that you need to worry because you don't want to overlook something, or because you think this is a sign of being responsible. But even if you recognize that worry doesn't work and that your worry isn't productive, what can you do to change?

We are going to look at a different way of "knowing" reality—separate from all of your interpretations, judgments, false alarms, implications, and predictions about the future. You will learn how to accept what really is and commit to change what you need to change in order to get what you want.

What Is Acceptance?

Acceptance is seeing things as they *really are,* not as you *think* they are. Acceptance literally means "receiving" what is here in the present and seeing reality transparently—not through the distorted lens of your worries.[1] Acceptance means being aware of what is real right now, not what could happen.

Take your breath, for example.

Before I mentioned it, you probably didn't notice it. Now focus your mind on your breath. What do you experience? Are you breathing in or out? In this moment, what do you notice? Focusing on your breath, whether you are meditating or simply stopping to notice, means that you are now mindful. You are aware *in this moment* of this experience.[2] You might also notice, as you focus on your breath, that you are having thoughts that are interfering with simply being aware, being mindful, being present.

You may have thoughts that you are breathing too rapidly, or that you have to catch your breath, or that focusing on your breath won't help with your worry problem. Rather than simply focusing on your breath, you are focusing on your *thoughts*. You are now *thinking about your breathing* in terms of "too rapid," "having to catch your breath," or "not helping with your worry."

All of these thoughts—these distractions—make it more difficult to simply be here in the moment with your breath. You are jumping ahead, and you may now find yourself trying to control your breathing. As you try to control your breathing, you notice that you cannot do so and that things are getting more and more out of control. You are no longer accepting and being mindful and aware. You have begun to worry.

As I've noted, acceptance of something doesn't mean you like it or say it's OK; it means you know it is what it is, and that is where you start from. Let's say that you are worried because you have gone through a breakup and are now alone. You keep changing from being angry about the breakup to being depressed about being alone. You say to yourself, "This is terrible. I can't live with this!"

Psychologist Marsha Linehan at the University of Washington suggests that "radical acceptance" of reality—looking at reality and seeing it for what it is—can help us when we are frustrated, angry, depressed, or anxious.[3] For example, you have broken up with your partner and you do not know how long you will be alone. Radical acceptance means that you are going to look at reality *not the way you demand that it has to be but the way that it is.* This is an important distinction. You may say to yourself, "I can't stand the fact that we broke up. I demand that things be made right!" You might feel like stomping your feet. You might spend hours complaining to your friends. You waste time ruminating and dwelling on it and asking endlessly, "Why me?"

None of this will do you any good. Radical acceptance means that you recognize that there is a reality that you are going to live with: "OK. We broke up. That is the reality. I don't like it. That's where I have to start from." The advantage of radical acceptance is that it gives you a place to start from.

What Is Commitment to Change?

Commitment to change means you can identify what you really value and really want, and that you choose to do the difficult things to make yourself happy. Worry is not included in commitment to change. In fact, worry is a struggle against accepting what you don't like, a protest against reality, and a refusal to accept uncertainty and limitation.

Worry is not action. *Action* is action. Solving problems means actually solving a problem—not worrying about it. And one way to solve a problem is to accept that the problem exists. Protesting, struggling, demanding perfection, trying to eliminate uncertainty, criticizing yourself, and setting off false alarms never solve problems.

What would it mean to accept a breakup and commit to change? It could mean that you say, "The reality is that we broke up. Protesting and being upset won't change things. If I accept that this is a fact, then maybe I can make my life better. I can commit to seeing friends, dating, and getting involved in different activities. But I also may have to accept for now that I will be lonely."

Accept Reality

Mindfulness

But how can you first learn to accept reality?

Psychologists Zindel Segal, Mark Williams, and John Teasdale have found that people who are more likely to become depressed tend to describe their experiences in general and abstract terms—"I'm a loser" or "I need success"—whereas people who are less prone to depression describe their experiences in concrete and specific terms—"I am working on a project" or "I want to do well on this test."[4] Relying on general and abstract concepts makes you more likely to jump to conclusions about the future in negative and self-critical ways. In a series of studies Segal, Williams, and Teasdale trained people who had prior episodes of depression and who were thus likely to have reoccurrences of depression. The training they provided these patients was in *mindfulness*. Mindfulness is a technique derived from Buddhist teachings whereby you concentrate on the immediate present experience rather than "escaping" to thoughts about the future, generalizations about the experience, judgments about what you are doing, or attempts to control your experience. Mindfulness is the ability to attend to and stay with what is currently present in your experience.

Acceptance of experience includes mindfulness: rather than trying to control your experience or predict the future through worry, mindfulness allows you to stay with the current experience in concrete reality, without struggling to control or judge it. When you worry, you become overly attached to your thought—focusing on your thought, thinking that you must do something, and treating the worry as if it is an experience that must stay with you until a problem is solved. In contrast, with mindfulness, you learn how to attend to or become mindful of your thought (or sensation), but you also gain distance from your worry because you do not respond to your worry by collecting information, solving problems, or predicting the future. You become more of an observer, simply noticing the thought and allowing the thought to be. Let's look at some specific aspects of mindfulness—gaining distance, describing what is in front of you, suspending judgment, and taking your self out of it—and see how you can apply them to your worry.

GAIN DISTANCE

Your worries involve what you *think* reality is. What does this mean? Your thoughts are internal experiences that change every second and are different from someone else's thoughts. For example, your thought "I might end up alone forever" is not reality, is it? You don't really know what is going to happen. It's simply a thought.

Another thought could be "This is a dog." Maybe this animal is a dog, but the *thought* is not the dog. I need to observe, to see, to check it out. I need to be aware—right now. A dog is a dog; a thought is not a dog. I can't pet a thought, and thoughts don't bark. Thoughts are not reality.

But your worries are thoughts that you treat as if they were reality. You believe that if you have a thought—"I could be alone forever"—then you have to pay attention to it, do something about it, and get rid of it. This is what psychologists call "cognitive self-consciousness" or simply "monitoring your thoughts."[5] When you monitor your thoughts, you examine your mind for unpleasant thoughts or feelings and then dwell on them. As you monitor these internal thoughts, you turn away from reality—what is actually right in front of you and what is happening right now. People who engage in this thought monitoring, wrapped up in their thoughts, are far more likely to worry—and to stay worried.[6]

Gaining distance from your thoughts means standing back and noticing that these are thoughts. You can try this by taking each of your worries and observing that you are *simply having a thought*. Try the following:

I am simply *having the thought* that I will always be alone.
I am simply *noticing that I have a feeling* of sadness.
I simply *had the thought* just now that I am a loser.
I am simply *having the thought* I need to do something right
    now.

Your thought that you will be alone is not the same thing as your future. Your future will be your future—and it may be very different from your thoughts. You become overly attached to your thoughts and worries because you have the following equations:

Thought = future
Thought = reality
Thought = responsibility
Thought = only thought possible
Thought = forever

Your thought that your savings will be wiped out is not the same thing as your bank balance. It's a thought, something you can observe: "I have the thought that my bank balance will run out." Now notice that you can also have another thought: "I notice that I can also think that my savings may increase." Nothing has changed about reality; only your thoughts have changed.

Gaining distance from your thoughts can mean recognizing that your thoughts—your worries—have often been wrong about reality. The worry that you had last year, that you would always be sad, turned out to be false. Reality was that you were sometimes sad and sometimes happy. Your thought that you would fail that exam—also turned out to be incorrect. And you also had thousands of thoughts and feelings that you thought you would always be concerned with. You thought, "I will always be bothered by this thought" or "I will always feel this way." You aren't and you don't. Your thoughts and feelings changed, so the worry about things always being the same was a thought, a guess, a false alarm. It was not reality.

Gaining distance from your thoughts also means recognizing that your thoughts can be experiences that you observe and then let go. Take a pile of index cards. On the back of each card write out a worry. Try to get as many worries as you can onto these cards. When you have all of these worries written down, shuffle the deck, with the worries facing away from you. Then pick up the cards one at a time, look at each one, and then toss it into a wastepaper basket.[7] After you finish with this exercise, walk away.

Gaining distance means learning how to walk away from a thought.

DESCRIBE WHAT IS IN FRONT OF YOU

Your worries seem to leap far beyond the information that is in front of you. You are sitting at your desk in your office, looking at the work that you have to do, and you begin to worry. You jump to conclusions: that you will never get all the work done, that your boss will get angry with you, and that she will fire you. Then you worry that you won't get another job for months, your savings will run out, and you'll go deeper and deeper into debt.

Notice how these worries have nothing to do with *what is in front of you right now*. What is in front of you right now is the work on your desk. Think of how you would describe it: "There's a folder with some memos that were written by my boss and my colleagues." What else is in front of you? "My desk has some other papers—a printout of some data. There's also my phone and my laptop."

Now describe what happened right before this.

"I got an e-mail from my boss, Carol, saying she wanted a report tomorrow morning."

What did she say?

"She said, 'Have the report in by nine tomorrow.'"

Describe what you have done already.

"I've looked over the material a few times and outlined some of the things that I want to write up. I looked at the data and other reports."

When we *describe* something, we do not jump to conclusions: we are not trying to read Carol's mind to find out what she "really thinks," we are not gazing into a crystal ball to see if we will get fired, and we are not labeling ourselves as failures. We stay with the description of the actual facts. *Describing*, rather than jumping to conclusions, allows you to place yourself in reality as it is—and keeps you from worrying about all the possible realities that may never be.

SUSPEND JUDGMENT

Think about the various worries you have—not getting all your work done, not finding the right partner, what someone thinks of you, whether your health is deteriorating. All of your worries carry *judgments* about what is good or bad, essential or unnecessary. "I must get all my work done, and if I don't, I have failed." Two judgments right there—what you must do and that you are failing. Or you worry about finding the right partner. Another two judgments there—that there is a "right partner" and that you must find him or her. In the worry "This could be skin cancer and I absolutely must know for sure it's not" there are two more judgments—classifying some symptom as skin cancer and saying you have a responsibility to eliminate all uncertainty immediately.

Try to find the judgments in each of your worries. Your judgments about reality might be that you label someone else ("He's a liar" or "She's unfriendly"). Or your judgment might be "This could be cancer" or "I am ugly." These judgments are not reality—they are what you think reality might be or should be. And they make you more anxious and more worried.

For example, rather than judging reality, describe it in terms of color or sensation. Or describe the behaviors that you actually see. For example, rather than judge yourself as a failure because you don't have a special partner right now, you might suspend judgment and simply observe: "I am sitting in my apartment. It's 9:25 p.m. On the table is some pizza I have not finished. It's a little warm in here right now." Rather than label a mole as cancer—another judgment—you might say, "I notice a mole on my arm. It's a little dark. I notice that if I touch it, the skin around it gets red."

TAKE YOURSELF OUT OF IT

Notice that each of your worries seems to have *you in the center*. "I am worried I will never find someone. I must do something about this." Or "I worry that she is angry at me. What did I do?" Or "This work will never get done. I must have really messed up." Your worries are almost always about how *you* see things and what *you* must do about them. There are eight billion people in the world, and everyone thinks at one time or another, "This is all about *me* and what I have to do right now."

Can eight billion people be wrong?

Yes.

Let's imagine you are sitting in your apartment worried that you will never find the partner of your dreams: "I will never find the right person for me." This has become all about *your* dreams—the only dreams that *you* can imagine having—so you think these dreams are the only ones you could have. You think that being alone tonight says something about *you*. (Perhaps there are two billion other people sitting at home tonight—what does this say about *them*?) *You* think that *you* have to do something to find the partner of *your* dreams. *You have to do something.*

Or you worry about your elderly mother. You think that *you* have to make her feel comfortable. *You* have to make sure she is all right. *You* have to check on her every hour. Your love for your mother is not enough for *you*—because *you* have to guarantee that nothing bad will ever happen to her.

Take yourself out of it for a moment.

If you are sitting at home thinking that you are alone, think about the fact that you are not unique. In fact, it is likely that almost everyone in the world at one time sat alone and thought they might not find someone to love forever. You are not alone.

Or if you lost money in the stock market, take yourself out of it. You are not alone. Millions of other people have lost money.

Or if you worry about your mother's health, take yourself out of that, too. Not that you don't love your mother, but her health is not about *you*; it's about *her*.

DISAPPEAR TO SEE REALITY

If you have taken yourself out of it, you can imagine taking a bolder step. You can imagine disappearing completely. Think about what you are worried about right now. Something has to get done, something might go out of control, some part of this vast world that we live in might not work exactly the way it should work. Now, imagine that *you do not exist*. You are not here. Time and events flow on without you. Tomorrow comes and you are not here. People move around, the sun rises, the cars flow through the streets. You have disappeared.

If you have disappeared, if you no longer exist, then there is nothing to worry about, is there? The people who might not have liked your talk? Well, you don't exist now, so why does it matter? The bill that might be late? How could you care, because there is no "you" to care? You are no more.

Now, this might sound like the dark side of spirituality, but it really is the nature of almost all of reality. There are eight billion people in the world. How much of this space do you really occupy?

Where are you in this space of humanity—one in eight billion? One way of getting balance about the things that you worry about is to try to remind yourself that the world is not *about you*. You are not the world.

Imagine a vast beach that stretches for a thousand miles and is fifty miles wide. The wind blows, and a single grain of sand falls two feet from where it used to be. That is you. You are a grain of sand. You struggle against the landscape, pushing and complaining about how all the other grains of sand get in your way. But stand back for a moment and look at the larger view.

The beach still exists. The tides come and go.

Now try this. Imagine that you are worried that you won't find your perfect partner. Your worries are making you depressed and anxious; you can't sleep. *You* have become your sole preoccupation right now—what *you* can do to find the perfect partner. You feel you are getting nowhere.

Well, do just that. Try going *nowhere*. Imagine that you have disappeared. You are looking down at the earth. You observe the building you live in. You pull back farther and farther. Your neighborhood is like a patch of color you see from an airplane. You have given up any fantasy of control because you are disappearing for a moment. You cannot touch the reality that you yearn to control.

Once you can take yourself out of it—imagine disappearing, describe what is in front of you, and suspend judgment—you are ready to accept reality. And once you are able to accept reality by observing it, you can do something about these worries.

But what gets in the way of accepting reality?

Accept Limitations

Along with your unwillingness to accept reality as it is—because you refuse to give up your worry and your struggle and your protest—is your unwillingness to accept your limitations. You feel you have to know everything, plan for everything, solve all the problems that could possibly exist in the future. You refuse to accept the limitations of what you can do and what you can control.

I once had a patient, a successful lawyer, who told me that he had been a nationally recognized basketball player when he was in college. The team he played for had been nationally ranked, but he was surprisingly short, in my opinion, to have been that successful as a basketball player. I mentioned this to him, and he replied, "I've been successful in different areas of my life because I know my limitations. I learned to play around being shorter."

There are a number of limitations that we need to accept in order to give up worrying about things. We can accept that we don't like what we see rather than protest about it or worry about it. We can accept that there may not be *the* answer, so we can live with ambiguity and complexity. We can accept that we can settle for less than we want, in order to appreciate more of what we have. We are continually finding that we cannot control everything, and if we don't accept some loss of control, we will worry about having no control. And we can accept that some problems may not be solvable and that we will just have to live with them, or as the basketball-playing lawyer would say, "play around them."

Accept Uncertainty: Know What It Is That You Can Never Know

Worriers equate the unknown with danger. However, uncertainty is actually *neutral* with regard to outcome. I do not know what the weather or the stock market will be like next week. I do not know what my friend will say to me when I meet him for lunch. I do not know what my next patient will find troubling. But simply because I do not know what these events will be, it does not follow that they will be negative. They are simply unknown.

I also do not know the positive outcomes that will occur.

Rather than focus on the unknown and equate it with danger or bad outcomes, you should focus your attention on the actual facts that you do know. If you think that the problem to solve is to solve problems about the unknowable, then you will feel helpless.

Why do you have to solve problems about the unknowable? If something is unknown or unknowable, it may never be a problem.

UNCERTAINTY TRAINING

Intolerance of uncertainty is the core issue for most worriers. Psychologists Michel Dugas and Robert Ladouceur found that worriers cannot tolerate not knowing something *for sure*. In fact, one worrier told the researchers that he would rather know a negative for sure than be uncertain about a positive.[8] Worriers keep looking for a perfect solution, an answer to every possible question they can ask, and a clear prediction for every possible what-if. In the absence of this certainty, they keep worrying until they find it.

Worriers also avoid confronting the emotional impact of their experiences. This is because worriers seldom get to the point of actually facing their worst fears. Moreover, since worriers are trying to *think* about how to solve all the problems, they do not use visual images, which make you *feel the emotion*. Feeling an emotion is one way of finding out that you can tolerate reality.

Now, as I pointed out earlier, when people are engaged in worry they are actually less anxious. This is because worry is abstract and linguistic, and when people rely on this abstract thinking, they do not experience visual images of bad outcomes. Since they avoid these highly emotional visual images, continuing to worry keeps them from experiencing anxiety. Thus, worry—and searching for certainty—is a form of *emotional avoidance*.[9] It's as if the person is thinking, "I will continue to search for certainty in order to avoid having that terrible image of a possible bad outcome." *Searching for certainty becomes a way to avoid emotion.*[10]

The more you can tolerate uncertainty, the less worried you will be. In fact, uncertainty training is highly effective in reducing worry and anxiety in a relatively short period of time, significantly helping 77 percent of chronic worriers.[11]

Step 1. Examine the Costs and Benefits of Accepting Uncertainty

We can identify unproductive worry because it involves unanswerable questions, chain reactions, unsolvable problems, things that are unknowable, demands for perfect solutions, relying on anxiety as a guide, and the demand for total control. For example, consider the worry "It's possible that I have a brain tumor, even if the doctor says I'm healthy." This worry includes a number of the elements of unproductive worry—it's an unanswerable question ("It's possible"), it's based on a chain reaction ("My health problems will go misdiagnosed and I will end up with a serious problem"), it's not solvable (you cannot eliminate possibility), it's unknowable (if it's continually misdiagnosed, then you cannot eliminate future misdiagnoses), it demands a perfect solution (absolute certainty), and it demands that you control the outcome ("I have to get complete reassurance"—something that is impossible). This worry qualifies as an unproductive worry.

We now can examine what the costs and benefits are of accepting uncertainty for your unproductive worry. For example, if you think, "I might have a brain tumor," you can ask yourself,

"What are the costs and benefits to me of accepting that this is possible?" The benefits are that if you accept it as possible—and accept that you cannot eliminate possibility—then you don't have to take action on it. You will worry less and give up trying to control something you cannot control. The costs are that you may immediately feel a bit more anxious and think you are letting your guard down. If you experience this reaction, then ask yourself, "Exactly what action can I take *today* that will really help me?" Since the worry is about an undiagnosed tumor (after having seen several doctors), the only action available is to continue seeing more doctors. This is an endless enterprise.

Step 2. Flood Yourself with Uncertainty

Uncertainty is reality. I don't know for sure what will happen tomorrow or the next day. I can make an educated guess, but I cannot say for sure. When you do not tolerate uncertainty, your thoughts are something like the following: "It's not certain that things will be OK; if I don't know for sure, I should worry until I do know for sure; I've been worrying and I still don't know for sure, so I should keep worrying until I am absolutely certain it will be OK." In contrast to worry, which is the search for certainty, in uncertainty training you practice having the thought thousands of times that "I don't know for sure" or "It's always possible that something terrible could happen."

Nancy thought that she might have HIV even though there was no real evidence that she did. She had not engaged in any high-risk behavior. But she began having this intrusive thought anyway. So she worried and checked her body for any of the early signs of AIDS. I had Nancy practice repeating for twenty minutes each day, "It's always possible I have AIDS." I told her to do nothing to neutralize this thought—not to try to reassure herself, just practice having the thought "It is always possible." As expected, her anxiety went up—and then it went down as she repeated this thought hundreds of times. Whenever she had the thought, "I wonder if I have AIDS," I had her repeat it two hundred times. She began to realize that having a thought about what is possible could be tolerated. In fact, it became boring.

Now think about how this is different from the technique of thought stopping. As we've seen, thought stopping involves noticing that you have an unwanted thought and then yelling at yourself, "Stop!" The idea is that you *cannot stand* having this thought. Thought stopping does not work and it actually can make things worse, because you believe that the thought—"It's possible I have AIDS"—is a thought that you need to fear and get rid of.[12] In contrast to this, *thought flooding* about uncertainty teaches you that you can have thoughts about what is possible, yet do nothing to neutralize the thought. You can experience the thought thousands of times and do nothing but invite it back in to bore you again by repeating it.

Accepting uncertainty is a core strategy in dealing with your worries. Once you accept that you can never know for sure, then you can recognize that continuing to worry to gain certainty is a total waste of time. Practic-ing flooding yourself with uncertainty thoughts—repeating them endlessly without doing anything to gain certainty—helps you recognize that you can live with uncertainty. It's like getting on the elevator thousands of times. You will no longer fear it because it has become boring.

But accepting uncertainty does not mean that you have given up participating in real life, because it may be necessary for you to make some changes. Let's see how you can commit to change.

Commit to Change

The Power of Doing What You Don't Want to Do

What is personal empowerment? Let's define it as *the ability to do what has to get done*. It's your ability to set healthy goals for yourself and follow a plan of action. It's your ability to stay on course, stay on task, and not get distracted. It's your ability to keep your goals in front of you and to do what you *need* to do and not what you *want* to do. Being able to do what you do not want to do is the way to overcome procrastination, worry, low frustration tolerance, depression, and anxiety. You will have to do things that you find unpleasant. The hard work comes before the payoff.

This is not simply a motivational pep talk. Overcoming your intolerance of frustration—your desire to dodge discomfort—is the central component in all of the exposure exercises in this book. If you worry, there are many things that you avoid doing or thinking about.

There are three steps in personal empowerment. Imagine that you are twenty pounds overweight and want to lose weight. If you are honest with yourself, you do not want to exercise or diet. The essential thing in losing weight is to make a *choice,* commit to *successful imperfectionism,* and practice *constructive discomfort.*

THE POWER OF CHOICE

This involves three questions for you to ask yourself:

What is my goal?
What do I have to do to get it?
Am I willing to do it?

When I ask you, "What is your goal?" I am referring to what you want the *outcome* to be. In this example, your goal is to lose weight. But it's not going to happen unless you make it happen. Ask yourself, "What do I have to do to get it?" In order to lose weight you have to decrease your calorie intake and increase your exercise. Forget about fancy, frivolous diets or mechanical devices that will manipulate your muscles for you. Losing weight means simply decreasing calorie intake and increasing calorie burn-off.

This means that you will have to be uncomfortable. It's not the end of the world, but it actually involves your answer to this question: "Are you willing to do what needs to be done? *Are you willing to be uncomfortable?*"

What are the costs and benefits of being able to do what is uncomfortable? What will you be able to do if you are willing to do what you don't want to do? How will you be able to face the things that you are worried about if you can consistently do what does not feel good? Doing what you don't want to do means making a choice to do it.

You might say, "I need to be ready" or "I need to have the motivation" or "I need to know that it will work out." If these are your guidelines, then you will not do what needs to be done. But, in fact, every day you do things that you are not "ready" to do, for which you lack motivation, and about which the outcome is uncertain—say, at your job, when you go to a meeting you don't feel ready for, don't feel particularly motivated to go to, and don't know the outcome of. How did you do it? You made a personal choice.

TABLE 5.1	
PERSONAL CHOICE: SAMPLE	
What is my goal?	Lose ten pounds.
What do I have to do to get it?	Increase exercise and decrease calorie intake.
Am I willing to do it?	I'm not sure. I like cake and I don't like exercise.
Conclusion	Maybe I won't lose weight.

Try the personal choice table for yourself. Ask yourself if you are really willing to pay the cost to make things happen. Are you willing to make that phone call to the friend who you think might be unhappy, or approach someone you want to get to know better, or complete some work that you are putting off, or see the doctor?

TABLE 5.2
YOUR PERSONAL CHOICE
What is my goal?
What do I have to do to get it?
Am I willing to do it?
Conclusion

SUCCESSFUL IMPERFECTION

The next step is to become *successful at becoming imperfect.* This sounds like a contradiction, but if, say, you want to lose wieght, you probably will not look like a bathing beauty next week. Success for you will mean carrying out behaviors that will not have a perfect outcome. It means *progressing* through imperfect steps. Every imperfect step you take forward—every exercise that you do imperfectly—will take you in the right direction. You don't have to become an Olympic athlete to lose some weight— you just have to get out there and start exercising.

We have already seen how perfectionism makes you worry in order to find a perfect solution. Perfectionism also may underlie your procrastination. You may think, "What's the use of exercising today? I won't be in shape tomorrow." You don't need perfection—you need *progress.* You need to become successful at being actively imperfect on a daily basis. So if you exercise and then look in the mirror and don't notice any changes, you are making progress. Commit to the behavior now—not to having the outcome at your fingertips. The behavior—exercise and refusing that chocolate cake—is the right commitment.

Ask yourself if there are some things that would be a step forward toward your goal. Let's say that your goal is to lose weight. Would you be willing to do any of the following: walk fifteen minutes more a day, give up one dessert, set aside 20 percent of your food and not eat it, keep track of what you eat, and give up an evening snack? Each step is imperfect. Are you willing to take imperfect steps to become more successful?

CONSTRUCTIVE DISCOMFORT

As we have seen, a great deal of worry is an attempt to avoid anxiety or other unpleasant emotions. The same thing is true with procrastination, the avoidance of discomfort. In order to do things that you do not want to do, you will need to change your attitude toward discomfort by *making discomfort your goal*. You will not make any real progress unless you are uncomfortable. If you procrastinate, then you are a "discomfort dodger," constantly avoiding things that make you uncomfortable.

If you plan to solve some of your problems, you may have to do some things that you find uncomfortable. Let's take a look at your attitude toward discomfort. Do any of the following sound familiar to you?

- I cannot stand being uncomfortable.
- I should wait until I feel ready.
- I shouldn't have to be uncomfortable.
- I'll just run out of energy.
- This discomfort will go on forever.

When you think of exercising, you say, "It's too uncomfortable." You think, "I cannot stand that discomfort" and "I'd rather do something else." But imagine if you were to choose to engage in uncomfortable behavior on a regular basis. Your initial instinct is to avoid discomfort, but by pursuing uncomfortable (but healthy) behavior, you can learn that things that you thought were going to be uncomfortable at the 95 percent level for two hours might actually be 25 percent uncomfortable for fifteen minutes. Overcoming low frustration tolerance and learning how to build resilience will require doing things that are uncomfortable.

Jose was constantly worried when he was around people he did not know well. He hesitated to approach women when he was anxious because he was afraid of being rejected. He learned to rely on alcohol to calm down, but this destabilized his moods. I asked Jose to consider identifying some things that he wanted to accomplish—like meeting new women and speaking assertively to an old girlfriend. I suggested that he commit to do something every day that is uncomfortable but healthy.

Every day when he noticed he was feeling anxious about making eye contact with a woman, he decided to jump at the opportunity to do something that made him uncomfortable. Jose would come back at the end of the week and tell me all the things he'd done that were uncomfortable: starting conversations with women in stores, asking a woman out, asserting himself with his former girlfriend, and going to a party without having a few drinks. Jose began to solve his problems by developing a new habit—even a goal—of being uncomfortable.

Your Discomfort History

You may think it's a good idea to list all of your positive qualities. But try this instead: list all of the things that you have done that were uncomfortable. Joan, who was divorced and had a seven-year-old girl named Hannah, had been worried about breaking up with Jason, who never seemed to know what he wanted and didn't have enough time for her. She thought, "But he'll get angry" and "If we break off, I'll be lonely." Being lonely, she thought, meant that she would have to be uncomfortable—which she already was with Jason. It meant she would have to go out on dates with new people, and that might not be so great.

So we decided to look at things that she had done in her life that were uncomfortable. Joan's list of uncomfortable but healthy things included the following: studying for exams in college, jogging, losing weight, giving birth to Hannah, asserting herself with her ex-husband, getting divorced, going on interviews, getting a job, dealing with clients, living on a budget, and asserting herself with a friend. The question then was, "How did you feel about yourself *after* you did these uncomfortable things?" Joan said, "I felt proud of myself." Joan was using *constructive discomfort*—the road to getting things done.

One way of confronting discomfort is to take an inventory of uncomfortable things that you have done in the past that were helpful to you. This might include studying for exams, exercise, ending an unhealthy relationship, moving to a new house, solving difficult problems, achieving goals at work, or asserting yourself. In some ways, your current and past problems involved one thing that they had in common—you had to do things that were uncomfortable.

Let's take your discomfort history. Using the chart below, write out things that you did that were uncomfortable but which you thought would be helpful to you in accomplishing goals. Then list the outcome—how you felt after you did these things, and what you accomplished. How were you able to do things that were uncomfortable and unpleasant?

TABLE 5.3

DISCOMFORT HISTORY

Things I did in the past that were uncomfortable or unpleasant	Outcome

Your Discomfort Diary

Let's list some uncomfortable things that you know might be steps toward a better life and which you can do now. Recording your discomfort will help you do the things that you don't really want to do.

First, take a look at Maggie's discomfort diary below. Each day she listed some healthy behaviors she knew she didn't want to do. She then kept track of them—noting when and if she did them and how uncomfortable they actually were. Then she noted how she felt after doing them.

TABLE 5.4

MAGGIE'S DISCOMFORT DIARY

Uncomfortable healthy behaviors	When I did them and the degree of actual discomfort (0–100%)	How I felt about myself afterward
Exercise at health club	Monday 7 p.m. (70%)	Sweaty, proud, like I got something done
Don't eat desserts at meals	Monday 8:30 p.m. (75%)	Frustrated, annoyed, more in control of myself
Don't snack on sweets in between meals	Monday 11 p.m. (80%)	Frustrated, hungry, a little anxious, getting control
Walk home from work	Monday 5:15 p.m. (30%)	Bored, interested, pressed for time, better about myself for doing something

As you can see, some of these things were quite uncomfortable—and after she did them she did feel some frustration and annoyance. But she also felt she was more in control. She began feeling more pride. As she began doing uncomfortable things every day, she found that the amount of discomfort decreased. This increased her ability to do other things that were uncomfortable—like being more assertive at work and doing things in her personal life that needed to be done.

Constructive discomfort works two ways. First, we start with making discomfort your goal—on getting into your *discomfort zone*—to do things you don't want to do. Second, discomfort becomes a *means to an end*—it helps you accomplish your other goals. Making discomfort a daily goal is the key to making progress. It's far more productive to do things that are uncomfortable than to worry about never doing them.

Now work on your own discomfort diary. Every day it is important to do things that you don't want to do. These are the uncomfortable things that can help you make progress. Write down a list of uncomfortable healthy behaviors, when you did them, how uncomfortable the behavior actually was, and how you thought about yourself afterward.

TABLE 5.5
DISCOMFORT DIARY

Uncomfortable healthy behaviors	When I did them and the degree of actual discomfort (0–100%)	How I felt about myself afterward

You may learn that discomfort is not as bad as you thought it was. By committing to doing what you do not want to do—by choosing to do things that you need to do in order to get things done—you will find that there is less to worry about (see Table 5.6). In fact, worry is always about the future—about what might happen. By confronting the things that you are avoiding, you may find that what you worried about is now in the past. It's something that you finished—one less thing to worry about.

You can make progress by embracing successful imperfection and by seeking out constructive discomfort. You may learn that discomfort is not as bad as you thought it was—it can lead to a sense of relief and even pride.

TABLE 5.6

COMMIT TO CHANGE: THE POWER OF DOING WHAT
YOU DON'T WANT TO DO

1. The power of choice
2. Use successful imperfection
3. Commit to constructive discomfort
4. Take your discomfort history
5. Keep a discomfort diary

Summing Up

Acceptance is the opposite of worry, since worry is a struggle against what is real and what is possible. We have seen how you can practice acceptance by becoming more mindful: staying in the present, describing rather than judging, and letting go of control.

Knowing your limitations helps you feel more in control. As you give up your frustrating worry and search for the answer to unanswerable questions, you begin to surrender control. As you give up the demand for *the* truth or *the* answer, you recognize that what is in the here and now—what is in front of you—is the place to start from. Finally, we have seen that once you have accepted what is, you can then choose to commit to change. Change does not mean doing what you want to do—in fact, it usually means doing what you don't want to do. Change and progress in your life involve successful imperfection and constructive discomfort—doing what you have been avoiding because of your worries.

6

Step Three: Challenge Your Worried Thinking

IN THIS CHAPTER we will examine some simple and powerful techniques that you can use that help you confine your worry to a specific time and place so that the remainder of your day becomes relatively worry-free. We will also set up your worries as thoughts and predictions to be tested and refuted. These techniques will help you put things in perspective, examine the logic and the actual evidence or facts, and draw your own conclusions. We can call this the *power of realistic thinking*.

Keep Track of Your Worries

Keep a diary of your worry—when you worry, where you worry, how much you worry, and what the effect is. By identifying the situations, experiences, or emotions that precede your worry, we can begin to plan for these "trouble times." For example, if your worry seems to be triggered by thoughts of seeing a friend, then you can plan some strategies specifically about that issue. For example, you might be concerned your friend will be angry because you haven't called him in a while. Your solution could be to say when you call, "Gee, I hope you aren't annoyed I haven't called." Or you might worry more when you are alone on weekends. Your solution could be to make sure that you have plans for the weekend and that you are more active. Sitting around worrying will simply feed into your anxiety and depression. If your worry is triggered by trying to fall asleep, then you can utilize some plans for dealing with these insomnia-producing thoughts. For example, you could practice what we call "sleep hygiene"—going to bed and getting up at the same time, planning an hour of cooling-down time before going to bed, getting out of bed and doing something else if you are having difficulty falling asleep.

Second, you can examine how you feel after you worry. For example, does your worry lead you to take action, or does it lead to more and more rumination? Imagine that you find that your worry leads to overeating, which temporarily distracts you from your worry. You would find the following:

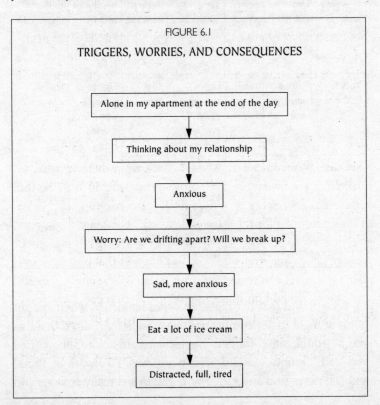

FIGURE 6.1

TRIGGERS, WORRIES, AND CONSEQUENCES

Alone in my apartment at the end of the day

↓

Thinking about my relationship

↓

Anxious

↓

Worry: Are we drifting apart? Will we break up?

↓

Sad, more anxious

↓

Eat a lot of ice cream

↓

Distracted, full, tired

Your Worry Record

A worry record is a helpful way to identify your worries. Look at Betsy's record below.

TABLE 6.1

BETSY'S WORRY RECORD

Day/ time	Events going on	How I feel right before I'm worrying	My worry	How anxious or sad did I feel? (0-100%)	What did I do next?	How did I feel then?
Monday 7:15 pm	Got home from work walked into empty apartment	Sad, empty, afraid	I'm all alone. I'll always be alone. I'll never have relationship.	70% anxious 80% sad	Ate three doughnuts and a piece of chocolate cake.	Stuffed tired. disgusted
Tuesday 6:30 p.m.	Walking home from work	Tense	I have nothing to do. Will I ever find someone?	50% tense	Looked at a couple who seemed happy	Jealous, ugly
Saturday 9:45 a.m.	Waking up	Sad	What will I do? There's no one here. Will I always be alone?	80% sad	Went back to sleep	Didn't feel anything, I was asleep

Betsy found that her biggest worries happened when she got home at night to her empty apartment. So Betsy realized that this was a "trouble time" for her. The feeling right before she worried was "sad," "empty," "afraid." Her worry was "I'll always be alone" and "I'll never find anyone." She began to feel really anxious and sad. What did she do next? She ate some doughnuts and had some cake. For Betsy, her worries were tied to her binge eating.

Once Betsy was able to identify the triggers, thoughts, and consequences of her worry, we tailored a self-help program for her. For example, she had the thought that she would always be alone when she got home. We handled this in several ways. First, she was able to challenge the thought that because she was alone right now she would always be alone. In fact, she had a lot of friends and had a history of several relationships. Second, we developed a social calendar plan, with Betsy scheduling in advance time with friends and time for dating. Whenever she had thoughts of always being alone, she could refer to her social calendar and see what was in store. Third, we worked on planning to improve her time alone by planning rental movies, books to read, bubble baths, and wonderful music to listen to. Finally, she also planned to delay binge eating for one hour, during which time she would do the first three things listed here.

A lot of times our worries lead us to do things that make matters worse. This could include binge eating, drinking too much, calling up ex-lovers who are better left in the past, looking for information about all the possible diseases that we can have, or sitting looking out the window at all the people whose lives we think are perfect. What do you do after you worry? Does it add to your problems?

Use the worry record form in Table 6.2 to keep track of your worries for one week. At the end of the week ask yourself the following questions:

- What times and places are you most likely to worry?
- Are there certain events that trigger your worry?
- What feelings do you have right before you worry?
- What are you predicting will happen that upsets you?
- What do you tend to do right after you worry?
- How did you feel then?

TABLE 6.2

WORRY RECORD: KEEPING TRACK OF YOUR WORRIES

Day/time	Events going on	How I feel right before I worry	My worry	How anxious did I feel? (0-100%)	What did I do next?	How did I feel then?

You might find that you worry more at night if you are alone, or you worry before you go to work, or you worry more on the weekends if you feel you have nothing to do. These trouble times may symbolize important themes or issues in your life. Typical issues that are represented by worries include being alone, feeling rejected, offending people, losing money, failing, being humiliated, getting taken advantage of, getting sick, someone else experiencing harm, leaving things undone, and being overwhelmed. I will explain how you can handle these specific issues when I describe how to handle both your negative thoughts and your core issues.

You may do some things right *after* you worry that can cause other problems. Some people who worry about rejection will have a few drinks. If you do this, then you will have two things to worry about—rejection and alcohol abuse. Or you might binge-eat after you worry, to get those unpleasant thoughts and feelings out of the way, and then you will worry about gaining weight on top of everything else.

List the dysfunctional things that you do after you worry (for example, overeat, drink, make foolish phone calls, overspend, overuse the TV or Internet):

DYSFUNCTIONAL BEHAVIORS AFTER WORRYING

_____

_____

_____

_____

Why is it important to identify these behaviors? Simply because they keep you from dealing with your worries and add to your problems. Once you have identified these dysfunctional behaviors, you can begin to focus on how to eliminate them. For example, examine the costs and benefits of a behavior (e.g., binge eating). Try to delay the behavior for at least one hour. During that time, carry out the exercises in this book that focus on your worries and your emotions. Your dysfunctional behaviors will interfere with your self-help, so you need to make a choice to commit to the self-help in place of the dysfunctional behavior.

Set Aside Worry Time

You may believe your worry is out of control and that it pervades every moment of the day. To challenge this, *assign a specific time and place for worry*. It may seem counterintuitive to you.[1] You probably think that practicing your worries will only increase your worry, and you will be overwhelmed. However, worry time allows you to set aside worry until a specified time, write out your worries, recognize that your worries are limited and repetitious, and gain a sense of control.

Try using worry time every day for two weeks. Set aside a specific time and place—let's say thirty minutes in the early evening. Sit down at a desk and write out your worries as they occur to you. Don't challenge them and don't reassure yourself—just worry. The rest of the time, if you have more worries, jot them down on an index card but put off the actual worrying until your assigned worry time.

For example, let's say your worry is "I won't be able to pay my bills." Write it down and put it aside until seven-thirty tonight. Then go over any other negative thoughts that you might have, like "I can't pay my credit card bill," "What if I lose my job?" or "What if my stocks lose even more value?"

After you have been practicing worry time for a while, you'll find that it gives you more of a sense of control over your worries. You begin to realize that you can put off your worries and that your worries are *repetitive*—you always have the same thoughts. It's not ten million worries—it's ten worries. In fact, some people say, "I get bored during worry time. I don't have enough things to worry about." This is a very common experience with worry time—people eventually find that they cannot fill the thirty minutes with worries, because they realize it is almost always the same things coming up over and over again.

Ten Ways to Defeat Your Worries

Now that we have identified your worries—and when they occur and what you are predicting—we can start using some powerful cognitive therapy techniques to take the power and meaning out of these thoughts.

1. Identify the Distortions in Your Thinking

When we are worried, depressed, or angry, we are inclined to think in a biased and distorted way. Cognitive therapists refer to "cognitive distortions," or thinking distortions, that may make you prone to look at things in the worst way possible.[2] In order to identify some of your own distorted or biased ways of thinking, examine the list of typical cognitive distortions in Table 6.3.

TABLE 6.3
TYPICAL COGNITIVE DISTORTIONS

1. *Mind reading.* You assume that you know what people think without having sufficient evidence of their thoughts: "He thinks I'm a loser."

2. *Fortune-telling.* You predict the future—that things will get worse or that there is danger ahead: "I'll fail that exam," "I won't get the job."

3. *Catastrophizing.* You believe that what has happened or will happen will be so awful and unbearable that you won't be able to stand it: "It would be terrible if I failed."

4. *Labeling.* You assign global negative traits to yourself and others: "I'm undesirable," "He's a rotten person."

5. *Discounting positives.* You claim that the positives that you or others attain are trivial: "That's what wives are supposed to do, so it doesn't count when she's nice to me," "Those successes were easy, so they don't matter."

6. *Negative filter.* You focus almost exclusively on the negatives and seldom notice the positives: "Look at all of the people who don't like me."

7. *Overgeneralizing.* You perceive a global pattern of negatives on the basis of a single incident: "This generally happens to me. I seem to fail at a lot of things."

8. *All-or-nothing thinking.* You view events or people in all-or-nothing terms: "I get rejected by everyone," "It was a waste of time."

9. *Shoulds.* You interpret events in terms of how things should be rather than simply focusing on what is: "I should do well. If I don't, then I'm a failure."

10. *Personalizing.* You attribute a disproportionate amount of the blame to yourself for negative events and fail to see that certain events are also caused by others: "The marriage ended because I failed."

---

11. *Blaming.* You focus on the other person as the source of your negative feelings and refuse to take responsibility for changing yourself: "She's to blame for the way I feel now," "My parents caused all my problems."

12. *Unfair comparisons.* You interpret events in terms of standards that are unrealistic—for example, you focus primarily on others who do better than you and find yourself inferior in the comparison: "She's more successful than I am," "Others did better than I did on the test."

13. *Regret orientation.* You focus on the idea that you could have done better in the past, rather than on what you can do better now: "I could have had a better job if I had tried," "I shouldn't have said that."

14. *What if?* You keep asking a series of questions about what if something happens, and fail to be satisfied with any of the answers: "Yeah, but what if I get anxious, and can't catch my breath?"

15. *Emotional reasoning.* You let your feelings guide your interpretation of reality: "I feel depressed, therefore my marriage is not working out."

16. *Inability to disconfirm.* You reject any evidence or arguments that might contradict your negative thoughts: "I'm unlovable—my friends hang out with me only because they must feel sorry for me."

17. *Judgment focus.* You view yourself, others, and events in terms of evaluations of "good" and "bad" or "superior" and "inferior," rather than simply describing, accepting, or understanding: "I didn't perform well in college," "If I take up tennis, I won't do well," "Look how successful she is. I'm not successful."

Consider the following typical worries and the cognitive (thinking) distortions involved:

- I wonder if he thinks I'm a loser. (Mind reading)
- I think she's in a bad mood because I said something stupid. (Personalizing)
- It would be awful if I didn't do well on the exam. (Catastrophizing)

- I may have done well on these exams in the past, but that doesn't mean I know this material now. (Discounting the positive)
- I don't think I know anything at all. (All-or-nothing thinking)

Look at table 6.3 opposite and see if you can categorize the following worries:

1. I'm going to end up a complete failure.
2. I'll never do anything right.
3. I could never be as successful as the president of the company.
4. She hasn't called, so she must no longer be interested.

I would categorize them as the following:

1. Fortune-telling, all-or-nothing thinking, labeling
2. Fortune-telling, all-or-nothing thinking, overgeneralizing
3. Fortune-telling, unfair comparisons
4. Mind reading, personalizing

If your worry is "I will never meet someone," then you are using fortune-telling. If you worry that your boss is disappointed in you, then you may be engaging in mind reading and personalizing. If you worry that the plane is going to crash but you say, "I just feel nervous—I think it's dangerous," then you are using emotional reasoning. Keep in mind that even though we call these "cognitive distortions," it does not necessarily mean that you are incorrect in your worries—your boss *could* be angry with you, or your relationship *could* fall apart.

Is there a pattern to your cognitive distortions? If there is, then you can challenge these negative patterns of thinking using specific techniques that I will outline below. These techniques can include testing out your predictions, looking at the evidence for and against your worry, considering the advice you would give a friend, or putting things in perspective. The key is to recognize that you may be using the same thinking distortions over and over. For example, if you are predicting catastrophes, then you can put things in perspective by testing out how often nothing really bad happens. If your worries tend to involve mind reading ("He thinks I am a loser"), then you can plan to challenge this by examining the evidence for and against your assumptions—you can even ask the person what he or she thinks about what you have said or done.

2. Determine How Likely It Is That What You Are Worried About Will Actually Happen

Betsy may have a lot of different thoughts in her head—thoughts about never finding someone, never being happy, always overeating. Let's take the thought "I'll never find someone." Betsy is feeling particularly down when she writes this in her diary and says that she believes this 90 percent. It seems quite hopeless to her. But what if we were to break it down into smaller steps? Let's look at the predictions above and ask her to predict the probability that any of these things will happen. Here are Betsy's answers:

Someone will smile at me this week. (90%)
I'll introduce myself to someone this week. (75%)
I'll get onto Match.com this week. (80%)
I'll answer some singles ads this week. (30%)

If we look at the steps involved in meeting someone, it turns out that a lot of these things are quite probable—even in the next week.

As another example, take the worry "I might run out of money." Susan kept worrying about her finances, even though she had a job and some small amount of savings. When she said that she might run out of money, she gave this a rating of 85 percent likely. However, when we broke it down into smaller steps in order to examine predictions for less extreme outcomes, we got the following:

- I will keep making a salary for the indefinite future. (90%)
- I will start keeping a budget. (65%)
- I will try to save a little bit of each month's check. (50%)

As a result of breaking down her predictions to these smaller steps, Susan's worries about running out of money dropped from 85 percent to 20 percent, according to her own ratings of her worry.

3. Determine the Worst Outcome, the Most Likely Outcome, and the Best Outcome

You are almost always thinking about negative outcomes—sometimes the worst outcome. But you should also think about other *possible* outcomes. You are thinking of failing the exam (the worst outcome), but there are other possible outcomes, such as doing very well on the exam, barely passing, and doing better than average. Betsy could think of the worst outcome when she was home alone, feeling down—"I'll never meet anyone that I love"—but she was able to come up with other *possible* outcomes. These included "I'll meet someone who is absolutely wonderful and we'll get married" (best outcome) and "After dating some guys I am not that crazy about, I'll meet a guy and we'll get married" (most likely outcome).

When Susan worried about running out of money (the worst outcome), she would get stuck ruminating about this. We examined the best outcome ("getting rich through speculating in stocks") and the most likely outcome ("having to go on a budget but gradually saving money"). This helped reduce her worry about catastrophes such as ending up homeless.

4. Tell Yourself a Story About Better Outcomes

When you think about bad outcomes, you are telling stories about how everything will end up badly, filling your imagination with details. These stories actually make the bad outcome seem more likely. This is because stories are easier to remember, they seem real, and they make negative thoughts more accessible to you—that is, you can more easily retrieve negative thoughts if they are part of a negative story. The reason for this is that we are much better at placing ourselves in a story than trying to remember specific facts. If we are going to aim for a better outcome, we have to have a story that leads to positive outcomes.

Betsy and I came up with a good story about meeting a guy and hooking up. Here's Betsy's story: "Well, the first thing I do is I decide to be more outgoing. I join the health club (I can stand to lose a few pounds). I sign up for a course and see if there are some nice guys there. And I get onto the computer dating thing. So I start answering ads and I meet this guy and we have coffee and then we find that we have a lot of things in common. We date—we go to movies and restaurants and take long walks through the city. And we fall in love."

Susan's story about a better outcome for her finances was the following: "I start to keep a budget, keeping track of unnecessary expenses—restaurants, cabs, things I don't really need. I begin to commit to saving a small percentage of my check every month. I gradually watch my savings grow, and I always think twice about making any large purchases. As my savings grow, over time I begin to feel more secure financially."

Another way of making your positive story seem more achievable is to find out about people who actually have accomplished the goals that you want to achieve. For example, if Susan wants to become more financially secure, she can think about people in a similar position—say, people making the same income that she makes but who are more financially secure. Alcoholics often benefit from going to AA meetings and hearing stories about how heavy drinkers became sober and remained sober, and the same is true for worry. Role models are invaluable for giving you ideas about how you can change—and the likelihood of changing.

5. List the Evidence That Something Really Bad Is Going to Happen

Betsy's thought that she would never meet anyone was a strong emotional experience for her. But like any thought that we have, we can ask if there is any evidence for it. What evidence was she using to support such an unpleasant thought? Betsy said that the evidence that she would never meet anyone was that she was alone right now, there weren't any good unattached men in New York, and her friends were single.

What is the logic behind this "evidence"? The fact that she is alone right now cannot be evidence that she will always be alone, since all married people were once single and alone. Being alone can be a temporary state of affairs. Or consider the thought that there are no unattached nice guys in New York—a city of eight million people. It's unlikely that she has met more than a couple hundred men. How could she generalize millions of people she's never met? And the fact that her friends are single is no evidence that she will never have a committed relationship. If her friends were married, would that mean that she was going to get married soon?

We decided to examine some reasons why she might meet someone. We came up with the following: Betsy has had several relationships with men in the past, men find her attractive, most people eventually get married, she is willing to do things to meet people, and she has something to offer.

I thought we might spend a moment on "something to offer." I asked Betsy what she wanted in a man, and she said, "Someone who's honest, who doesn't play around. He would have to be

smart enough, someone I can do things with. Someone I can talk
to, who's a good listener. Good-looking—but he doesn't have to
be classically handsome." And then I asked her what her friends
liked in her. She said they saw her as a good friend who cared
about them, who wasn't judgmental, and whom they could
laugh with. I asked Betsy to think about the fact that what she
was looking for in a man is what she had to offer to other people.
She was looking for someone like herself. Betsy smiled and said,
"Well, I don't want to get conceited," and I replied, "It's better
than worrying, isn't it?"

6. Test Your Predictions

Let's see if the future is really as bad as you think it's going to be.
Let's take some likely worries:

- I won't be prepared for the test.
- I'll fail the test.
- Bill won't call.
- I won't get any sleep.
- I won't be able to pay my bills.
- Angelica is going to get angry with me.
- I'll be depressed all weekend.

Come up with your own list of worries, write down your predictions in your worry record, and then go back to them every
seven days and examine the outcome. For example, Jennie had
all of the predictions above, and she went back to them for the
next two weeks. Here's the outcome:

- I got motivated and studied for the test.
- I did OK on the test—not great, but well enough.
- Bill called—but a couple of days after I expected him to.
  Maybe he's not right for me anyway.

- I didn't sleep as well as I'd like, but I got some sleep. Even though I was tired the next day, I got through it.
- I wasn't able to pay the entire balance on my credit card.
- Angelica wasn't angry with me. She just had some problems with her work. I was taking her moods too seriously.
- I was down on Saturday morning, but then I went to the health club, and later Angelica and I went for a walk in the park.

Let's look at how one person tested his predictions.

		TABLE 6.4	
		TESTING YOUR PREDICTIONS	
Date/time	Prediction	Actual outcome (time)	How I felt afterward
January 18 4:30 p.m.	I'll never get this writing done	I wrote three pages (8 p.m.)	Relieved, relaxed
January 19 11 a.m.	I'll be late for my appointment	I was ten minutes late, but so were they	Relieved

The two predictions that were driving his worry were that he would never get his writing done and that he would be late for an appointment. But the actual outcomes were that he did get a few pages written and he was only ten minutes late for his appointment. In both cases, the outcomes made him feel relieved.

You can test out your predictions by using Table 6.4 to write out the actual outcomes that you predict and what outcomes actually occur. How did you feel after it was over?

If you are like many worriers, you have been making worried predictions for years, perhaps thousands of negative predictions. But 85 percent of the predictions that worriers make do not come true.[3] Moreover, worriers continually underestimate their ability to handle negative outcomes, since they tend to cope quite well with negative outcomes—even outcomes that they had not foreseen.

Let's take the current worry that Susan has, that her money will run out. As Susan and I looked back on her prior worry history, she indicated that she had worried about exams and papers in college, about getting into accidents, about air travel, about getting a job, and about her performance on her job. In fact, not one of her negative predictions ever came true. Despite this, she would continue to worry each day.

If almost all of your past worries proved to be false, maybe this is just another one of those false alarms.

7. Put Predictions in Perspective

A lot of our worries are predictions that are completely out of sync with reality. We often worry that a catastrophe will happen, that something rare will be almost certain to occur, that we will start slipping down the slope to chaos, or that we will suddenly fall through a trapdoor. Let's see how you can put your predictions into more realistic perspectives.

DON'T TURN WORRIES INTO CATASTROPHES

Imagine the following. I ask you to walk twenty feet across a board that is twelve inches wide and two feet off the ground. I'll give you a thousand dollars to do this. You say, "That's easy. I'll take the bet." But what if I tell you I've changed my mind and the board is going to be a hundred feet in the air. You pass it up. One mistake and you would fall to your death.

The same thing is true with the first worry in the sequence. Betsy thinks, "I'll never meet someone. I'll never get married. I could never be happy if I don't get married, I'll end up alone and miserable." She is worrying about a *string* of bad things, each worse than the preceding one. Another example of this kind of string of negatives might be "I lost 20 percent of my money in the stock market. I'll keep losing money. I'll go broke. I'll end up homeless." The string of negatives gives us an idea of why the current thing that you worry about seems so bad.

But the fact is that none of the things in Betsy's string of events has happened. In fact, the only thing that has happened is that she is alone tonight. Betsy is viewing this experience as a catastrophe—but in fact it is simply an inconvenience. None of the "awful" and "final" things that she predicts have actually occurred—and none is likely to occur.

USE REALISTIC PROBABILITIES

One way of challenging this is to ask yourself what the probability of each event is.[4] Let's take the example of losing 20 percent of your money in the stock market:

I'll keep losing money.	Probability = .50
I'll go broke.	Probability = .01
I'll end up homeless.	Probability = .001

If we multiply .50 × .01 × .001, we get .000005—or five in a million. From these estimates, the chance of ending up homeless depends on this sequence of probabilities coming true—a very unlikely occurrence. However, when we worry, we don't think about probabilities in a rational way. In fact, we often think, "It's possible, therefore it is likely to happen."

GET OFF THE SLIPPERY SLOPE

A lot of us worry about what will happen if the present situation gets out of hand. The investor worried that her 20 percent loss could spiral down into homelessness. Another person worried that a discoloration on his nose (which turned out to be nothing) was a sign of cancer, that this would turn into full-blown melanoma, that it would metastasize, and that he'd end up dead in a year, so his thought was "I've got to catch it early." He was always looking for signs of cancer or other life-threatening illnesses. His older sister died at the age of twenty-two from cancer, and this made him overly focused on this problem for himself. But is what you're worrying about really a slippery slope? Or is it just a little more noise?

DON'T FALL THROUGH YOUR TRAPDOOR

Some of us worry because we believe that we will be caught by surprise by a sudden catastrophe. I call this the trapdoor phenomenon. You feel that you are walking along peacefully in life and that everything is just fine, but if you let your guard down, you'll fall through a trapdoor into hell. Some people who are extremely jealous feel this way. They think they have to constantly get reassurance, check up on their partner at every moment, and become the only person of any interest to their partner. Of course, this just leads their partner to push them away, leading to further demands for reassurance. The jealous person is afraid of trusting someone only to be betrayed in the end.

Now, there may be trapdoors in real life, but if you fall through them, you'll almost always be able to recover. One woman who was very jealous and constantly demanded reassurance was in fact betrayed by her husband. Part of it was due to the fact that she was too demanding and hostile, but another part of it may have been due to the fact that he'd done the same thing with his three previous wives. After her initial hurt and anger over his betrayal, she realized that she had spent her marriage living in fear of the inevitable—that he would betray her—and that she was now free to pursue a relationship with someone who was more trustworthy. The trapdoor that she feared turned out to be less of a free fall into oblivion and more of a difficult period in her life that created some new options with better alternatives.

8. Think of How You Could Cope if the Bad Outcome Actually Happens

Worriers underestimate how well they can cope with unforeseen or anticipated negative outcomes. Of course, some of these outcomes that are predicted—"The plane will crash"—do not leave much room for coping. However, other worries allow us to consider ways in which you could cope. For example, let's imagine that Betsy actually never gets married. What would be some ways she could cope with this? Since this may actually be an outcome—and consider that it is an outcome freely chosen by millions of people throughout the world—examining how she could cope with this is not unrealistic. One thing to think of would be the costs and benefits of being single, rather than simply looking at this as a total disaster. There might be certain benefits worth considering.

Another worry would be the string of thoughts leading someone to think, "I'll go bankrupt." Imagine if that did occur. Again, millions of people survive bankruptcy—in fact, bankruptcy is often a fresh start on life, free-ing people of the burden of debt and allowing them to keep all future earnings—and, in some states, allowing them to keep certain personal property, including one's house. Many of the "disastrous" outcomes that you may worry about are real-life conditions that millions of people contend with and are able to transcend.

9. Imagine the Advice You Would Give a Friend Who Had Your Worries

We are generally a lot more rational and balanced with friends or strangers than we are with ourselves. For those of us who have demanding standards for ourselves and expect perfection at everything, it is useful to ask, "If my friend had this problem, what advice would I give her or him?"

Betsy was very harsh on herself, thinking that she would never find a partner because she wasn't the richest, most beautiful, most famous person around. I thought, "Maybe she should go down to City Hall in New York City to see the people who have filed for a marriage license." That would be a sobering experience. It's not the rich and beautiful and famous who are getting married.

I asked Betsy to imagine that her friend Catherine was going through this down period and was thinking, "I'll never find a partner and I'll always be alone." I suggested that she think of Catherine as having exactly the same experiences and qualities that Betsy has. Then I asked Betsy to give Catherine advice:

Betsy (to Catherine): "You have already had several relationships. In fact, you're even getting more desirable—you're more stylish, more interesting, you have more to offer. You're feeling down right now, but your friends and men who meet you find you very appealing. You just have to get yourself in a position where people meet you."

I then asked Betsy why she would be so much more reasonable with Catherine than she is with herself. Betsy indicated that she thought that she needed to worry in order to motivate herself. But the fact was that her worries were actually making her more likely to avoid people and to act shy when she met men. Betsy's homework assignment was to imagine advising a friend who had the same negative thoughts that she had. This helped her ease up on herself.

10. Show Yourself Why This Is Not Really a Problem

Our typical worries are often focused on rather trivial issues that other people think are not worth thinking about. For example, when you tell other people that someone might be annoyed with you, you don't have a date, your significant other hasn't called, you are not prepared for an exam, you might not get some work done, or you worry about your health but the doctor says that you are fine, you often find that people in your life say, "What are you worrying about?"

A rather powerful technique that I have used with people who worry about some of these things is to ask, "Tell me why this is *not* a problem." This technique can help you challenge the idea that simply because you are currently upset about your worry, it means that there is something very important in your apprehensive thoughts.

Let's consider Betsy, who worried that because she was not currently in a committed relationship, she would end up miserable in her life. I asked her to tell me why this was not a problem. At first all Betsy could think about was that she was all alone, but I pointed out that she had friends and colleagues and a family. And then I asked, "Are there some things that you can still do even if you do not have a husband?" She could go to work, see her friends, travel, go out to the theater, go dancing, date different guys. Then I said, "I want you to finish this sentence— and I want you to do it over and over again. The sentence is, 'I don't have a husband right now—and this is not a problem because . . .' " Betsy continued, "Because I can still do everything I want to do. It's not a problem because I have a good job, I don't need someone to support me, I can date other guys, I don't have to put up with someone else's issues, I can see my friends, I can read and not be disturbed. And I might end up with a husband in the future, anyway."

Summing Up

Monitoring your worries, looking at the dysfunctional behaviors that follow after your worry, and using worry time can help you gain some control over your worry. The ten techniques outlined in this chapter will help you defeat your worries. Use the following table to help you identify and challenge your worries.

TABLE 6.5

TEN WAYS TO DEFEAT YOUR WORRY

Question to ask yourself	*What to do*
1. What thinking distortions are you using?	List the thinking distortions (mind reading, fortune-telling, etc.).
2. How likely (0–100%) is it that this will actually happen?	If you were placing a bet, how likely do you think it is that this event will actually occur? 0%? 10%? 50%? 70% 100%? Why would you give it this probability?
3. What is the worst outcome? The most likely outcome? The best outcome?	Describe different possible outcomes. Worst: Most likely: Best: Look at what you listed as the most likely outcome. Why would it be the most likely?
4. Tell yourself a story about better outcomes.	Use a separate sheet of paper to write a short story where things work out for you. What are the steps that you might need to take in real life to make this story come true?

Question to ask yourself	What to do
5. What is the evidence (for and against) your worry that something really bad is going to happen?	If you had to divide 100 points between the evidence for and against, how would you divide these points? (For example, would it be 50–50? 60–40?) Points: evidence for = Points: evidence against =
6. How many times have you been wrong about your worries in the past? Give examples. Is there a pattern?	
7. Put predictions in perspective.	Don't turn worries into catastrophes. Is what you're worrying about the end of the world or merely an inconvenience? Use realistic probabilities. How likely is this, really? Get off the slippery slope. Are you predicting a chain reaction that is not likely? Don't fall through the trap-door. Are you expecting that the bottom will fall out—or is it more likely that this is a bump in the road?
8. What are some things that you could do to cope if the bad outcome actually occurred?	
9. If someone else were facing the events that you are facing, would you encourage that person to worry as much as you do? What advice would you give him or her?	Put yourself in the shoes of giving advice to your bestfriend. If your friend was predicting all of these negative things and worrying a lot about them, what would you say to him or her? What if you said this to yourself? Is there some reason you treat yourself worse than you treat others?
10. Indicate why this is not really a problem.	This is not a problem because . . .

7

Step Four:
Focus on the Deeper Threat

WHY DO YOU WORRY about some things but not others? In Chapter 3 we identified your personality style, and from that we can determine the core beliefs that drive your worries.[1] Examples of such beliefs are:

- Abandonment—people will leave me.
- Defectiveness—there is something really wrong with me.
- Responsibility—I have to be ethical and moral in everything.
- Specialness, uniqueness—I need to be viewed as superior.
- Helplessness—I can't take care of myself, I can't make anything good happen on my own.

These beliefs underlie your personality style.[2] For example, if you are overly conscientious (obsessive-compulsive personality), then you will believe in demanding standards, responsibility, and control over events. You might worry that you are not working hard enough, that you are not responsible enough, or that things are not as orderly as they should be. Or if you are a dependent person, then you will worry about being abandoned, because you fear that you are helpless on your own, that you will not be able to take care of yourself, and that you can never make yourself happy.

Your Core Beliefs

To help identify your specific beliefs, look at some of them in Table 7.1, below. Do you see yourself in any of these beliefs and worries? If you have a negative belief, for example, you think that there is something defective about you, and you will try to adapt to this by avoiding certain things. Or you might try to compensate. For example, if you believe that you are really boring and incompetent, you would avoid opening up to people until you are absolutely sure you can trust them. If you have a belief about demanding standards—you won't settle for less than perfection—then you will work yourself to death. You will worry about being less than perfect because you equate this with being a loser.

TABLE 7.1

PERSONAL BELIEFS AND WORRIES

Personal beliefs	Example	Worries	How you adapt to your belief
Defective	You think that you are incompetent and inferior.	"If they get to know me, they'll reject me. No one wants defective people."	You avoid letting people really get to know you. You avoid taking on challenging tasks or relationships. You try to please other people so that they won't see that you are really "inferior."

Personal beliefs	Example	Worries	How you adapt to your belief
Abandonment	You believe that people will leave you and that you will end up alone and miserable.	"My partner is no longer interested in me. Other people are more appealing. If I am on my own, I can't be happy."	You continually seek reassurance that you are loved and accepted. You check on your partner to see if your jealousy is valid. You don't express your true opinions because you are afraid people will leave you.
Helpless	You think that you can't take care of yourself.	"If he/she leaves me, I won't be able to make myself happy or take care of myself. I won't be able to survive."	You stay in unrewarding relationships or jobs because you are afraid of making a change that will result in being alone and helpless.
Special	You think you are superior and deserve a lot of attention and praise.	"If I don't excel, then I am just inferior and worthless. If people don't respect my outstanding qualities, then I can't stand it. Maybe I'll just end up ordinary. I might be humiliated."	You surround yourself with people who need you so that they will tell you how great you are. You break the rules so that you can get your way. You demand that others give in to your needs.

Personal beliefs	Example	Worries	How you adapt to your belief
Responsible	You take pride in being rational and diligent and getting things right.	"If I make a mistake, it means that I'm careless. I might forget something. Things might get out of control."	You exhaust yourself with work so that you can feel you are doing the right thing. You review what you do to make sure you didn't make mistakes.
Glamorous	You focus on being attractive and impressive to other people.	"If I have any imperfections in my appearance, then I won't be loved and admired."	You spend considerable effort trying to be physically attractive or fascinating. You flirt with and seduce people. You check the mirror.
Autonomous	You value your freedom to do things your way.	"If someone intrudes on my time and space, then I will have no freedom at all."	You put up barriers to people having authority over you. You refuse to comply with others' requests. You insist on doing things your way.
Caretaker	You think you are responsible for making everyone feel comfortable and happy.	"Did I say something that hurt her feelings? Have I disappointed them? Could I do something to take care of them?"	You constantly sacrifice yourself for the needs of other people. You apologize and play the part of someone who is always pleasing and cooperative.

Let's take a closer look at two personality types and see how your beliefs determine them.

Avoidant—Sensitive

The avoidant style of personality is marked by low self-esteem and sensitivity to criticism. These individuals can form relationships with other people and open up with them—once they have established that they can trust them. Their beliefs about themselves are that they are incompetent, uninteresting, and defective and that other people are rejecting and critical and feel superior. Their typical worries are "Others will see that I am boring or defective. They will criticize me." People with these beliefs of being incompetent and defective often withdraw into themselves, relying on solitary activities (hobbies, the Internet, reading) and retreating into fantasy. Because of their fear of negative evaluation and fear of negative feelings, they are highly likely to have significant interpersonal anxiety. Their avoidance of negative feelings is reflected not only in their withdrawal from social activities (where they fear being evaluated) but also in their intense fantasy life where they dream of escaping or of feeling more successful. Sometimes this fear of negative feelings is expressed in substance abuse—especially alcohol and marijuana abuse.

Dependent—Devoted

People with this style will often cling in relationships and do a lot to keep the relationship going. They are concerned about being abandoned and left alone. They often feel that they cannot function without someone else in their lives—often someone who they feel will take care of them. They can be very devoted and loyal.

The personality style of devoted and dependent is often related to underlying personal beliefs about the self as weak, helpless, needy, and incompetent. In addition, other people are idealized as nurturing and supportive or are viewed in a negative way as abandoning and unreliable. Typical worries are "People will leave me and I won't be able to take care of myself. I need to please others in order to keep them. I can't assert myself too much."

Consider Miriam, who feared that her husband might leave her. We can see that she has many of these dependent features. She viewed herself as needy, helpless, and not particularly competent, and she worried her husband might be unreliable and abandon her. Initially, Miriam said, she idealized her husband as a "protector"—someone who was "very steady and sure of himself." But she came to view his "independence" as a potential threat to their marriage.

Think about your own core beliefs. Do you tend to worry about abandonment or not being a special person? How are your core beliefs related to your childhood experience? To the values that you were taught? To the losses that you have experienced in your life?

Why Are These Core Beliefs Important?

Your worries result from these core beliefs. Knowing this, you will be able to focus on these underlying issues and undermine the worry more easily. If your worries are recurrently about living up to your demanding standards, then modifying this need for demanding standards—or perfectionism in performance— can reduce your worry substantially. A belief is like a lens through which you look at experience. The lens makes you select out certain information, weigh it or value it in a certain way, and it excludes conflicting information. For example, if you believe that you are either totally responsible or totally irresponsible (the overly conscientious personality), you will be a perfectionist, predict that you will make irresponsible mistakes, and expect catastrophic consequences for these mistakes. Similarly, if you believe you are basically unlovable, then you'll think people don't like you, you'll feel easily insulted or rejected, and you'll expect to get rejected and abandoned.

Look at Figure 7.1 and you can see how experience can be filtered through a core belief.

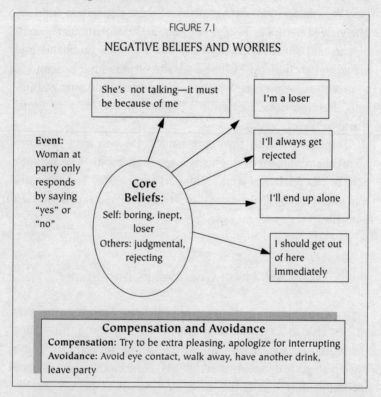

FIGURE 7.1

NEGATIVE BELIEFS AND WORRIES

Event:
Woman at party only responds by saying "yes" or "no"

Core Beliefs:
Self: boring, inept, loser
Others: judgmental, rejecting

She's not talking—it must be because of me

I'm a loser

I'll always get rejected

I'll end up alone

I should get out of here immediately

Compensation and Avoidance
Compensation: Try to be extra pleasing, apologize for interrupting
Avoidance: Avoid eye contact, walk away, have another drink, leave party

Let's say someone doesn't seem to respond to you at a party. She answers your statements with only "yes" or "no." If you have a core belief that says that you are a boring person, you'll interpret her behavior as reflecting how boring you are. The other thing you'll notice is that you might try to compensate for being a boring person by trying to be extra pleasing or by apologizing, which can make people think that you are a bit strange or insecure. Or you can avoid rejection by avoiding eye contact or leaving early. These attempts to compensate or avoid will maintain your worries, because you won't find out that you can be accepted the way you are and that people don't generally expect someone to be fascinating at a party. Now look at Figure 7.2. This indicates how you might respond if you had a positive belief about yourself and other people.

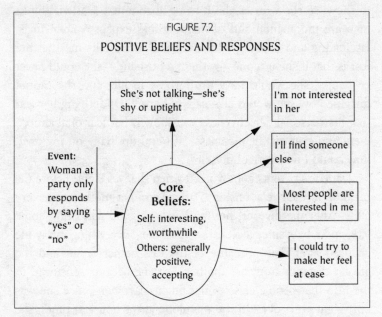

FIGURE 7.2

POSITIVE BELIEFS AND RESPONSES

She's not talking—she's shy or uptight

I'm not interested in her

Event: Woman at party only responds by saying "yes" or "no"

Core Beliefs:
Self: interesting, worthwhile
Others: generally positive, accepting

I'll find someone else

Most people are interested in me

I could try to make her feel at ease

Your experience with the woman who responds with "yes" and "no" would be quite different. You might not care how she responds or what she thinks. Your belief will determine whether you are worried or indifferent.

Examples of Negative Beliefs and Worry

Darlene and Jeff have been dating for six months, and now Jeff isn't calling as frequently as he used to. Although Jeff says he is busy and stressed out at work, Darlene worries that Jeff is losing interest in her. She thinks, "Maybe he'll find someone else. If he breaks up with me, I'll end up all alone. Who would want me? I'm not as interesting and successful as the other women I see."

Darlene's belief about herself is that she is not interesting and not lovable. This is a belief about personal defectiveness. She worries that her "boring and unlovable" qualities are beginning to show, so she worries about being abandoned. Darlene thinks men are judgmental and demanding and expect women to be fascinating and exciting all the time. Darlene tells me that her fear is that if she is alone—without a husband—she could never be happy, she would have no purpose in life, and she cannot imagine how she would take care of herself. Underlying her fear that her personal defectiveness will show is her fear of abandonment and eventual helplessness: "If I end up living on my own, how could I take care of myself?"

Darlene's parents got divorced when she was eight. Before the breakup in their relationship, Darlene and her mother were very close. After the divorce, her mother took a job and came home late, and a babysitter took care of Darlene: "Everything in my life changed after that." Because of the loss of her father and the greater distance from her mother, Darlene became sensitized to the idea that people close to her might leave her. Since she was only eight years old and she was alone in the house at times, she feared that something terrible could happen to her. Thus, in Darlene's mind, being alone was potentially dangerous. Darlene harbored the sense that she might have been the cause of the divorce. "I don't know if it sounds like it makes sense now, but I thought then that if my mother loved me enough and if my father wanted me, they wouldn't have broken up. And I thought that my mother preferred going to work—and eventually dating new men—to spending time with me. I began to doubt myself."

Steve is a young lawyer in a large firm. It's a very competitive environment, and he's not getting along with his boss. Steve knows that he could always get another job, but he worries that if he doesn't make it at this prestigious law firm, then he won't realize his true potential as an outstanding lawyer. He won't be *special.* For Steve, not being special is the same as being a failure. He can't stand the idea of being ordinary.

Steve has demanding standards—he believes that he has to excel to be worthwhile. Steve worries about not getting a job done at a superior level—he believes that he must be better than everyone else at everything. His underlying fear is that he is going to end up mediocre and that this will mean that his life has been a waste. Because of this belief about needing to be special, Steve worries not only that he will not make partner at the law firm but that he cannot keep up with the level of material consumption of the people he socializes with. He worries that his apartment is not nice enough and that his wardrobe is not fashionable enough, so people will view him as just an average person. His beliefs about others are that they are inferior and mediocre and can be used for his own gain. When he thinks about his relationship, he basically worries that others won't think his partner is as attractive and prestigious as he wants her to be—that she will not live up to his standards and what he wants people to see him as being.

Underneath his fears of being mediocre are Steve's own doubts about himself. He grew up in a working-class family, his parents fought all the time about money, and his father was often unemployed. He was fortunate to get a scholarship to a prestigious school, but he always felt out of place, one class down from the other people there. He is constantly worried that people will see that he "doesn't really belong."

Changing Your Core Beliefs

You won't be able to change your core belief in a few weeks.[3] You have spent years developing strategies of avoidance and compensation to keep you from facing your core fears. For example, if you have demanding standards, you may have been avoiding challenging tasks that you could fail on, and you might be compensating by being a workaholic. Thus you seldom really face your core belief of demanding standards and the fear of being a failure or a lazy person.

Indeed, the core belief is so familiar to you that you may never even think about it. How could this be? If you have demanding standards and fear being lazy and irresponsible, you may be working extremely hard to prove that you are responsible—and, on the surface, you may actually believe that you are responsible. But why do you worry so much about living up to your responsibilities? Steve worked excessively but worried that he would fall behind in his work, even though this almost never happened. He would increase his effort, skip lunch, forgo exercise and time with his friends, and work long into the night. On the surface he viewed himself as highly responsible and quite productive—but he continually worried that this might all slip away from him. He fantasized about escaping to a deserted island and never working again. This fantasy was appealing at times, but it made him anxious that he was losing his motivation. When we examined his worries—"What would happen if you didn't get all the work done?"—his thinking led to the following: "I would worry I would fall behind even further. My work would become mediocre. I would then become lazy and irresponsible." He believed, he said, that he had to drive himself extra hard to prevent this from happening.

Would he really become lazy and irresponsible if he did not drive himself so hard? Attempts to modify your core belief often meet with resistance. This is because you see the core belief—let's say "I need demanding standards"—as actually preventing another belief from being activated—"I am lazy and irresponsible."[4] You often view your core belief in all-or-nothing terms—"Either I am totally responsible or I am totally irresponsible." You have almost no tolerance for shades of gray. You see even the slightest chance of experiencing the core belief as threatening to send you into the oblivion of your worst fears. But there are a number of techniques that have proven useful in modifying the core belief.[5]

Craig is a successful businessman who has acquired enough money that he could retire with his wife and never have to work again. However, he believes that his work is a sign of responsibility, and he will not consider early retirement. But there is less demand for his company's product in the current market, so Craig's productivity in sales has declined in the last two years. Although Craig knows that market conditions are bad throughout the industry, he will not use this as an "excuse." He worries he'll be late on assignments, that he will not cover all the details adequately, and that sales will fall further. Craig's father was a rigid and cold man who criticized Craig when he was a boy. "Nothing was ever good enough for him," Craig said. "There wasn't a lot of love or warmth growing up."

Craig wasn't a worrier in college or business school, since he felt he knew what was expected of him and was in control of what he had to do. His worries began after business school, when he began to work in sales. Craig felt he had no way of knowing for sure how sales would go. Interestingly, nothing really bad happened on the job. In fact, he continued to have success, but the uncertainty began to plague him.

Craig's worry has foreclosed promotion for him. He believes that he must be in control, so he sees taking on more responsibility less as an opportunity and more as a burden. Craig felt that taking on more responsibility would mean a greater risk of failure—even though he hadn't failed before. His thought was, "If I failed, it would show that I'm really lazy." I asked Craig how this fear of being lazy tied in with his worries. He said, "I sometimes think that I need to worry to keep myself from being lazy."

If we look at Craig's core issues, childhood history, and worries, we can see that he compensates for his fear of not being totally responsible and productive by being work-absorbed and working excessively long hours. These are shown in Figure 7.3. Indeed, Craig views his worry as something that prepares him and motivates him to do his best. Furthermore, his fear of not being totally responsible—and his reliance on worry and self-criticism—has led him to avoid new and challenging tasks, for example, taking on a promotion or looking for a more challenging position elsewhere.

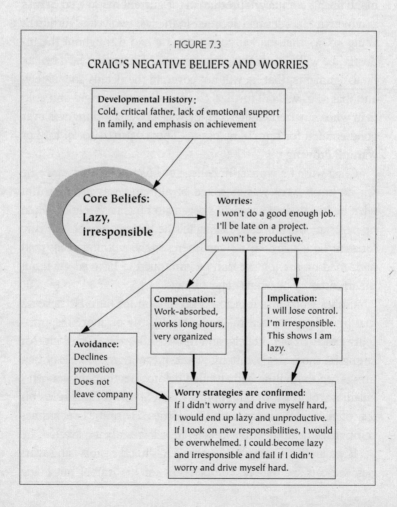

FIGURE 7.3

CRAIG'S NEGATIVE BELIEFS AND WORRIES

Developmental History:
Cold, critical father, lack of emotional support in family, and emphasis on achievement

Core Beliefs:
Lazy, irresponsible

Worries:
I won't do a good enough job.
I'll be late on a project.
I won't be productive.

Compensation:
Work-absorbed, works long hours, very organized

Implication:
I will lose control.
I'm irresponsible.
This shows I am lazy.

Avoidance:
Declines promotion
Does not leave company

Worry strategies are confirmed:
If I didn't worry and drive myself hard, I would end up lazy and unproductive. If I took on new responsibilities, I would be overwhelmed. I could become lazy and irresponsible and fail if I didn't worry and drive myself hard.

The following techniques will help you modify your core beliefs. Keep in mind, however, that these beliefs have been affecting you for many years.

Identify Your Beliefs About Yourself and Other People

As we discussed earlier, you can identify your core beliefs by examining your response to the Personality Beliefs Questionnaire in Chapter 3.[6] Take another look at Table 7.1, "Personal Beliefs and Worries," on page 116, to see which beliefs and worries fit you.

How Are Your Beliefs Related to Your Worries?

Let's go back to our discussion of Craig, who had these demanding standards he thought he needed to live up to in order to prevent himself from becoming lazy and irresponsible. Consequently, he engaged in a lot of fortune-telling ("I won't get the job done"), selective negative filtering of information ("I still haven't finished the last part"), all-or-nothing thinking ("I've got to get the whole job done now or it's a total waste of time"), personalizing ("It's entirely my responsibility"), discounting his positives ("The part that I've done doesn't matter if the whole thing isn't done the best way it can be"), and catastrophic thinking ("It would be intolerable if I didn't do the best job. I couldn't stand it").

Because Craig's beliefs predispose him toward looking for any signs of laziness and irresponsibility, he often will worry that he won't get enough sleep and that the next day he will not be as productive. Consequently, he has insomnia. He also focuses on the smallest details, ignoring the larger picture that he has accomplished a lot. In order to keep himself highly motivated, he keeps changing his standards—he keeps raising them so that he is never satisfied.

Ask yourself if your beliefs lead you to do any of the following:

- Am I fortune-telling bad things?
- Do I mind read what people will think of me?
- Am I not counting my positives?
- Do I think it would be catastrophic if something happened?
- Do I use a double standard to evaluate myself and other people?

Examine the Costs and Benefits of These Beliefs

Craig felt that his belief in demanding standards accounted for a good part of his success in life: "If I didn't have these standards, I would never have done as well as I have done." He also believed that it made him into a conscientious and reliable person. However, he also could see the downside to these demanding standards. He was often worried, he had insomnia, he could never relax, he was never satisfied, and he was always somewhat pessimistic. He said, "I never live in the moment." But Craig, like most people, was reluctant to "give up" on his core beliefs: "I don't want to become complacent and mediocre." Craig believed that he could not relax any part of his standards or else he would quickly sink into "laziness." Like many worriers, he believed that his fears and perfectionism motivated him. I asked Craig to examine the costs and benefits of living up to 85 percent of his standards rather than 100 percent. He said that he worried whether 85 percent would motivate him enough, but he thought it was worth a try.

We often think that our core beliefs may give us an edge. Darlene feels that a benefit of believing she is boring and people will reject her is that she won't be caught by surprise: if she finds she is boring, she can try to be more interesting, and if she believes that someone is going to leave her, she can ask for reassurance and feel better. The downside, of course, is that she is worried, anxious, depressed, self-critical, and insecure in her relationships.

Has your belief led you to take jobs that were not as demanding or to avoid trying to move forward in your career? Has your belief led you to make poor choices in partners or friends or to stay in unrewarding relationships?[7] Has your belief contributed to your insecurity around new people? If you never had this negative belief, would you have made different choices, felt differently about yourself, been less anxious? What would your life have been like if you had more positive beliefs about yourself and other people?

What are the costs and benefits of your belief?

Belief	Costs	Benefits

Are You Viewing Yourself in All-or-Nothing Terms?

Craig views himself (and others) as either "responsible" or "irresponsible," "hardworking" or "lazy." The result of this all-or-nothing way of seeing things is that Craig cannot enjoy "mostly successful" or "good enough." He has a hard time seeing growth or learning as important experiences, focusing instead on the bottom line. For Craig, if everything does not go perfectly well, he discounts his successes and selectively focuses on the one small detail that is not completely right.

Darlene thinks, "Either I am fascinating or I am boring." I suggested that almost no one is fascinating for more than a minute.

Most of our interactions are small talk—"What did you do today?" "I went shopping and then I worked on the project for two hours. We ordered in for dinner." If you view yourself in black-and-white terms, you will miss a lot of the gradations of gray. For example, if you think, "I'm either a winner or a loser," you miss the fact that while you may not be the world's best at everything, you are relatively successful at various things. Sometimes you are interesting, sometimes you are not. If you view your appearance in black-and-white terms, then you may miss some of your better features and will focus excessively on slight imperfections.

Try to think in terms of "sometimes," "to a degree," and "relatively," and think of yourself in different situations with different people. You might be more relaxed and more expressive of your ideas with close friends, but with a total stranger you might start off being a bit reserved. Think of how you change across time and situations. Then fill in this chart.

Belief	Seeing myself as more complicated
Examples of my all-or-nothing thinking:	How am I more complicated?
	Are there shades of gray?
	Does my behavior vary at different times and in different situations?
	How do other people see me?
	What would happen if I viewed myself in less extreme terms?
Conclusions:	

What Is the Evidence Against Your Belief?

Let's consider Craig's belief that he is really lazy and irresponsible. Craig's "evidence" for this was that he sometimes didn't feel like working at all, and he had fantasies of escaping to the islands and not coming back. But Craig was able to come up with a lot more evidence that he *wasn't* lazy: "I always work hard. I have ignored a lot of my family's needs—which I really shouldn't do. I have gotten a lot of recognition at work. My boss has told me over and over again how much he thinks he can count on me." He concluded that the evidence was 90 percent that he was not lazy.

Since Darlene believed she was boring, she seldom registered information that people found what she said interesting or worthwhile. But when we looked at the evidence, it was clear that her friends often laughed along with her, confided in her, and listened to her stories; she had good advice to give, and she was intelligent. I asked her to view herself from the point of view of her friends, and she said that none of them would say that she was boring. Think about your core beliefs—that you are "boring" or "stupid" or "irresponsible." What would be some examples of things you could do that would be the sign of not being boring, stupid, or incompetent? For example, if Darlene viewed herself as boring, she could look for evidence that she was sometimes interesting to people. Examples included people who laughed at her jokes, asked her questions, wanted to see her, wanted to talk with her, or called her up. Look for evidence that contradicts your belief.

My negative belief: _____	
Evidence for:	*Evidence against:*
Conclusions:	

Would You Be as Critical of Other People?

Craig tends to be tougher on himself than he is on others. I refer to this as a double standard. I asked Craig what he would think of someone else who worked as hard as he does. He said, "I'd tell him to lighten up on himself. I would say, 'Look, you have made a lot of money for this company, so why drive yourself crazy?' " Craig said his justification for being harder on himself was to keep himself from becoming lazy.

Similarly, Darlene is a very understanding and accepting person. I asked her to think about other people using her demanding and negative views that everyone had to be fascinating all the time. Darlene said that people are human and they don't have to be fascinating. I asked her why she wasn't as tolerant of herself. She smiled and said, "Because I am so boring." But then she said, "I am always harder on myself than I am on other people."

This is a major problem with beliefs. We tend to see other people much more realistically and objectively than we see ourselves. You can ask yourself why you would be so tough on yourself but not on other people. Imagine looking at yourself as if you were a friend thinking about you. Would a friend be as tough on you? Maybe a friend—or even a total stranger—would be more realistic, fairer, and less judgmental.

How I would see someone else	Is there a good reason for me to judge myself differently?

Is There Some Truth in Your Belief?

A lot of these core beliefs are stated in all-or-nothing terms—"Either I am never lazy or I am always lazy." As you know, there are times when all of us are lazy, irresponsible, boring, unattractive, annoying, or any other negative trait that you can think of. One problem with these sorts of beliefs is that they are so absolute and inflexible. I have found it quite useful to find *some truth* in every negative thought. Maybe Craig *was* lazy at times. He immediately agreed: "Oh, definitely. I can sit in front of the TV flipping channels and watch one senseless game after another. Totally lazy." I asked Craig to imagine that we got a pie and cut a piece of the pie that represented the percentage of time during the week that he was lazy. Carl said that "the lazy part" would be about 10 percent.

Or let's consider Darlene, who thought that she was boring. Sometimes Darlene *is* boring. When she feels anxious, she acts in a boring way. She avoids eye contact, puts a dumb smile on her face, and answers with one-word responses. When she is comfortable and knows that she can trust you, she is easy to talk to, has opinions, seems relaxed, and says interesting things. When I pointed this out to Darlene, she was both puzzled and relieved. She knew that she is boring at times, but this was only because she tries to compensate for her anxiety by being self-conscious and avoiding saying anything that might seem dumb. How ironic that while she thought she was basically boring, she isn't—but to compensate for her "fundamentally boring nature" she acted in a boring way! This is another example of the use of "safety behaviors," behaviors that you utilize to make yourself feel secure but which can sometimes backfire and reconfirm your worries.

Act Against Your Beliefs

Craig's all-or-nothing belief about being lazy and irresponsible was driving him to work excessively and demand the highest standards on everything. Consequently, we decided to examine what it would be like to experiment with intentionally planning some lazy time to see if allowing himself a little slack would lead to his becoming lazy and irresponsible. The question for Craig was, "Is it possible to be a little lazy on a regular basis in small doses and not become a total oaf?" I asked him to plan "goof-off time" when he would intentionally do nothing productive. We gradually increased the goof-off time to sixty minutes total per day, in chunks of fifteen to thirty minutes during the day. This actually made his work seem less oppressive, and he worried a lot less because he found that he was able to step back from work and get a better perspective. Experimenting with a little of the negative belief is empowering.

In order to challenge her belief that she is boring, I asked Darlene to take the initiative in conversations with new people by turning herself into an interviewer. Since the majority of people think that the most fascinating conversation is always about themselves, Darlene's job was to ask other people all about their interests and themselves, and then ask them more about themselves. She didn't need to say anything about herself. When she began to do this, people really warmed up to her. They were thrilled to find someone who took such an interest in them. This made Darlene refocus away from herself to focus on other people. Of course, they thought she was interesting.

Develop a More Positive Belief

Many of us go around with these negative, maladaptive beliefs for years. We worry that people will not find us interesting, attractive, or successful enough. We try to compensate for our inadequacies by avoiding certain relationships, seeking reassurance, working harder than we need to, aiming for perfection, and staying in bad relationships. Every day we worry that what we believe to be true about ourselves—say, that we are boring and inadequate—will be exposed as reality. Something will happen, we fear, that will reveal what losers we really are. We worry to prevent that from happening.

An alternative would be to develop a more positive and more realistic belief about yourself. This can include adaptive, flexible beliefs such as the following:

- I am a human being with positive and negative qualities.
- I am just as good as other people.
- I can learn from my mistakes and the mistakes of other people.
- I can appreciate myself even if I am not perfect.
- People can be accepting and forgiving.
- It doesn't make sense to measure people.
- There are lots of different ways to enjoy life—there's no one "right" way.

Think about the benefits of having these new, humane beliefs about yourself and other people. These are ways of seeing yourself as a complex person with flaws and virtues—someone who is learning, growing, and experiencing things.

Craig was able to develop new, more flexible, and humane beliefs about himself. His new positive beliefs are shown in Figure 7.4. These included the following:

- I work hard most of the time, but I don't have to drive myself crazy.
- I have the right to relax once in a while.
- I should treat myself as well as I would treat other people.
- I am better off rewarding myself for my positives than criticizing myself for my negatives.

Let's consider Darlene's new beliefs. She was worried that she had to be interesting all the time. She also believed that having a relationship with a man was essential. Applying these new beliefs—these new ways of thinking about herself and other people—freed Darlene from the tyranny of her maladaptive beliefs. Rather than worry about what Jeff was thinking of her, Darlene could see herself as having both positive and negative qualities and as being just as good as other people. She can begin to see that other people do not demand perfection—that they can be forgiving and accepting. She can think of herself as a person with complex qualities that are ever-changing, rather than as someone who is measured, found wanting, and then discarded. She can think of herself as a process of continuing development, rather than a finished product for sale.

How Changing Negative Beliefs Affects Worry

Let's go back to how changing Craig's negative beliefs might affect the way he would worry about work and his productivity. In Figure 7.4 I show a new way for Craig to think about his worries, utilizing the changed belief.

When we look at Craig's new, more realistic, and humane belief, we can see that changing the belief has a dramatic impact on his worries, his needs to compensate and avoid, and his belief that if he does not worry and drive himself hard, then he will become totally lazy.

And let's return to Darlene, who noticed that she has some lines on her face. She looks in the mirror and thinks, "I'm getting old. Jeff will leave me." Darlene has a perfectionistic standard for beauty—either you are perfect or you are ugly. I asked her if Tom Cruise and Nicole Kidman are perfect-looking. She said, "Some people might not think so." In any case, Darlene's belief about herself is that she is physically defective and unlovable and that men are extremely demanding of perfect looks.

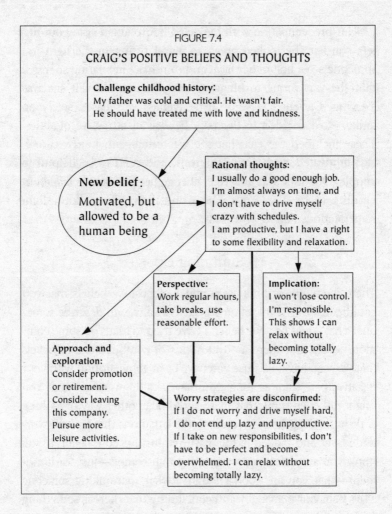

FIGURE 7.4

CRAIG'S POSITIVE BELIEFS AND THOUGHTS

Challenge childhood history:
My father was cold and critical. He wasn't fair.
He should have treated me with love and kindness.

New belief:
Motivated, but allowed to be a human being

Rational thoughts:
I usually do a good enough job.
I'm almost always on time, and I don't have to drive myself crazy with schedules.
I am productive, but I have a right to some flexibility and relaxation.

Perspective:
Work regular hours, take breaks, use reasonable effort.

Implication:
I won't lose control.
I'm responsible.
This shows I can relax without becoming totally lazy.

Approach and exploration:
Consider promotion or retirement.
Consider leaving this company.
Pursue more leisure activities.

Worry strategies are disconfirmed:
If I do not worry and drive myself hard, I do not end up lazy and unproductive.
If I take on new responsibilities, I don't have to be perfect and become overwhelmed. I can relax without becoming totally lazy.

I asked her a number of questions. First, were there men who found her attractive? Yes. Second, when she went to a party, did men approach her and try to find out more about her? Yes, definitely. Third, was she attractive enough to turn men on? Absolutely. Fourth, were there women less attractive than she who had relationships? Yes, all around her.

Her preoccupation with looks led her to avoid going out unless she felt she looked great, to avoid sitting in the light lest someone see a line in her face, and to restrict her eating so much that she was prone to bingeing later because she felt she was starving. Darlene's view of attractiveness was based solely on looks—so I decided to diversify her list of attractive qualities. These included the fact that she was intelligent, funny, caring, and motivated, had lots of interests, and tried to be helpful to people. Once she was able to challenge her personal belief about needing to be glamorous, she would worry less about slight imperfections that all of us have.

Summing Up

There is an almost limitless number of positive beliefs that you could consider. Think of an adjective or a way to describe someone. That could be your belief. I have tried to focus on some common beliefs, but there are thousands of combinations of beliefs that you can have. Because you have been going around with your negative beliefs for so long, you may take them for granted. You might not even think that there could be another way of looking at things. But imagine if you took the situations that you are worried about and looked at them with a positive core belief. If you think you are defective, imagine if you assumed—just for a moment—that you are good enough. Rather than taking someone else's behavior personally and concluding that there is something wrong with you if everyone isn't enthusiastic about everything you do, you could conclude that you are just as good as everyone else. And just like everyone else, you don't have to be perfect.

Use the nine techniques we've covered to challenge your negative beliefs. (See table 7.2, opposite)

You can use form 7.3, opposite, to examine some of your negative beliefs and see if you can modify them by using the techniques that I have outlined. This will take practice, since you have been living with these negative beliefs for years. But, as the slightly revised saying goes, practice makes progress.

TABLE 7.2

CHALLENGING YOUR NEGATIVE BELIEFS

1. Identify your beliefs about yourself and other people.
2. Examine the costs and benefits of these beliefs.
3. How has your belief affected you in the past?
4. Are you viewing yourself in all-or-nothing terms?
5. What is the evidence against your belief?
6. Would you be as critical of other people?
7. Maybe there's some truth in your belief.
8. Act against your belief.
9. Develop a more positive belief.

TABLE 7.3

CHALLENGING YOUR PERSONAL BELIEFS

Technique	Response
Identify personal belief	
Degree of belief in belief (0–100%)	
Cost and benefit	Cost: Benefit:
Evidence for and against your belief	
How has this belief affected you?	
Would you be this critical of someone else?	
View yourself on a continuum—not in all-or-nothing terms	
Act against your belief	
Conclusions	

8

Step Five:
Turn "Failure" into Opportunity

ALL OF US WORRY about how things can go badly. You could try to trick yourself into feeling good by affirming that everything will work out and that you will always be successful, but that's nonsense and you know it. You will make mistakes, you may fail at something—but trying to "think positively" is not the answer. You can undermine the power of worry by learning how to handle mistakes and how to step beyond failure to the next stage.

Yale psychologist Robert Sternberg has noted that our education does not train us how to face failure and deal with it productively. In fact, psychologists distinguish between "mastery models" of learning, where the goal is to achieve success as much as possible, and "coping styles," which focus on how you respond to frustration and failure. Do you give up and criticize yourself, or do you persist? Consider the fact that most dating relationships will eventually come to an end. If you play sports, you are likely to lose as many times as you win. If you invest, you will likely lose money some if not most of the time. Sternberg observed that many of the articles that he submitted to scholarly journals were rejected.

If we can learn how to face failure and take the sting out of it, we will have less to worry about. In order to make this point I have outlined twenty things that you can say to yourself if you fail that can help you dramatically reduce the negative impact of failure—and, if you are fortunate, turn failure into new opportunities. Since failure is inevitable in life, and since you worry about failing, it is essential to develop a strategy for failure.

"I Didn't Fail, My Behavior Failed"

Let's imagine that you have taken a test and you get your grade back. It's an F. Would it be fair to say that *you, as a person*, failed? Or should we say that your *performance* on that test failed? What's the difference? The difference is that if you think that you as a person failed, then you will label yourself a failure and generalize this to other tests and other situations. You will feel helpless and hopeless. This is the point that psychologist Martin Seligman makes in his theory of learned helplessness: If you attribute your failure to something *stable and internal* about yourself—your ability—or you as a person—then you are more likely to be depressed, give up, and generalize your failure to other situations.[1]

The other problem with saying "I failed" is that it simply isn't true. Let's say you're a woman who is thirty-five years old, has a full-time job, is married with two children, has friends and hobbies, has taken many other courses that she *did* pass, is the daughter of Sylvia and John, and is Ralph's sister. When you failed on the exam, did you fail on all these other behaviors and relationships?

Behaviors fail, not people.

The advantage of attributing your failure to specific behaviors is that you can change your behaviors, but it would be very difficult to imagine what it would mean to change who you *are*. Let's imagine that you are a single man at a party. You want to meet Pam, who is standing over there having a drink. You are not sure what to say to start the conversation, but you go up to her and say, "Haven't I met you before?" Pam, to your surprise, says, "No," and abruptly walks away. Did *you* fail? Or did your *comment* fail? Think of who you are: someone with a job, friends, family, interests, knowledge, hobbies. Did all of those fail when Pam walked away? Or should we say that this particular comment failed in that particular situation at that particular time?

Think of yourself as *a collection of actual and potential behaviors*. How many behaviors did you engage in when you saw Pam, walked over to her, and asked her a question? I just named three, but there probably were about fifty others. You had to notice her, categorize her as Pam, identify what was desirable about her, label the situation as appropriate for an introduction, identify that it was you who would walk over and talk, select what you were going to say, and so on. This sounds like a lot of behaviors. Which behavior failed? And which ones succeeded? How many other behaviors do you engage in during a day, week, month, or year? Thousands? Millions? If one behavior doesn't pay off, doesn't that seem rather trivial?

Finally, if it's one behavior that failed, then how many behaviors do you have left that could succeed? If you segment out the behavior that failed in this specific situation at this particular time, you can still consider the many thousands of potential behaviors in the future that could potentially succeed in different situations at different times. Limiting your failure to a particular time, situation, and behavior allows you the flexibility to pursue successful opportunities in the future.

"I Can Learn from My Failure"

Imagine that you focused on the goal of making a profit, but a year later you have lost all your money. Isn't this failure? Well, there's a story in business, probably apocryphal, of a young executive who is handed a project by the president of the company. A year later, the project is scrapped after millions have been spent. The president calls the young executive into his office. The executive is worried: "Will I lose my job? I failed on this enormous responsibility. He's going to think I'm a loser." However, the president says, "Dan, I've got a new project for you. In fact, it's even bigger than the last one." Dan is relieved but a bit confused, and he says to the president, "I'm really happy to get this new project. But, to be honest with you, I expected you to fire me after I failed on that last project."

"Fire you? Hell, I wouldn't fire you after I've spent millions on your education!" What the president is focusing on is what the young executive learned and how he can apply it on the next project.

Observe a child working on a jigsaw puzzle. She tries to put pieces into places where they don't belong. Is she failing or learning? Or in working on the crossword puzzle, you find that the word you wrote in doesn't fit. Did you fail or did you learn? What did you learn and how can you use it now?

The term *failure* has the connotation of finality—"It's all over. You failed." But *learning* is forward-looking and empowering.

There's an even more efficient way of using "failure" as learning: learn from someone else's failures. When businesspeople consider a marketing plan, the first thing they examine is how someone else succeeded and how someone else failed. A friend of mine was planning on setting up his own private practice. He went out and spoke with very successful practitioners and very unsuccessful practitioners. He wanted to find out what worked and what did not work. *Failure is information.*

The behavior that "failed" gives you more information than you had before about what you can and cannot do in order to obtain your goal. Children and adults who persist or even increase their efforts after a failure are using their failure as a learning experience to drive them forward toward different—and potentially more effective—behaviors.

But we are often *ashamed* of our failures and we do not want to look at them again. We also degrade failure as containing nothing of any value. I would suggest that in looking back at your failures you ask yourself what important lessons can be learned.

"I Can Be Challenged by My Failure"

Another way of responding to frustration is to view it as a *challenge.* Carol Dweck, who studies children's motivation, tape-recorded what children say to themselves after they fail on a task. She studied two different groups of children: children who give up when they fail (helpless children) and children who persist or improve when they fail (persistent children). The children who are helpless say, "I'm just not any good at this sort of thing. I'm not much good at anything. I may as well give up." In contrast, the persistent kids say, "Hey, this is great. I love a *challenge!*" When kids reframe failure as *challenge,* they are energized and try harder. They reflect on their "failure" in terms of what they can learn.[2]

A few years ago my wife and I decided to take up windsurfing. I felt reasonably confident as I approached the lesson, since I had been sailing for a few years. I figured, incorrectly, that I could easily transfer those skills to windsurfing. Much to my surprise and dismay, my performance for the first three days was an abysmal failure. I think that I was able to stand for an average of half a second, and I probably fell at least 150 times. To add to the problem, all the people on the beach who were watching enjoyed laughing at me and ridiculing my lack of skill. And the icing on the cake is that my wife, who had never sailed, did not fall a single time.

In any case, I did not give up. I felt challenged. I looked out at the bay and saw other people windsurfing. I had found sailing on a lake rather boring because it had gotten too easy, so I thought it would be a real accomplishment if I could overcome these enormous failures and learn how to windsurf. I approached my lessons with the humility I had so richly earned.

What does this story suggest? Like the children Carol Dweck studied, you can make a choice about your *response* to failure: you can choose to give up because you think it is too hard (or you think you are permanently incompetent), or you can become motivated to try harder. Psychologists refer to "competence motivation" or "effectance motivation" to indicate that we are often motivated to overcome obstacles that make our tasks more difficult.[3] Indeed, persistence in pursuing challenge and difficulty can actually increase our resilience to deal with other difficulties—a process known as "learned industriousness."[4] According to Eisenberger's theory, people differ in their history of being reinforced for trying hard, persisting in the face of failure, and using self-discipline (rather than only relying on external rewards). If you are reinforced only for outcomes (success or failure), then you may be undermined by failure experiences. In contrast, if you are reinforced for effort, you will persist in the face of failure. In fact, research by psychologists Quinn, Brandon, and Copeland found that people who scored higher on measures of learned industriousness are less likely to rely on smoking and substance abuse to handle their frustrations.[5] Failure experiences are opportunities to feel challenged and to develop this learned industriousness—an ability that you will need to handle the other failures and frustrations that are inevitable in life.

"I Can Try Harder"

There are several causes that you can point to when you fail at a task. You can attribute your failure to your lack of ability, bad luck, a difficult task, or lack of effort. If you explain your failure by referring to your lack of ability (for example, "I'm stupid"), you are likely to become depressed, give up trying, decrease your learning, and give up on other tasks. Research by psychologists Martin Seligman and Lynn Abramson indicates that it is not failure alone that leads to depression, but rather *how you interpret that failure.*[6]

Let's say that you fail on the first exam in a course and there are three more exams. If you attribute your failure to lack of ability ("I'm just not good in chemistry"), you might give up. You will feel helpless and depressed. On the other hand, if you attribute your behavior to lack of effort, you will think that you could try harder the next time. Perhaps you can study more, get some help, organize your material more effectively, or talk to the professor. Seligman studied the explanatory styles of failure among insurance salespeople—a profession with an enormous attrition rate during the first two years. He found that those salespeople who persisted—who did not give up when they failed—tended to respond to their failure by saying, "I'll have to try harder on the next call" or "It's a numbers game. The more calls I make, the more likely I'll be successful" or "Everyone gets turned down at times at these calls. Maybe the next one will pay off." Because they were able to attribute failure to an *unstable cause,* such as lack of effort or specific qualities of the person they were calling ("He already has an insurance policy"), they did not give up or become self-critical. As a result, they eventually experienced some success, which further reinforced their effort to try in the next situation.

Dweck's research on young children indicates that some children (whom she labels "helpless"), when confronted with an insolvable task, simply give up. They say to themselves, "I'm just not good at this." Other children are "persistent" and actually improve their performance following failure, because they say to themselves, "I'll have to try harder" or "Let's see what I did wrong." In fact, this difference may be the reason why girls often give up on mathematical tasks. They tend to say, "I'm just not good at math," and they then give up. In contrast, boys tend to say, "I can do this. I just have to stop and think. I'll have to try harder this time."[7]

Attributing your failures to internal stable factors such as lack of ability is predictive of depression in the future.[8] If you are a worrier and tend to attribute your failures to personal defectiveness or incompetence, you will worry all the more about possible failure in the future. In contrast, if you attribute failure to lack of effort, task difficulty, or even bad luck, you will worry less about failing in the future because you can always try harder after a failure.

"Maybe It Wasn't a Failure"

It is also possible that you did not fail, even though you think you did. Let's take divorce, an experience many people equate with failure. Irene had been married for ten years to Phil when she began to suspect that he was having an affair. She confronted him, but he denied it. She had tried for two years to get Phil to participate in marital therapy, but he blamed all the problems on Irene. It turned out that he was having an affair, and he finally left Irene to move in with his new lover. Irene began to feel like she was a failure because she hadn't been able to keep Phil.

I asked her why she thought it was her sole responsibility to keep Phil in the marriage. After all, hadn't Phil taken a vow of fidelity when they got married, and therefore, hadn't he failed to keep his word? Furthermore, wasn't Phil responsible for at least half of the relationship, and therefore, wasn't he at least half as responsible for the relationship ending? Perhaps we could even say that Phil was largely responsible for the dissolution of the marriage, and if that is so, shouldn't we conclude that she had not failed? Irene began to feel less critical of herself and more angry with Phil.[9]

Failure implies an all-or-nothing evaluation of your performance. In the case of divorce, seldom is there an all-or-nothing cause. Both parties contribute to the problems. Moreover, a marriage ending could also be a positive outcome. Ann's husband was often drunk and abusive toward her, threatening her on a continual basis. He refused marital therapy or rehabilitation for his substance abuse problem. Consequently, when Ann finally left him she was encouraged to view the termination of the relationship as a successful achievement for her.

"I Can Focus on Other Behaviors That Can Succeed"

We often have tunnel vision, focusing exclusively on the single behavior that does not pay off. When we worry about something in the future, we tend to think that this one set of behaviors is the only thing that counts. This selective focus can make it seem like everything is hanging on one decision and one outcome. Let's return to the party described earlier. The young man approached Pam, but she rudely walked away from him. Are there any other behaviors that he can engage in that are rewarding? Perhaps there are other people at the party who might be interesting to meet. When he leaves the party, he might return home and read an absorbing book or watch a film on television. The next day at work there might be some challenging things to work on. He can call a friend and make dinner plans. Or he could go to a health club and work out. Interacting with Pam was only one behavior out of *an infinite number of possible rewarding behaviors*. Even though he cannot interact with Pam, there are still millions of other potentially rewarding behaviors that he can engage in.

Let's take Ben, whose girlfriend broke up with him. He felt sad and dejected, so I asked him what his thoughts were. Ben said, "I can't be happy without her. I'm waiting for her to call." We examined the evidence that he could be happy without her:

he had been happy many times in the thirty-six years before he had even met her, and even when he had been in the relationship with her, he was often happy doing things on his own. We listed twenty things that he could do on his own, with friends, or with other women that could be rewarding. By focusing his energy and time on behaviors that were rewarding, he gradually lost interest in his ex-girlfriend, and he began feeling better. Two months later he was involved with another woman. When his ex-girlfriend called him, he had far less interest in seeing her. He had found alternatives that were more rewarding and less costly.[10]

"I Can Focus on What I Can Control"

Ben was obsessing about rewards that someone else controlled— that is, rewards his ex-girlfriend controlled. Consequently, he placed all the power in her hands and disempowered himself. I asked, "What rewards are within your control?" When we focused on *what he could do for himself,* he no longer felt helpless. As he felt less helpless, he felt like he needed her less. Focusing on the behavior of someone else is a common problem during breakups— you sit around waiting for someone else to do something.

Sam had come to see me after having been depressed for several years. In fact, he described himself as so shy that he predicted that cognitive therapy could never change him or help him overcome his depression. As I got to know Sam, it became apparent that he was still hung up on his ex-girlfriend, who had broken up with him three years before. He described how their relationship had fallen apart after he told her he would not marry her simply because she was pregnant, although he professed his love and devotion to her. At that time, he had known her for only a few months. He described her as critical and uncommunicative throughout most of their relationship, but he still hung on to the belief that she was the only woman who could make him happy.

Sam had put himself in a helpless position by believing that only Judy could make him happy. He decided to call her and arrange to see her for dinner—to test out his idea that there might still be something there. They met for dinner, but Judy still remained cold and aloof and owned up to no responsibility for the relationship ending. Right around this time, Sam met another woman who seemed far more interested in him and with whom he had a lot in common. I suggested that he could always keep Judy in mind as a possibility, should she change her mind, but that he could also begin to concentrate on this other woman, Iris.

Sam and Iris began dating more frequently. As he began to focus on Iris, he lost interest in Judy. He realized that when he tried to rekindle his relationship with Judy he was helpless, since getting back together wasn't her goal, and consequently she prevented him from getting what he wanted. By focusing on dating Iris, Sam was in greater control. Eventually Iris and Sam married.

The point to this is that we often may fail at things we do not control. Learning how to give up on a goal that is not working for you can be seen either as another failure or as an opportunity to focus on what you can control. When you worry about something not working out, you might explore behaviors that you can control that may not involve that particular goal. *Giving up creates opportunities.*

"It Wasn't Essential to Succeed at That"

When you worry, you have tunnel vision—you focus on one goal to the exclusion of all other goals, and you view that goal as essential. My view of this is that nature is wise—*what is essential is not left up to chance or volition.* It is essential that your blood circulate, that you breathe, that you digest your food. If you fail at these things, you will die. They are so essential that they are automatic. However, it is not essential to get a good grade, make a lot of money, or meet the man or woman of your dreams today.

Wally is a businessman who is worried that he might get fired at any minute. We examined the evidence, and it did appear that there might be some chance that he would get fired. I told him a story, reported by psychiatrist Isaac Marks, about a patient who continually worried that he would get a sexually transmitted disease. After months and months of therapy (which failed to affect the patient's obsessions), the patient did indeed contract syphilis. Much to his surprise, he felt relieved: he recognized that it was treatable, and he participated in group therapy with other people with STDs. After hearing this story, Wally and I explored the possibilities that might be available to him should he get fired, such as private consulting. The next week I got a phone call from Wally: "Bob, guess what? I got syphilis!" I asked him what he meant. "It's just like that story you told me. I got fired, and I decided to do my own consulting. I called up some people, and got a few clients. I feel like a tremendous burden has been taken off my shoulders." The job was not essential.

Almost every goal that you tried to achieve—including those you did achieve—will probably (in hindsight) prove not to be essential. If you view the goal as less important, then you may feel less bad about it.[11] Getting into a particular school, passing a particular exam, getting someone to like you, getting to an appointment on time, and looking your best are probably all goals you thought were essential. But you can ask yourself, "How different would my life have been if I had not achieved some of those goals?"

"There Were Some Behaviors That Did Pay Off"

When you don't attain your goal, you might conclude that everything you did in that situation failed. Does this make sense? Imagine that you had a job for a year, and then you got fired. Would you conclude that *everything* you did on the job was a failure? Sean had been working for a rather shaky company for about a year when the company's financial problems caused them to lay him off. He became self-critical and depressed, labeling himself a failure. I asked him to draw up a detailed description of what his job had entailed during the previous year. I asked him to give himself grades, from A to F, for each role on his job. As he examined the evidence, he realized that he had been very successful at almost every aspect of his job. We looked further at what new skills, information, and professional contacts he had acquired on this job. He realized that he was far more experienced now than he had been a year earlier. I suggested that he had gotten an excellent education and had had the benefit of being paid for it. He liked this idea. A month later he interviewed for another job and was offered a position that he took. His previous experience was an important criterion for his acceptance.

We often believe that if we do not accomplish something *perfectly,* then nothing has paid off and it was a complete waste of time. For example, you may worry that your relationship might not last forever—and it is possible it might not. But does this imply that everything was a waste of time if your relationship ends? Since 50 to 70 percent of marriages end in divorce, concluding that a relationship that did not last forever was a failure would mean that almost everyone has failed.[12] This kind of all-or-nothing thinking about relationships (or work, or anything else) is entirely illogical, since there are thousands of behaviors involved in relationships that are pleasurable and meaningful, even if the relationship does not last forever. Eventual outcomes may be uncertain, but viewing life only in terms of a "perfect score" may lead you to discount the importance of the process and experiences of your daily life. Indeed, if you followed the logic of this thinking, you would have to assume that every relationship is a waste until you find out it has lasted forever—which would be the last day of your life.

"Everyone Fails at Something"

One of the consequences of failure is that you may feel all alone—you think that no one else has failed at this except you. The failure becomes *personal, not universal.* You think of yourself as qualitatively different from, and inferior to, all other people, whom you view as total successes at everything that they do.

Sharon felt devastated by a recent failure at work. She worried that others would find out about her failure and not want to have anything to do with her. I asked her to list five people she knew well and admired. Then I asked her to tell me if any of them had ever had any problems or failures that she knew about. I role-played with her as one of her friends who had failed at something, and in the role-play I asked her to talk to me about my feelings of failure. After the role-play she said that when people shared their failures with her she respected them more and felt closer to them. This proved two things to her: first, that everyone fails, even people she admires; and second, sharing failure with a good friend can bring us closer. (In fact, sharing success can drive some people away.)

When Fred was in college a professor gave him a C on an economics term paper. The paper was a proposal for a private mailing service for overnight mail that would compete with the post office. The professor—at Yale—thought this was unrealistic and foolish. Two years after graduating from college, Fred Smith founded Federal Express. Henry Ford's first company went bankrupt. The founders of Standard Oil drilled and failed and drilled and failed again before they finally succeeded. R. H. Macy failed several times before succeeding with his department store.

Successful people build their success on their failures. Everyone falls when they're learning how to walk, everyone loses at tennis, and every stock investor has lost money—in fact, the bigger the winnings, the bigger the losses.

Our culture places too great an emphasis on success and not enough emphasis on endurance, persistence, resilience, and humility. I have yet to see a television ad or a self-help book that seriously addresses the inevitability and universality of failure. *Failure is normal;* it is part of relationships, working, playing sports, investing, or even caring about someone. If we can normalize failure—understanding that it comes with the territory—then we will have less to worry about, since we can see it as part of the process of living and participating in events.

"Maybe No One Noticed"

You may worry that everyone notices your failures and is talking about them, remembering them, and judging you forever. You may worry that your failures will seem so dramatic to others that they will be preoccupied with thinking about them. Think of what an egocentric fantasy this is: that other people have nothing better to do than to sit around talking about your problems. Our worry is a form of exaggerated self-reference.

I go to psychology conventions with my graduate students and present our papers at different symposia. There might be a hundred people in the audience. Teri, who was presenting her first paper, told me that she was worried that everyone in the audience would notice that she was nervous. She worried that someone would ask a question to which she wouldn't have the answer and she would look like a fool. I asked her how anyone would notice she was anxious—what would they see or hear? She worried that they'd hear her voice quaver and see her hands shake. I asked Teri how many speakers she had heard at the conference so far. It was about fifteen. And what did she recall about their anxiety? Nothing. This is interesting, since it's fair to assume that most of the speakers were anxious. Maybe people don't notice—or remember—mistakes or problems or failures.

Or let's take Don, a television news broadcaster, who was sure that people could see he was anxious and made mistakes when he was on the air. I asked him what information the viewer would use to determine his anxiety. He realized that he was basing their judgments of him on his *subjective experiences* of himself. That is, because he felt anxious (and was always aware of his own anxiety), he concluded that everyone watching had the same information. He suffered from "anxiety transparency"—he thought everyone could see his anxiety. His homework assignment was to watch himself on television and see if he could tell when he felt anxious and what the signs of his anxiety were. He wasn't able to see any signs of his anxiety, especially on a small television screen.

"Did I Have the Right Goal?"

Helplessness is the inability to attain your goal in a given situation.[13] If you are a worrier, then you probably blame yourself when you don't achieve your goal ("This just proves what an idiot I am!") and you believe that the goal is essential ("I really needed that!"). You end up discounting even the positives that you accomplished on the task you failed at, and you discount other positives that you have accomplished or will accomplish.

Alison was giving a presentation on her research in an area that might have challenged some of the work of another researcher, Tom. Tom had gained quite a reputation as a leader in the field. At Alison's talk, during the question-and-answer period, Tom got up to question Alison's work. Tom sounded sarcastic and even had the nerve to turn to Alison's audience as if he were the speaker. After the talk Alison told me that she was furious at Tom. "Who the hell does he think he is? Why can't other people be more supportive? It's just not fair!" I told Alison I could understand all her feelings—she felt personally attacked. But I added that I could see that her anger was really eating away at her. I asked Alison what her goal had been in giving the talk. "Were you trying to persuade Tom of the value of your work? Were you trying to make yourself as famous as Tom? Or were you trying to communicate information about your research?"

Alison realized that what had gotten her upset was not really that Tom had attacked her work. Rather, it was that she seemed to have had the goal of *trying to get Tom's approval.* I suggested that not only was it almost impossible to get Tom's approval, but there would always be other Toms who are competitive and want to grab the floor. This was not something that she could control. She also could not guarantee that this talk, or any talk, would make her famous—so that was another goal that was out of her hands.

On the other hand, if she changed her goal to communicating her work to the audience, rather than winning approval, then she had considerable control over the situation. She could prepare her lecture, use audiovisual aids, and speak honestly about her research. In fact, she had already achieved the goal of communicating her work. And after all, everyone there, *including Tom,* had come to hear her speak.

The other issue for Alison was what was so essential about Tom's approval. If Tom didn't approve of her work, did that necessarily mean that Alison's work was no good? And since Alison's research was based on helping people, hadn't she already achieved her most important goal: helping other people? Certainly, as Alison thought of it, helping people was the reason that she got into psychology in the first place. She could control whether she did her work with her clients and she could control whether she prepared for her lectures. In fact, Tom and everyone in the audience had nothing that Alison *needed.*

"Failure Is Not Fatal"

Do you say to yourself, "That's awful. What a terrible thing. I failed"? If you do, you are treating failure as if it were a fatality. Let me give you an example of this. Larry is a young Wall Street investor who made some investments for a fund that went sour. They lost a couple of million dollars. He felt hopeless and self-critical, and he thought of suicide. Larry was convinced that his failure to invest the money wisely was a terrible thing and that, given the fact that he was such a failure, life might not be worth living. I asked him how bad it felt to him, on a scale from 0 to 100. He answered that it was a 100.

I asked him to draw a horizontal line and label the left part 0 and the right part 100. I told him that we would call this the Negative Events Scale, with 0 corresponding to the absence of anything negative and 100 corresponding to the worst event that could happen to anyone. Next I asked him to label various points on the scale with events he thought matched the degree of negativity. The first few points weren't hard for Larry to label—100 was nuclear holocaust, 90 the death of family members, 80 serious sickness for self or family members. However, as we got below 80 and tried to label the other points, Larry grew uncomfortable. It was hard for him to see various degrees of negativity. I asked him where he would put loss of a limb, or armed robbery, or less serious sickness of a family member, or loss of a friend, or imprisonment, or tight shoes. He was able to see that there were many other negative things that could happen that were worse than losing some money for the fund, and a few events that were not as bad. He decided to change his estimate of negativity for the loss to 40. I asked him why. "Well, I still have my family and my health and my job. And, after all, everyone who invests makes mistakes. I can absorb the loss." This seemed like a key concept: He could absorb the loss and go on. It wasn't fatal.[14]

Our research shows that people who worry about making a mistake, losing, or failing often believe that they will have no fallback position. They believe they will not be able to absorb the loss. Thus, they are extremely cautious in considering any changes in their behavior, often requiring excessive amounts of information. But successful investors—who may invest millions of dollars at a time—view a failure in an investment as part of the process of being a player. The important point is cumulative gains—how much you gain over a long period of winners and losers. Failure is not fatal if you are still in the game.

"Were My Standards Too High?"

Henry was an investor who had made several million dollars and enjoyed a rather privileged lifestyle. Since he and his wife had two kids in private school and a large mortgage, his investment strategy had grown more conservative in recent years. He was not going for the big killing, which was associated with high risk, because he wanted to protect his assets. However, Henry began to think of himself as a failure because he wasn't making the percentages on investments that he used to make. He would compare himself to the wunderkind characters on Wall Street who were making millions more.

Henry's problem was his perfectionism and his inability to see that he was actually achieving his most important goal—protecting his assets. In this sense, his behavior was successful. The greater financial success of someone else proved not that he had failed, but only that others could make more money. We also examined the evidence that he had more assets than 99 percent of the people in the United States, which is certainly evidence against failure. Because of his perfectionistic standards, Henry had discounted his positive achievements.

Perfectionism is usually the result of illogically linking your self-worth to your performance. Gail claimed that she experienced tremendous pressure at work. She said that she wanted to impress her boss with her performance, so she would work in the office for twelve to fourteen hours a day. I asked her to trace the sequence of her automatic thoughts, and this is what she came up with:

1. I need to do a great job.
2. I need to be the best.
3. I need to be perfect.
4. If I'm not perfect, I'm a failure.
5. If I'm a failure, then I'm worthless.
6. Life is not worth living if you're worthless.

Clearly, Gail's perfectionism was based on the assumption that if she was not perfect at work, then she was worthless. We examined other interpretations: "If I'm not perfect, I can be human," "If my performance is not perfect, it can still be excellent," "Maybe my boss isn't as much of a perfectionist as I am—maybe I don't need to be perfect," "If he wants perfection, then that's his problem," or "My work is good enough."

Perfectionism is a key component of depression and anxiety.[15] Perfectionistic thinking leads to negative self-evaluations of performance at work, appearance, sexual behavior, relationships, and health. It reveals a disparity between real self-image (how you see youself) and ideal self-image (how you would like to be).[16] People with a greater disparity between real and ideal self-image are prone to becoming depressed and anxious, often believing that they can never attain their demanding standards and goals. Perfectionists often take pride in their high standards, assuming that having such standards implies that they are not mediocre. In fact, the problem with perfectionistic standards is that they are never attained (or at least not for very long), thereby leading to continual dissatisfaction and worry.

Moreover, perfectionists believe that they have to evaluate and measure experience rather than simply *have* it. Perfectionists often believe that they are in a contest with other people and that they are at risk of falling behind. Moreover, the perfectionist has a receding reference point, since no matter what he achieves, it is never good enough.[17] Although the perfectionist may claim that his standards motivate him, these demanding expectations are just as likely to disable performance.

What are the real costs and benefits of these standards? What would happen if you expected 80 percent of those standards rather than 100 percent? How have these standards—which you made up—become *requirements*? What was your life like before you had these demanding standards? Do you believe that these demanding standards help you feel more pride in yourself, or have these standards simply added to your self-criticism and worry?

I often ask people to practice refraining from evaluating the "goodness" or "badness" of their behavior and simply describe the facts and their experiences. Perfectionists often find that this exercise is illuminating, since their focus has been almost exclusively on their *evaluation* of experience. When Gail described the behaviors on her job rather than evaluate them, she began to feel less anxious and less worried. In fact, describing behaviors—monitoring them on a daily schedule—rather than measuring them allowed Gail to see that she was actually doing a variety of things on the job that she had overlooked.

"Did I Do Better than Before?"

Gail began to challenge her perfectionism, but she still had doubts about her performance. This was a new job for her, and she felt as though she had to perform exceptionally well. I suggested that we think of this as a *learning curve*—that is, you start off knowing very little but show cumulative gains over time. Since she had been on the job for a month, we were able to see that she had made substantial improvement since the first week. If she extrapolated from this and continued to grow in knowledge at this rate for the next year, she would be extraordinarily successful.

Carol Dweck has found that people who are undermined by frustration or failure have a "theory of mind" that leads them to view abilities as fixed and permanent traits.[18] Thus you are either good or bad at a task—you either have the ability or you do not. This theory that abilities are immutable and perhaps inborn leads some people to give up quickly—"I guess I'm not good at math, so why bother?" In contrast, other people have a more fluid or cumulative theory of mind—that you can acquire abilities through experience, challenge, and learning from your mistakes.

Ed is another example of how the idea of "doing better than before" can be effective against worry. Ed had not had a date in three years. We began to work on a social skills program to increase his positive interactions with both men and women, with the eventual goal of helping him get a date. I had him keep track of any positive interactions he had with other people. One day he came in complaining that he had talked to several women in a shopping mall on Saturday afternoon but had not gotten a date. He also had gone to a party during that week and had met several new people. I pointed out to him that he had made considerable progress since he first began treatment: "What were you doing six months ago?" I asked. "Sitting at home doing nothing," he admitted. He was doing much better compared to before. I suggested that he think of this as making progress, not perfection—a concept of fluidity and progress.

Ed began to view his social skills as a *learnable* set of behaviors rather than as a fixed quality that could never be changed. In fact, a major part of helping him overcome his worries about failing was to have him keep track of how he was doing with specific behaviors. Rather than comparing himself to some abstract standard of perfection, we focused more on comparing him with himself. This also led to a discussion of his theories about other aspects of himself—as someone who couldn't learn new skills. The goal now was to change from a fixed assessment of his performance to viewing his performance as an accumulation of experiences and learning new behaviors. This significantly decreased his worries about failing.

"I Can Still Do Everything I Always Did, Even Though This Failed"

Do you worry, "If I fail at this, it's going to be awful" or "I can't stand failing at this?" Labeling an experience as "awful" means that it is intolerable, that there is almost nothing left for you, and that life will be miserable from now on. Let's take the fear of rejection: "I can't start a conversation with her because if she rejects me then it would be awful!" Let's imagine that you go to a party and see someone you find attractive. You go over to that person and say, "Hi, my name is Gerald." But this very attractive person is unfriendly and walks away from you. Doesn't that sound devastating? Fortunately, this doesn't have to be awful. A simple technique that you can use is to ask yourself, "What can I still do even if this did happen?"

Even though this stranger, whom you have never seen before, walks away from you, does this mean that your life is now totally empty of rewards? Let's make a list of all the things that you can still do even though he or she was rude to you. *You can still do everything that you could do before you met this person.* There is not a single behavior that you can't engage in as a result of the other person's rudeness. As a consequence, you might view his or her behavior as totally insignificant.

Another way to see this is to adapt a simple learning theory approach that stresses the importance of seeking positive behaviors. This approach is now referred to as behavioral activation theory.[19] In other words, when faced with a behavior that did not work, rather than sitting around ruminating, think of something else to do that is rewarding. I like to think of this as the "Italian restaurant solution." Let's say that your favorite entrée is veal. But in this restaurant, tonight they don't have any veal on the menu. What do you do? Do you whine, "I want my veal," or protest that you will not eat because there's no veal? Do you call the owner in and ask him to give you a full explanation of why there isn't any veal? Do you sit and think of how fortunate all the other people in other restaurants are because they can eat veal? No, you don't do those things. You look at the menu and *select something else.*

If you fail at something, you should ask yourself, "What can I still do?" Think of the menu. There are twenty-five thousand entrées on this menu of rewarding, challenging, and interesting behaviors. You can choose something else, or you can ruminate. When we worry or get overly focused on a particular goal or outcome, we become rigid and inflexible. This narrows our options and makes us feel even more constrained about our course of action. Flexibility—"all the other things that I could still do"—places the outcome in a broader perspective.

When Todd was worried because his business had been losing money for several months, we examined some constructive things that he could do to generate new business, but we also examined all of the behaviors that he could do both within his business and outside of his business that had nothing to do with the current problem. As Todd became more flexible he worried less about things that he had previously thought were essential.

"Failing at Something Means I Tried.
Not Trying Is Worse"

We have already discussed the idea of "learned industriousness"—that is, taking pride and pleasure in exerting effort toward your goals. People with learned industriousness are not simply focused on outcomes and are less likely to dichotomize experiences into "success" or "failure." Consequently, these people are less depressed, less anxious, and less likely to rely on substances such as alcohol and drugs to handle their emotions.

Marcy complained of lack of pleasure, depression and hopelessness. I had her keep track of her activities for every hour of the week and rate each activity for pleasure and mastery (that is, how effective or competent she felt). When she brought her activity schedule in, we noticed she was spending almost all her time sitting around ruminating about her depression. She felt considerably better when she interacted with her husband or with friends, but she had decreased her activities with them since she had become so depressed. I suggested she start scheduling more activities with other people and to explore some interests on her own. She had a strong interest in photography, so she began taking photographs. At first she didn't think her work was all that good (a fairly typical negative filter for a depressed person). But simply trying to do something, putting the effort in, made her feel somewhat better. She said, "You know, I feel better just knowing that I tried." I explained my rule of thumb: "The environment is a natural reinforcement for positive behavior." In other words, there would be people and activities out there in the environment that would reinforce her effort. The more she tried, the better she felt. This also reinforced her belief that she had some control over her moods, because she could see that her moods varied with the behaviors that she tried. Eventually her depression lifted. Marcy shifted from outcome evaluation in her thinking to learned industriousness—taking pride in trying.

"I've Just Begun"

Let's imagine that you are thirty-three years old and I ask you to look back at every complicated and challenging skill that you have learned in your life. This might involve learning a sport, learning a language, or mastering a new subject. Were there any failures or frustrations along the way? There must have been many times that you felt frustrated and perhaps even felt like giving up, but you persisted anyway. You may think that if something does not work out, then you are finished. I view it as *you have just begun*.

When I was in college, my friend Lawrence and I would go to the gym to lift weights. Every week a different young man, who was overweight and out of shape, would come to the gym, start lifting lots of weights for a long period of time, pressing himself to his limits, and then leave. I would comment to Lawrence, "Well, we won't see him again. He'll go home in so much pain that he'll never want to come back." This turned out to be a certain bet.

What these lifters were doing was operating under the New Year's resolution model: "This year I'm going to get into shape. And I'm going to start today. I'm going to throw myself into it." Like virtually all New Year's resolutions, this one would fail. The reason is that the best way to establish a new behavioral pattern is through the process of *shaping*—that is, very gradual small increases in the frequency and intensity of behavior. If you want to take up jogging, you should probably walk briskly for five minutes on the first day and gradually build up to brisk walking and then very slow jogging over a couple of months. You need to get into shape, and the same is true of your behavior. Starting off with high-intensity, high-frequency behavior may give you one day of the illusion that you are committed to your program, but it is a sure guarantee that you will give it up in the near future. *Consistency makes progress.*

Look at your behavior as the beginning step in a long process of evolution, self-modification, and change. If you expect immediate results and don't get them, then you can say to yourself that you have just begun. And if you have just begun, then you have a lot to look forward to.

"Tomorrow Is Another Success"

Psychologist Martin Seligman has advanced a new kind of psychology that he calls "positive psychology."[20] Seligman has proposed that people differ from one another in the degree to which they pursue positive goals and embrace a more optimistic view of life. The individual with "positive psychology" welcomes challenge, growth, change, excitement, and independence, and is open to new experiences. Part of this optimistic, growth-oriented way of thinking—a way of thinking that is in contrast to the pessimistic worrier's view of the world—is that tomorrow is another opportunity for success.

Consider the following proposition: *every failure is followed by a success*. This may sound initially like a rather naive statement, but it is almost always true—unless you believe that you will never again have any positive or successful experiences in your life. If you look back on failure experiences that you have had, each one eventually was followed by some positive and successful experiences. Let's take Karen, a therapist, who was feeling depressed because several of her patients at the clinic she worked in were dropping out of treatment. She concluded that she was a failure. She believed that another therapist there, whom she admired, was having close to 100 percent success with her patients.

First I told Karen that research on premature dropout indicated that between 40 and 50 percent of patients dropped out prematurely. Then I asked her if she would ever succeed at another behavior in the future—and of course she said she would.

Next I asked her if she would fail again—and she was sure she would do that, too. So I pointed out to her that she was saying that every failure will be followed at some time by another success at something. If she didn't do well with this next patient, she would probably do better with another patient later: "There will be other patients, other successes. You've just told me that." Karen smiled, but she knew it was true. She would fail, then succeed, maybe fail again. She felt energized, though, by the idea that tomorrow was another opportunity for success.

Perhaps one of the reasons why we overfocus on a specific failure is that we get "engulfed" by our experience. This means that we become so captured by our momentary experience that we have a difficult time standing back and viewing a series of thousands of points (representing our behaviors) over a long period of time. Karen was focusing on a single point—a point that is almost invisible when viewed from the perspective of this long series of points in a lifelong process of different experiences.

"Tomorrow Is Today"

Most worriers—and pessimists—live in a hypothetical future, full of what-ifs that almost never come true. In contrast, a behavioral activation approach suggests that there is no reason to wait another day or another hour to get rewards. There is always something to do right now. Let's say that it's Saturday afternoon and you live in New York City (or Boston, or Washington, or some other large metropolitan area). You say to yourself despondently, "There's nothing to do." You begin feeling tired, noticing aches in your joints you hadn't noticed before, and think, "I don't have the energy." This is the core experience for rumination and worry—focusing on your current dissatisfaction and delaying any concrete positive action. As Yale psychologist Susan Nolen-Hoeksema has found, this kind of rumination and avoidance prolongs depression and anxiety. It keeps you from taking action that can distract you from your negative self-preoccupation, and it reduces your opportunity for constructive action.[21]

What are the advantages of staying home, ruminating, feeling sorry for yourself? You might think it's safe—you risk nothing. Ironically, *you risk getting depressed.* Using behavioral activation to reduce your worry and rumination means that you could begin today by making a list of activities—going to a play, listening to a concert, strolling in an art museum, going to a bookstore, taking a walk, going jogging, calling a friend, taking a bubble bath, writing a poem, renting a film. If you are a worrier, then you might begin thinking about absorbing yourself in the present moment—what is going on right now.

I recall years ago making this decision when I was sitting in my apartment in New York ruminating about being single and bored. I chose to take a subway downtown. That's how I met the woman who would become my wife—on the subway going downtown.

Summing Up

In this chapter we examined twenty things that you can say to yourself to handle "failure." Not achieving your goal on a particular task is an event. Whether it leads to depression, helplessness, and powerlessness or energizes, challenges, or arouses you depends on how you interpret the event of "failure." Will you use the event to empower yourself by leading to curiosity, challenge, and learning? Or will you treat failure as more evidence of being powerless or controlled by hypothetical negative events that probably will never happen?

The twenty self-statements opposite challenge you to think in a different way about events in your life. Rather than thinking like a passive, complaining, self-critical person who sees yourself as a victim of circumstances beyond your control, you can empower yourself by taking control of your response to failure. You determine how you think and act following frustration. You may not control past events, but you do control the present and the future, and you do control what you will do with events.

TABLE 8.1

1. I didn't fail, my behavior failed.
2. I can learn from my failure.
3. I can be challenged by my failure.
4. I can try harder.
5. Maybe it wasn't a failure.
6. I can focus on other behaviors that can succeed.
7. I can focus on what I can control.
8. It wasn't essential to succeed at that.
9. There were some behaviors that did pay off.
10. Everyone fails at something.
11. Maybe no one noticed.
12. Did I have the right goal?
13. Failure is not fatal.
14. Were my standards too high?
15. Did I do better than before?
16. I can still do everything I always did, even though this failed.
17. Failing at something means I tried. Not trying is worse.
18. I've just begun.
19. Tomorrow is another success.
20. Tomorrow is today.

9

Step Six: Use Your Emotions Rather than Worry About Them

WORRY IS AN ATTEMPT to suppress and avoid unpleasant emotions by trying to think through a solution so that you will not feel too emotional *right now*. Worriers will say, "But I seem to be anxious all the time." When people are engaged in worry, however, they are actually less anxious.[1] It's as if you are thinking, "I will continue to worry, to try to find the perfect solution, in order to avoid having that terrible image of a possible bad outcome." *Worry becomes a way to avoid emotion.*[2]

Worry makes you avoid facing the emotional impact of your experiences because *you are thinking rather than feeling*. You have probably heard people say, "You think too much," but what they should also say is "You should allow yourself to feel more." As a result, worriers seldom get to the point of actually facing their worst fears. In fact, when psychologists ask worriers "What will happen next?" to try to get to the worst fears, worriers take longer than nonworriers to get to the worst fear. It's as if the worriers have so many intervening steps of worry between the first worry and the worst fear that they may never get to the worst possible thing that can happen.

Why is getting to the worst possible fear important?

Imagine you had a fear of getting on an elevator and took such small steps toward the elevator that you never managed to get there. Someone else takes two steps, gets on the elevator, and rides up and down. You have to get on the elevator and ride it to find out if it's safe. The worrier is like the person who takes minute steps and never quite gets on the elevator, but keeps worrying about it. In order to get over your fear of the elevator, you have to get on it. You have to experience the fear in order to realize that it is not really dangerous. *You have to go through it to get past it.*

Psychologist Tom Borkovec has found that the essential factor in this avoidance of emotion is that worriers do not form *visual images* of the things that they fear. Worriers worry in abstract sentences, using language rather than images. In one study, 71 percent of worries were thoughts and only 14 percent were visual images.[3] Borkovec and others have found that visual images of bad things happening are far more intense emotionally than are thoughts about bad things happening. Rather than have a visual image of being alone in your room crying, you think, "Maybe I will end up alone." Then you come up with a set of possible ways this can happen, and then you think of how you can avoid each problem. Rather than have the emotional visual image of being alone in the room, you engage in the relatively cold, abstract thoughts that constitute worry. Thus, your emotions are temporarily suppressed.

Imagine I say to you, "You might get rabies." How anxious does this sentence make you? Perhaps your heart rate has increased a bit. Now imagine I show you a film of you with rabies, paralyzed, unable to swallow, agitated, convulsing, near death. Well, as you know, a picture is worth a thousand words. Or, when it comes to worry, a picture is more upsetting than a thousand words.

This emotional avoidance theory of worry is supported by a number of other research facts. When worriers are confronted with a threatening stimulus, they show no increase in arousal (contrary to nonworriers, who show an increase in arousal). With the presentation of the threatening stimulus, the worrier engages in the abstract linguistic process of worry, looking for solutions. Abstract linguistic worry is nonemotional; literally, worriers think too much, rather than feel the emotional impact of a negative event.

But why is it important to feel the impact of something you fear? Research by a number of psychologists shows that in order to overcome a fear you have to *feel afraid*. You can't just think it through—you have to *feel* it through. As a result, worriers do not process the negative event, as evidenced by the fact that they do not become habituated to (less responsive to or more bored with) the negative stimulus. The negative stimulus does not, therefore, become less threatening. The worrier shows no decrease of arousal with repeated exposure to the threatening image.[4] There is a lack of emotional learning—that is, recognizing that the threat really isn't dangerous.

Worriers have greater difficulty identifying their emotions, they report greater fear of their emotions, and they have more negative views of unpleasant emotions.[5] For example, they believe their unpleasant emotions will last indefinitely, they feel less in control, and they believe other people don't have the same feelings.[6] Furthermore, evidence from EEGs indicates that chronic worriers show greater activity in the cortical (thinking) sections of their brains during worry, and suppressed activity in the limbic/amygdala (emotional) section of the brain.[7] This is in contrast to people with a specific phobia, who show the opposite pattern. Thus, worriers are relying on the nonemotional part of their brains (the cortical sections) to handle threat; they are thinkers rather than feelers.

For example, Jennifer was worried that her husband was losing interest in her. She began to think the relationship might end. Jennifer then thought about every possible way she could spot early signs of his loss of interest. She did not face her worst image: "I am alone and feel miserable." Thus, during her active worry, she was abstract and less emotional. Her potential for facing the intense emotion of being alone was temporarily suppressed. Because Jennifer was functioning during the worry phase in the abstract and relatively less emotional level of experience, she was less anxious. However, when her worry subsided, her anxiety rebounded as physical tension and irritability. Jennifer was trying to avoid the emotions that she would experience if she was alone—sadness, helplessness, anxiety.

In order to get rid of any fear or anxiety, you need to experience the anxiety in order to process it—in order to find out that what you are afraid of really isn't so bad. *You must feel afraid to overcome your fear.*[8] You must learn how to feel anxious.

Do You Repress or Express Emotion?

What happens when you don't accept your emotions or you try to inhibit them? If you use a technique researchers have labeled "repressive coping," then you believe that you cannot tolerate your emotions and that you have to get rid of them. Repressors minimize the importance of things, try to be rational all the time, and deny that they are upset. Some people with this repressive coping style have a difficult time even *labeling* their feelings; they can't say if they are lonely, sad, anxious, or angry.[9] In contrast, if you use the *expressive style,* then you recognize, accept, and use your emotions in a constructive way. In fact, if you are expressive, you may be sensitized to your emotions and aware of all your different feelings—you may complain more about how bad you feel, you may be more likely to cry or feel upset. A repressive coping style, the inability to recognize and label your emotions, and an overemphasis on rationality or antiemotionality are associated with longer-term physical problems, such as increased risk of hypertension, cancer, asthma, and general physical complaints.[10]

The Importance of Letting Your Emotions Out

Psychologist James Pennebaker had college students write stories about experiences they had that upset them—what happened and how it felt.[11] Right after they wrote out their stories the students felt *worse*. Does this mean that expressing emotions is bad for you? No. Several weeks later the students who wrote about their feelings felt *better* than another group of students who did not write about their feelings. Why would this happen? First, when you write out your emotions you begin to realize that you won't be overwhelmed by them. As a result, you become less afraid of these emotions. The second reason is that you realize that there are only a few things that bother you—it's not a million things, so maybe it's manageable. And finally, you begin to process your experiences—that is, you begin to put them in perspective ("Maybe it wasn't so terrible") and you think about how you can solve the problem. That's why writing out the feelings actually helped people feel better.

KEEP AN EMOTION DIARY

Write out a detailed description of what is bothering you now: what happened, what led up to it, what your feelings and thoughts are, and anything else that you think is important. Keep this emotion diary for two weeks. You can use the form opposite to guide you. In the left column list the date when you write this out and the events or situation that you are describing. In the second column write out a detailed description of what the experience was like for you, what happened, your feelings and any thoughts. Take about ten minutes to do this every day.

Examples of emotions include the following: happy, interested, excited, caring, affectionate, loving, feeling loved, compassionate, grateful, proud, confident, hurt, sad, regretful, irritated, angry, resentful, disgusted, contemptuous, ashamed, guilty, envious, jealous, anxious, afraid.[12]

TABLE 9.1	
EMOTION DIARY	
Date and situation	*Experience, feelings, and thoughts*

For example, look at the diary that Jennifer kept when she worried about her husband's loss of interest in her.

TABLE 9.2	
JENNIFER'S EMOTION DIARY	
Date and situation	Experience, feelings, and thoughts
Monday Joe is late coming	I am feeling angry and anxious and worried. I feel like I'm home not loved and that I must be boring. I can see myself getting more and more jealous and insecure. I feel tense in my body.
Tuesday Joe is reading the newspaper	I feel angry. I want to scream. I want to get out of here and just end it now before he gets tired of me and loses interest and finds someone else. I am afraid. I feel so helpless.
Wednesday Joe is watching television	I feel bored. I'm angry. I don't feel like I get any attention. I am feeling invisible. I see me by myself, lonely and unloved. I feel like I am falling apart. I feel so anxious and sad. I want to be angry, but I am just feeling anxious and sad. My stomach is feeling uncomfortable.
Thursday Joe is late coming home	I'm angry. I feel sad. When I think about being alone I feel afraid. How will I take care of myself? I must be worried that I won't be able to take care of myself and that I will spend the rest of my life alone. Pathetic.

As Jennifer continued keeping her emotional diary she noticed that her feelings kept coming up—and they began making some sense to her. She was equating Joe's absorption in work and the newspaper with being unloved and being ignored, personalizing his behavior. She was also afraid that if she was ever alone, she would be helpless and would never connect with anyone again. She viewed her current anxiety as a signal that she would become permanently alone and depressed. As she continued to write out these different feelings and thoughts, she began to put them more in perspective. She realized that Joe's absorption in work was not a sign that their relationship would have to end or that he did not love her.

The Meaning of Emotion

If you have a negative view of your emotions, you may try to eliminate unpleasant feelings by drinking, binge-eating, watching television, surfing the Internet—or *worrying*. For example, your negative view of emotion might contain the following beliefs about unpleasant feelings such as anxiety or sadness:

- These feelings will last forever.
- My feelings do not make sense.
- No one else has these feelings.
- I should not have these feelings.
- My feelings show that I am weak or inferior.
- No one would understand my feelings.

I have outlined in Figure 9.1 overleaf how you could think about and respond to your unpleasant emotional experiences. You can notice and label your emotions, consider them normal, believe you can express your feelings and be understood or validated, and perhaps learn from the experience. In contrast, you might try to escape from these feelings by binge-eating, drinking, or becoming overly absorbed in the Internet. This style of emotional avoidance reflects the beliefs that you cannot handle emotions, that emotions will overwhelm you, and that your emotions do not make sense.

For example, Christina was a chronically anxious person who worried about her job and her relationships. When she came

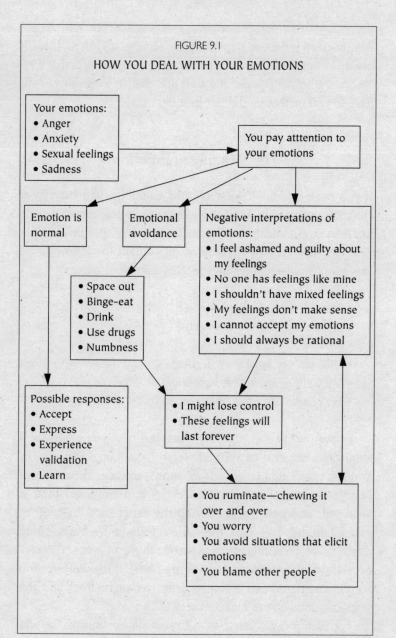

FIGURE 9.1

HOW YOU DEAL WITH YOUR EMOTIONS

Your emotions:
• Anger
• Anxiety
• Sexual feelings
• Sadness

You pay atttention to your emotions

Emotion is normal

Emotional avoidance

Negative interpretations of emotions:
• I feel ashamed and guilty about my feelings
• No one has feelings like mine
• I shouldn't have mixed feelings
• My feelings don't make sense
• I cannot accept my emotions
• I should always be rational

• Space out
• Binge-eat
• Drink
• Use drugs
• Numbness

Possible responses:
• Accept
• Express
• Experience validation
• Learn

• I might lose control
• These feelings will last forever

• You ruminate—chewing it over and over
• You worry
• You avoid situations that elicit emotions
• You blame other people

home to her apartment, she was flooded with negative feelings. However, she did not allow herself to stay with these feelings and examine them and her thoughts. Rather, she would start drinking or binge-eating, suppressing these negative feelings. This emotional avoidance and emotional numbing contributed to her general anxiety that she could not face reality.

We found that people who worry a lot believe that people would not understand their feelings, that other people did not have the same feelings that they had, and that their feelings did not make sense to them.[13] They also experienced guilt about their feelings and believed that they should not have conflicting feelings. They felt they had less control over their emotions, they displayed less acceptance of their feelings, and they blamed other people for their feelings. If you worry, you are intolerant of negative feelings.[14]

In addition, people who worried a lot focused more on how bad they felt, and they did not distract themselves with other activities. These findings indicate that negative beliefs about emotions contribute to worry. Finally, we also found that people who are dependent in their relationships (who fear abandonment) and people who are avoidant (who fear rejection) also had negative beliefs about their emotions.

Ten Ways to Handle Emotions

Use Your Emotions to Tell You About Your Needs

Professor Leslie Greenberg of York University in Canada has developed a comprehensive, humanistic approach to psychotherapy, called emotion-focused therapy (EFT).[15] Greenberg's model proposes that emotions are a source of information so that you can experience the *meaning* of events. Emotions are a window into what matters to you. Thus, like physical pain, emotions tell us what is bothering us and that something needs to be changed.[16] EFT emphasizes expression, validation, self-understanding, clarification, and recognition of needs that come from your emotional experience. *Emotions contain information.* Noticing that you feel anxious or angry may provide you with information that certain needs are not being met. Your strong negative and unpleasant emotions are not always a sign that you are irrational or neurotic—these emotions may be a signal that something problematic is going on and that you are not handling this well.

For example, Phil felt anxious when he was around his girlfriend, Geneva. However, rather than ask himself if his anxiety might be telling him something, he began to worry about his anxiety: "I must be getting sick. Perhaps I am really neurotic. Geneva is such a nice person, but I must be losing control if I am so anxious. I really need to pay attention to this anxiety so that I don't lose control and make a fool of myself." However, as Phil and I discussed the matter it became clear that he had a lot of reasonable reservations about Geneva, even if she was a nice person. There were lots of things missing in the relationship. He felt he could not communicate and get support from her, that things were superficial, and that he did not see a future. Rather than admit that she was not right for him, Phil began to worry that there was something wrong with him.

Phil and I discussed his fear of his emotions—his fear of feeling uncomfortable, his perfectionistic belief that he should always "accept his girlfriend the way she is," and his right to be dissatisfied. Phil's worries were focused on his intolerance of his emotions—in this case, his discomfort and anger around Geneva—rather than on using his emotions to point to what his needs are. Phil said, "I need someone I can be myself with. I need someone I can communicate with and feel like we really click together. I mean, I really like Geneva, but I don't feel she meets these needs."

Climb a Ladder of Meaning

Often psychologists focus on what is wrong with you and how you are thinking irrationally. But frustration and anxiety can often point to what is valuable and meaningful to you.[17] One technique that I use is called "laddering." I ask you to take what you are feeling anxious or worried about and climb a ladder of meaning that leads to your higher values. What does this mean? Let's take Jennifer, who worried that her husband had lost interest in her. I attempted to use the laddering technique to elicit her higher values, values that she could be proud of and could eventually learn to use to build a better relationship with Joe.

I asked Jennifer what it meant to her when she was ignored. We then began climbing the ladder: "I need him to pay attention because when he pays attention it means he cares about me, and this meets my need for love and affection and closeness, because if I have love and affection and closeness, I will feel that life is complete and I can give love, because I am a loving person."

Laddering allowed Jennifer to climb to a higher level—higher than anger, anxiety, loneliness, and feeling unloved. It points to what is good about her: she is a loving person and wants closeness. Of course, realizing that you have these higher values does not mean you will get what you want. Indeed, you can also feel sad recognizing that you strongly value something but may not be getting it at the present time. However, rather than feeling unloved and empty, the laddering technique allowed Jennifer to feel affirmed and validated in her needs.

Accept Your Feelings

Some people cannot accept the fact that they have these unpleasant feelings. They become alarmed by their emotions—feeling guilty, overwhelmed, confused, and ashamed. In fact, some people believe that if they accept that they have a feeling, it will mean they are saying it's OK and nothing can be done about it. But if you don't accept that you have a feeling, it will be hard to deal with it.[18] For example, if you are angry at your partner, you won't be able to do much about the anger unless you first accept that this is your feeling.

In Jennifer's case she had a hard time accepting she felt angry. She initially told me that she was frustrated with Joe, but that she primarily felt anxious and worried. When we talked about the fact that her emotional log showed that she was feeling a lot of anger, she pointed out that she was afraid of accepting her anger because she did not want to alienate Joe.

But if you don't accept that you have a feeling, you won't be able to do anything about that feeling. And if you don't accept it, you might struggle against it and make the feeling even stronger.

Notice Your Emotions

In order to accept your emotions you have to experience them. You can begin this process by noticing what emotions you are having. Most of our emotions are experienced through physical sensations: tension in the face, rapid heartbeat, tingling in fingers or toes, sweating. Do a body awareness check.[19] Close your eyes, lie back, and notice any tension or any arousal in any part of your body. Scan your body one section at a time. Start with your hands, then your arms, your legs, your feet, your butt, your stomach, your chest, your neck, your face. Where is the tension?

Wherever you feel the tension, try to *increase* it. This will tune you in to your emotions. As you begin to imagine the tension increasing, think back on what you are feeling emotional about. What feelings are you having? Don't just stop with one feeling. Try to list as many of the feelings that you are having. Here's a list of feelings that you might find useful: happy, interested, excited, caring, affectionate, loving, feeling loved, compassionate, grateful, proud, confident, hurt, sad, regretful, irritated, angry, resentful, disgusted, contemptuous, ashamed, guilty, envious, jealous, anxious, afraid, other feeling.[20] Try to find as many different labels for your emotions as you can.

Use Images to Create Feelings

As you experience emotions, try to form a visual image that goes with the emotion. These visual images can be about current experiences in your life, past memories, or just images that come to mind. For example, when Jennifer felt more and more physical tension, she formed the visual image of herself alone in a dark room, feeling abandoned and unloved.

You can use emotional imagery to change your feelings. I asked Jennifer to try to hold this image of herself alone and sad and allow herself to feel the painful emotions. I then asked her to try out some new images. First, I asked her to begin to change the visual image of being alone in the room to a visual image of holding Joe while they were both in bed. As she held this image, tears began to fall, and she said, "This is what I want." I then asked her to leave this image behind, put up a blank screen in her mind, and form a new image. This would be an image of talking with friends whom she loved and who cared for her. Her image was of walking on the beach with Elena, whom she had known for years, laughing and talking.

This technique of "imagery rescripting," or rewriting your images, is quite powerful.[21] The power behind imagery rescripting is that you experience the image of your worst emotional fears. However, as you experience and accept these emotions, you learn that you are not destroyed by them. Moreover, by rescripting the image, developing a new picture in your mind with a different and more positive story, your feared fantasy is modified. What you were afraid of ever imagining is now transformed into a new image that captures your hopes and dreams.

Feel Less Guilty and Ashamed

Jennifer felt guilty about feeling angry. She viewed herself as loving and understanding, and she believed that being angry was inconsistent with this view of herself. As a result, she was focusing on her worries and anxiety—which were important—but she could not allow herself to admit to the anger. Another factor in feeling guilty is equating having the feeling with carrying out the action. Jennifer was afraid that if she admitted to herself or to Joe that she felt angry, she would act out in a hostile way. She recalled that her parents always emphasized "being understanding and tolerant of everyone" and "not showing your anger because it is bad."

You can challenge your guilty and shameful thoughts about your feelings by asking, "Why shouldn't I have the feelings that I have?" Would anyone ever say, "You shouldn't have a stomachache" or "You shouldn't have a headache"? Let's say that you feel angry at your partner. You might have the (irrational) belief that you should never feel really angry at your partner. You might think, "I love him. I should always feel loving feelings." But you don't—you feel angry right now. Feeling angry does not mean that you are going to attack your partner—it's just a feeling. Imagine that you are feeling very sexually attracted to someone at work, but you are married. You think, "I feel so ashamed and guilty. I should never be attracted to another man." But being attracted doesn't mean that you will act on it. There is nothing evil or malicious about having a feeling. The problem is not that you have the feeling—it's in carrying out the action. The more you feel guilty and ashamed about your feelings, the more you will worry about them, and the more intense your feelings will become.

Some of us believe that our emotions will spin out of control and make us act in ways that could embarrass us or cause harm. For example, Oren was feeling tense about work and confused about his marriage. He noticed that when he was walking behind his six-year-old daughter, he had a strong feeling and the thought "Maybe I could push her down the stairs." Oren had never been mean or cruel toward his daughter, but he became afraid of his thought and his feeling. He began to believe that any negative thought or feeling about his daughter or his wife could make him lose control. So he began watching for more and more of these thoughts and feelings—and sure enough, he found them. Of course, this made him worry even more. Psychologists call this "thought-action fusion," because some people believe that their thoughts (or feelings) will lead them to take action. It's almost as if the thought and the action are the same.

I explained to Oren that many people who have obsessions believe that these thoughts will lead to action. He was confusing having a feeling (or thought) with the reality of carrying out an action. I asked Oren to repeat two hundred times in the session, "I want to push my daughter down the stairs," in order to demonstrate that having this thought would become more boring rather than more dangerous. Initially, he was highly reluctant to carry out this thought-exposure exercise, but with my encouragement he did, and his fear and guilt over this thought subsided.

Recognize That Almost Everyone Has These Feelings

We often feel that no one would have the same feelings we have and no one could understand our feelings, so we keep these feelings to ourselves. Sometimes we believe that our feelings are a sign of something worse—maybe we are going crazy, maybe there is something odd and disgusting about us, maybe we are just weird. Let's take Michael, who is sad and lonely because Mary has left him. How can we normalize his feelings? Well, don't a lot of people feel sad and lonely after a breakup? But they also can feel a lot of other things as well. They might feel angry. They might feel a bit relieved. There is no *one* feeling that people have after breakups—just lots of different feelings. Or how about Deanna, who was running from the World Trade Center on September 11? Later she felt afraid—she kept dreaming about crashes and explosions. Aren't those feelings that a lot of people would have?

Annalise believed her feelings of emptiness and resentment and her worries about being alone for the rest of her life were almost unique to her. Her husband had died two years before. I pointed out to Annalise that these were very difficult feelings to have, but that many other people unfortunately also had problems with anxiety and depression. Almost half of the general population has a history of depression, anxiety, or substance abuse problems. Because she was ashamed of her feelings, she never talked about them with other people. I asked her to consider how many of her family and friends had talked to her about their troubles. If no one else had these problems, then why were they turning to her so often to discuss them?

Accept Contradictory Feelings

Some people believe they should have only one feeling toward someone—for example, either like or dislike. Are people and situations really that simple? Can everything be reduced to just one feeling? I doubt it. Mixed feelings, complex feelings, contradictory feelings mean that we notice a lot more *complexity*. It's the difference between painting in black and white and painting with the colors of the most intense rainbow. If you believe that you should have only one feeling toward someone, then you will feel frustrated and confused. People who have this simplistic view often ruminate and worry that there is something that they are missing, a piece that will clarify things for them and reduce everything to a simple black-and-white picture. Since that black-and-white picture never lasts for very long—things are really complicated, after all—you worry and ruminate even more.

Let's say that you are going through the breakup of a relationship. What kinds of emotions could you have? Would it be just one feeling, or lots of different feelings? Could you have both positive and negative feelings? Some people believe that life should be simple—if you break up, you either hate or love the person. But very few people are so simple. Most of us have lots of different feelings—feelings that might seem contradictory. Accepting conflicting feelings is very important because it indicates that you are using more information.[22] For example, if you break up and have conflicting feelings, it means that you are using more information about how complicated two people can be together—or apart.

Accepting complexity may be difficult. You might believe that you need to clarify matters. It might be hard to balance all of these feelings. But if you accept that you will have mixed feelings, even conflicting feelings, then you will be a lot less likely to feel guilty, confused, and obsessed. You can simply say, "Having mixed feelings means that I am aware of how complex people are—and how complex I am."

Jennifer had mixed feelings toward Joe. She felt anxious, angry, loving, excited, and sometimes bored. She worried that her mixed feelings might be a sign that her marriage was falling apart—or that Joe's apparent mixed feelings (sometimes being interested and excited about Jennifer and sometimes being more wrapped up in his own things) meant that they were not right for each other. Jennifer's belief was that mixed feelings mean that there is something wrong that needs to be addressed immediately. I asked her to examine her feelings toward her close friends and toward other members of her family—did she have mixed feelings toward any of these people? Of course, as it turned out, she had mixed feelings toward everyone. I suggested that she view this as a sign that she was mature and intelligent and could recognize conflicting aspects of being human. Her worry was often driven by her need to, as she put it, "find out what is really going on"—which, for her, meant reducing everything to one feeling or one quality of a person.

Be Irrational

You may also believe you should be rational all the time. Everything should be "logical," everything should add up. You may view feelings as "messy" or "immature." For example, when you get upset about something, you might say, "These feelings are just self-indulgent and stupid" or "I need to be logical and rational about this." You try to distance yourself from people and experiences that arouse any feeling in you, since you think these feelings reflect a weakness in you. You might even get angry at people who "make you" feel things.

The problem with this emphasis on rationality to the exclusion of feelings is that *people evolved to have feelings* and *to use feelings to tell them what they needed.*[23] The more you insist on being rational all the time, the more frustrated you will be. This is like refusing to accept the fact that you are hungry because you think it is inconvenient. You can trace back to your childhood experiences how you learned these "antiemotional" beliefs. Sandra's mother, a doctor who spent most of her time taking care of other people who were sick, told Sandra she was selfish and manipulative when she cried. She told Sandra she should try to "put things in perspective" and "stop whining—you don't appreciate how good you have it." This disapproving emotional style led Sandra to believe she needed to be rational, and that her problems and emotions were just a sign of being immature. Ironically, she had sought out cognitive therapy with me because she thought we would not deal with her emotions.

Talking about her mother's attitude when Sandra was upset, Sandra recalled, "I felt devastated. I knew it would do no good to talk about it." I encouraged her to imagine that she had a six-year-old daughter, and I asked her how she would want to respond if her daughter were crying. Sandra hoped to be a loving, soothing, nurturing mother whose child would talk about her feelings and share them. I suggested that she imagine herself as this little girl and treat herself the way she had just described. In this way Sandra was able to stop being overly rational and start validating her own emotions.

Face the Worst Case

Usually when we worry about something in the future there is an upsetting image that is associated with that worry. As indicated in our discussion of worry as emotional avoidance, exposure to your feared image can be helpful in reducing your worry. The rationale behind this is that you are telling yourself you cannot stand having this emotional image, and so you need to worry to eliminate its impact on you. However, with prolonged exposure to the emotional image—without utilizing worry or other distractions—the image becomes boring and will no longer bother you. The analogy is to the fear of getting on an elevator, as I discussed earlier. If you get on an elevator a hundred times, you will become less afraid of elevators. The same thing proves to be true with practicing emotional imagery.

Close your eyes and try to come up with some negative outcomes. For example, in the case of worry about a brain tumor, you might imagine what it would look like if you were to die from a tumor. Get a visual image of your actual death. This sounds horrible, I know. But just take that image and repeat in your mind, "This is always a possibility." Hold that image for twenty minutes without distracting yourself. You will probably find that your anxiety initially goes up and then decreases until you are bored.

Gina had a fear of a brain tumor. I asked her to form a detailed image of what a terrible experience it would be to have this brain tumor and how it would end in her death. She had an image of having a headache, then of going to the doctor, who says it's nothing. Time goes by and she becomes disoriented, can't see well, and is incapacitated. In her image, she is lying in bed in the hospital, the pain in her head is unbearable, and people are standing around saying, "It's a shame, but now we can't operate."

I had her make a tape of this story and play back the tape over and over for twenty minutes each day. As a result of this repeated exposure, Gina was surprised to find out that her worries about the tumor became weaker. Most surprising to her was that repeating the feared image became so boring that she had a hard time concentrating on the parts that used to be most frightening.

Summing Up

We have seen that worry is often a way of avoiding your emotions. Unfortunately, if you do not recognize, experience, and go through your feelings, you may not learn what your real needs are, and you may not recognize that you can handle the fears that you have. As you suppress your emotions by worrying, you will experience a rebound in negative feelings later. The following guide provides common examples of the kinds of problems that you might have with your feelings and some questions to help you recognize and understand them better.

TABLE 9.3

A GUIDE TO DEALING WITH YOUR FEELINGS

Your problem	Questions to ask yourself
No one would understand my feelings.	Are there some people who accept and understand your feelings? Do you have arbitrary rules for validation? Do people have to agree with everything you say? Are you sharing your emotions with people who are critical? Do you accept and support other people who have these emotions? Do you have a double standard about feelings? Why?
My feelings don't make any sense to me.	What could be some good reasons why you are sad, anxious, angry, etc.? What are you thinking (what images do you have) when you are sad, etc.? What situations trigger these feelings? If someone else experienced this, what kinds of different feelings could they have? If you think your feelings don't make sense right now, what does this make you think? Are you afraid that you are going crazy, losing control? Are there things that happened to you as a kid that might account for why you feel this way? Are there people in your life right now who tell you that your feelings don't make sense?
I feel ashamed of my feelings. I shouldn't have these feelings.	What are the reasons that you think your emotions are not legitimate? Why shouldn't you have the feelings that you have? What are some reasons that your feelings make sense? Is it possible that others could have the same feelings in this situation?

Your problem	Questions to ask yourself
	Can you see that having a feeling (such as anger) is not the same as acting on it (for example, being hostile)?
	Why are certain emotions good while others are bad?
	If someone else had this feeling, would you think less of him or her?
	How do you know if an emotion is bad?
	What if you looked at feelings and emotions as experiences that tell you that something is bothering you—like a caution sign, a flashing yellow light?
	How is anyone harmed by your emotions?
I shouldn't have mixed feelings about someone. My feelings should be clear.	Do you think that having mixed feelings is normal or abnormal? What does it mean to have mixed feelings about someone? Aren't people complicated, and so you could have different, even conflicting feelings?
	What is the disadvantage of demanding that you have only one feeling?
My feelings don't tell me anything that is important.	Sometimes we feel sad, anxious, or angry because we are missing something that is important to us. Let's say you feel sad about a breakup in a relationship. Doesn't this mean that you have a higher value that's important to you—for example, closeness and intimacy? Doesn't this say something good about you?
	If you aspire to higher values, doesn't this mean that you will have to be disappointed at times? Would you want to be a cynic who values nothing?
	Are there other people who share your higher values?
	What advice would you give them if they were going through what you are going through?

10

Step Seven: Take Control of Time

JUSTIN DRIVES TO THE CITY from the suburbs every day, and his stress level spikes when he crosses the bridge in heavy traffic. His heart is beating rapidly, and he feels like he wants to jump out of his car and start yelling at the slow driver in front of him. The traffic is not any worse than usual, but he just can't stand these delays. Justin thinks about all the things that he has to do, and he worries he'll never get them done. He's blowing his horn at the guy in front of him, but nothing seems to change. He's trapped in the traffic again.

He parks his car at the garage and starts walking to his office. He just can't stand the fact that the man in front of him is walking so slowly. Doesn't he realize there are other people in the world? He waits for the elevator, again—this seems to be taking forever. As he gets off at his floor, he rushes past Maria, not even bothering to say hello. Maria looks at him and thinks, "Another day with Justin."

Where are the reports he wanted on his desk? He thought they'd be here right now—right when he sat down. He feels like flinging the mail across the room—"Can't anyone get anything right?" Oh—here's the report. But he had to waste a couple of minutes finding it. "How am I going to get all these things done today? Deadlines, so many different projects, and I can't rely on anyone."

He works feverishly throughout the morning—no time for lunch. "OK, maybe a sandwich while I work on these things. Did I get that report from Maria? Where is it?" Justin tells Maria all the things that she has to have done by tomorrow morning, but he's talking so fast about so many things, she can't follow everything he's saying. She's sure to miss something, and then he'll worry about getting everything done.

I Need It Right Now

You might recognize yourself in Justin. You feel that you're overscheduled, and you worry that you won't have enough time to get things done. You feel everything has to be done *right now,* because time is running out. If you don't have the true love that you want, you feel it has to happen right now—today or tonight at this party—or it will never happen. If your stocks have dropped, you worry that you have to recover your losses right now, or you will turn into a pauper. You've got to get the job right now, lose weight right now, find out you are cancer-free right now—*or it will never happen.*

Psychologist John Riskind describes this sense of time urgency in terms of "looming vulnerability."[1] According to Riskind, we feel anxious partly because we view a threat or danger as approaching rapidly and overcoming us so quickly that we will not have time to cope. For example, if you looked up and saw a train approaching you on the tracks at a hundred miles per hour and the train is fifty feet away, then you would feel that a catastrophe is going to happen. However, if you imagined the train approaching at twenty miles per hour and it was one mile away, you would feel you had enough time to get out of the way. In a series of experiments, Riskind has shown that this sense of rapidly approaching danger accounts for why a lot of us are anxious.

It makes sense. If we go back to Justin, who feels overwhelmed with projects and deadlines and impediments, we can see that he feels that events are happening to him rapidly and that threats are approaching faster than he can handle them. There is a continual sense of urgency, emergency, and imminent catastrophe. Justin worries in order to find ways to cope right now—so that the train doesn't hit him.

What's Your Sense of Time?

Your sense of time—and how it impacts on you and how you cope with it—will have dramatic effects on your stress and your worries. For example, ask yourself the following:

- Do you often feel pressured for time?
- Are you often thinking about things that might happen in the future?
- Do you have a hard time staying in the moment?
- Do you find yourself frustrated with how slowly things are going?
- Do you feel like rushing people through their conversation?
- Are you often worried about deadlines?
- Are you often overscheduled?
- Do you show up a lot earlier or a lot later than other people?
- Do you keep checking your watch or the clock?
- Do you get frustrated when you are behind someone in traffic or walking down the street?
- Do you feel you just can't stand waiting?
- If you think that something bad could happen, do you feel you need the answer right now?

These different pressures of time are almost all self-imposed. You may think that time is reality, just as gravity and space seem like reality to you. But can you point to time? Can you point to urgency? Can you point to "enough time"?

Of course, this seems absurd. Time is not an object, and it is not located in space—at least not for the average person like you or me. Time is a sense that we have, and it's related to what we are doing and what we expect to do. Our sense of urgency is entirely subjective: it's our individual sense of something that we think needs to be done. Urgency is in your head, not "out there" in reality.

Have you noticed that there are periods when time just seems to fly by? You got so absorbed in something that you didn't realize that the time had gone so quickly. Or have you noticed that time sometimes seems to drag? This sense of slowed-down time occurs when you are bored, depressed, or anxious, when you feel nothing is happening. In either case, the clocks haven't changed; your sense of time has. We tend to experience time in terms of the events that are occurring in our minds. If you sit and stare at a wall, time drags. If you are watching a fascinating movie, time seems to rush by.

If you think there are a hundred things that you have to do, and you think about them all at once, then time seems to be rushing in on you. It's the train—a hundred trains—coming at you at some land-speed record. But what if you thought of only one train coming ever so slowly? You would feel less time pressure.

In order to get a handle on time—and in order to reduce your worries—we are going to look at a number of things that you can do with time to help you. These are:

- Turn the urgency off
- Accept impermanence
- Appreciate each moment
- Improve the moment
- Stretch time
- Plan time

Turn the Urgency Off

Worry is always an escape from the moment and an attempt to control future time. Almost all worriers have a sense of time urgency—the sense that you *have to have the answer right now*. The man who worries about his health wants a diagnosis and a prognosis right now. The woman who worries about losing her job wants to know right now what her future history will be as an employee. What does it mean to you not to know right now? If you are a worrier, you probably believe that if you do not know right now, then the outcome will be terrible.

What are the costs of demanding an answer right now? You feel pressured, anxious, and out of control, and you overly focus on something that is currently unknowable—that is, the uncertain future. You may think that demanding an answer right now may help you get an answer, but that is generally not the case. There are many things that you cannot know until they happen. You cannot know if you are going to pass the test until you finish the test. You can't know if your relationship will work out until you go through your relationship. You can't know if your money will run out until you see what your expenses and income are in the future.

Demanding the answer seldom leads to the answer—in fact, it generally leads you to ask unanswerable questions, one sign of unproductive worry.[2]

You can test out whether an answer is available right now by giving yourself a time limit to find it. In many cases, if you examine the limited information available to you right now, you can readily conclude that you will not get an answer immediately.

Furthermore, you don't *need* the answer right now. This point is often a revolutionary one for worriers. Do you really *need* to know right now whether someone is annoyed with you or whether you will do well on the exam next week? Do you really *need* to know right now whether you will get married? Do you absolutely *need* to know if your investments will go up or down? Of course not.

Instead, live in the *present tense*—focus on your interests, your friends, dating people you like, exercising, work, your family, and the rest. Focus on living your life in the moment. Every time you have a sense of urgency to know right now about the future, bring yourself back to living in the present by saying, "What are some constructive and positive things that I can do right now?" If you can't get the answer to the questions that you "need to know," then take action on what you do know and what you can do.

Not only do you not need to know right now—but you may also not need to be any particular place right now. For example, you may find yourself worried about being on time. I am often amused when I am driving on the highway and someone cuts me off, zooming past me far beyond the speed limit. Where is that person going? What is the urgent appointment? What would happen if he or she drove slower?

Brandon is an intense driver who races as fast as he can on the highway. His wife finds it unbearable to be in the car with him. Brandon tells me that his sense of urgency on the highway is such that "I can't stand someone slowing me up." I asked him what it meant to be slowed up by someone, and he said, "It makes me feel like they are keeping me from getting to where I want to go." But is he really never going to get to his destination? Or is it simply a minor delay? I asked Brandon what about being delayed was so troubling. He answered, "It's wasting time. I can't stand wasting time."

Why not waste time? Even if I waste an hour, there are twenty-three more hours in the day, and another 364 days in the year. What if Brandon were to look at wasting time as a major goal—a benefit? Or to look at it as inevitable? We all waste time.

I asked Brandon to build in "wasting time" as part of his schedule: "Every day when you drive to work, I'd like you to drive slower than the slowest person on the highway. Find out what really will happen if you intentionally waste time and drive slower." Initially Brandon thought this was an insane assignment, but after he tried it for a couple of weeks, he realized he felt less pressure to "be on time." We then examined standing in line. Brandon felt that waiting in line was another example of wasting time. So his homework assignment was to go to a large department store and look for long lines—get in line, wait, and then leave the line right before his turn came. This was a "total waste of time," Brandon said at first, but he soon learned that wasting time was really of no consequence. Nothing really happened, and he wasn't really worse off.

Accept Impermanence

The Value of Impermanence

Carson thought that his anxiety and tension would last *forever*. It was as though this moment in time represented the rest of his life—completely overwhelmed with bad feeling. He couldn't step back and imagine how he would feel a couple of hours later. Carson's fear of negative feelings made him try to catch any negative feeling by worrying. I suggested that he might take a different strategy toward his emotions. He might accept that negative feelings are inevitable but also *impermanent*. You can't avoid having negative feelings, but the good news is that every feeling will pass by.

What is the negative feeling that you have right before you start worrying? Do you feel anxious, tense, irritable? Whatever the feeling you have, I will bet you that this feeling will eventually pass. Feelings are experiences in the present moment—and moment to moment, your feelings change. What was the best feeling you had last week? Whatever it is, that feeling has passed you by. You don't have that feeling right now. Did you ever have a panic attack? Chances are you are not having that panic attack while you are reading this book.

If feelings are impermanent, if they are transitory, then why worry about them? Imagine that you are really upset because you have just heard that your partner is leaving you. As terrible as it is, this feeling too is impermanent. Impermanence gives us hope, for feelings—and worries—are continually in process. Feelings and worries are like leaves on the surface of the water. Sometimes the water seems like it is standing still; at other times the current moves rapidly. It's only a matter of how fast the river flows. But it flows—and so do these feelings.

Observe Impermanence

Joanne is worried about her bills. She's overdrawn her checking account, and she doesn't get another paycheck for a few days. She feels pressured, anxious, and worried. I asked her to try doing *nothing* for an hour about these feelings, then to try describing these feelings without trying to change them. As Joanne described these feelings, she noticed that the intensity of these feelings changed. Over the course of the hour she felt them less intensely. They were not permanently intense.

One way of proving to yourself that your negative feelings do not last forever is to keep track of your feelings every hour of the week in a mood log. For example, Jennifer believed she was always anxious about Joe. I asked her to chart her emotions and keep track of what she was doing every hour of the week. To her surprise, she was hardly ever thinking about Joe, since she was at work most of the day, and even when they were home she was involved either in her own activities or in having rather pleasant interactions with Joe. As a consequence of segmenting her feelings, she became less worried about occasionally feeling anxious (or angry).

All emotions are temporary. Why use worry to try to change something that will change on its own? Step away from the feeling right now, and watch it gradually pass by.

Appreciate Each Moment

One way to help you step away from time is to appreciate and experience the present moment. I discussed mindful detachment in Chapter 5, but I now turn to taking control of time by experiencing the present moment the way it is. Ironically, you will feel less out of control in time if you give up trying to control time—give up urgency, give up (for the moment) the future—and appreciate each present moment. These ideas of mindful detachment—your mind stepping back and detaching to stay in the present moment—have been derived from techniques of Buddhist meditation.[3] Using this technique, you can observe, notice, and describe your feelings rather than demand that you get rid of them.[4] Rather than struggling with your feelings, sensations, or thoughts, you accept and observe them in the present moment. You are both mindful (aware) and detached (accepting).

The problem with worry is that we get caught up and distracted in all of the possible things that we try to control. We notice that we are uncomfortable or anxious, and we think we have to change that feeling immediately. We become attached to our goals of getting everything done and trying to control everything. But by using mindful detachment, staying in the present moment rather than focusing on trying to make the future happen right now, you can let go of the worry that drives your sense of urgency.

Let's imagine that you are stuck in traffic. You think, "I've got to get out of here *immediately*!" You are overcome with a sense of urgency that you think you have to eliminate completely. But let's imagine that you practice mindful detachment and appreciate the moment. Since you cannot control the traffic in front of you, you sit back in your seat and observe. You take yourself out of the picture of trying to control everything. When you are the observing, detached mind, you do not judge or push or strive or struggle. You observe that there is a green car, the sky is filled with clouds, and the clouds are shifting in the wind. You observe and detach, but you are completely in the moment. Any thoughts of "getting there on time" are pushed away from your thinking; you stay in the moment and observe the cars and the sky.

Practice mindful detachment when you are overcome by a sense of urgency that something has to happen right now—as if that train is coming down the track and you can't get out of the way. Just stand back from your urge to control and change things, and simply describe your response to it in the most minute details of your sensations—*staying in the present moment.* Concentrate on where you feel the tension and the urge. Stand back and watch it. See the tension rise, plateau, and decrease. Use metaphors to describe it—"It's like water flowing through me" or "It's like a needle sticking into me." Try to describe to yourself what you see and feel. As you stay in the present moment, notice that a new moment begins and also passes by. As you give up control and observe each moment, you will worry less.

Improve the Moment

If you are caught up in the moment and the moment is overwhelming, devastating, upsetting, and painful, what can you do? You can *improve the moment.* Whatever the moment is, it could be better.

What can you do to improve the moment right now?

Ask yourself, "What would feel good at this moment?" Perhaps a soothing bubble bath will feel good, or listening to some music, or reading poetry. You can take control of time by starting in the present moment. Get lost in the details of the present moment—what you see, feel, hear, smell. Walk outside and look around you. If there are trees and grass, look at them more closely. Notice the different shapes and colors of the leaves. Look up at the sky. Notice the clouds. Stay in this present moment— losing yourself as you improve the moment.

You no longer live in the future. You are now in the moment, which is getting better. You do not control the future, but you can make this moment better than it could have been. As you improve the moment, your worries vanish.

Make a list of ways to improve the moment: walking, working on a hobby, petting a cat, looking at photographs, watching a special movie.

Stretch Time

Your worries are like a narrow target on a specific time in the future. As you worry about something in the future, you are aimed at a target that makes the rest of your life disappear. All other time, including the present moment, all past moments, and all moments after, are no longer important. It's as if you have a telescope focused on one point, and the rest of your existence seems to vanish.

How can you learn to stretch time so that you place this moment in a perspective that makes it insignificant? If it is insignificant, then why worry? Think of your life as a time chart. How much space does this one moment take up? It takes up a single point—nothing compared to the space of years for your childhood, adolescence, young adulthood, and the many years remaining in your life.

Now examine how you might feel at different times in your life, stretching time beyond this single moment.

- How will you feel about this worry in a month? A year? Five years?
- What will you do five hours from now? The next day? The day after?
- What are all the positives that could happen between now and then?
- What are all the positives that could happen this moment? In a month, a year, in ten years?

Brianna felt upset about a conflict with her boss at work. How will Brianna feel about this in a couple of days, a month, or a year? Brianna acknowledged that she probably won't think about this next week. Why would she feel less concerned about this in a week? She said that there were a lot of other things in her life other than a few interactions with her boss. Then she added, "I always get over it." If you always get over it, then there are some good reasons that you will get over it. For example, Brianna gets over it because she has other things that occupy her thinking—her work, friends, dates, movies, health club, travel, sleep. She always gets over it because events overtake her worry and put things in perspective.

Take Elvin, who worries about his investments doing poorly. Right now he seems obsessed with his loss of money, and he projects disaster into the future. But the next time I see him—the next week—he is talking about having a good time with his wife, cooking dinner at home. Events take over, and the narrow focus on the worry is eventually lost.

Imagine getting into a time machine. Go into the future a week, two weeks, a month, or a year. Almost everything that you worry about today will seem trivial when you look back on it from the future. This is quite informative, because it tells us that many of the things that bother us now turn out to be unimportant.

Plan Time

Many of us have a hard time being realistic about our schedules. You may rush into a meeting a few minutes late, hassled by the pressure of not being on time. Although it may really make no difference if you are exactly on time, the pressure of not being on time becomes another source of stress and worry. Patrick was continually late for meetings with me—not very late, but always about ten minutes late. He would arrive in a sweat, apologize, and take a few minutes to settle down. It turned out his life was generally like this. He was always running a little behind. We examined what the source of this time pressure was, and a few things began to emerge that contributed to his worries and stress. These included his tendency to overschedule, procrastinate, and underestimate how long things would take, and his expectation that things would run as smoothly and efficiently as possible. Things almost never run that smoothly, and so any unexpected glitch would throw him further behind time.

We decided to take control of time by doing five things:

1. Develop a time plan.
2. Give yourself enough time.
3. Keep track of positives.
4. Learn how to say no.
5. Use someone else's time.

Let's look at how this worked.

1. Develop a Time Plan

Patrick did not use a personal organizer to list all the things that he had to do and when he had to do them. At his best, he had a list of things to do—but no time scheduled to do them. The time plan included time to get up, have breakfast, shower, watch the news, get to work in plenty of time, and get organized. We also built in time to relax, go to the health club three times each week, spend time with his wife and son, and watch television. Whenever he felt overwhelmed, we looked at his time plan and scheduled in some of this work. We examined his "off-task" activities that ate up time. Patrick's major time-waster was surfing the Internet. So his rule then became "I have to get three hours of work done before I can spend fifteen minutes on the Internet." This gave him more time and more control.

2. Give Yourself Enough Time

Patrick often underestimated how long things would take, partly due to his illusion that everything would run as smoothly as possible—and, of course, there were always unexpected problems that ate up time. The other part of his underestimation is that he often put in more time on things than they were worth. Patrick was something of a perfectionist and had difficulty prioritizing how much time an activity really deserved. The first thing we did was establish that he continually underestimated time needed to travel and time needed for specific work projects. Second, we worked on prioritizing which things were really important and which things deserved less time. Third, Patrick planned on giving himself enough time by starting things earlier and trying to get them done before the deadline. Giving himself more time was part of his need to accept his limitations and recognize that he would not be able to get everything done at the highest level in the shortest amount of time.

3. Keep Track of Positives

Part of Patrick's time pressure and worry was that he continually focused on the work he did not get done. He seldom looked back and recognized the work that he did do. I asked Patrick to keep a daily list of activities that he completed and to examine this list every day with the intention of giving himself credit for his accomplishments. Patrick did this for the first two weeks and came back quite pleased and less stressed: "I never realized how much I really do get done. I was always worrying that I was rather lazy because I was always thinking that I hadn't gotten everything done." Keeping track of your behavior may help you realize that you really are using most of your time effectively. It can also tell you how you do not use time effectively, so you can plan time to work for you.

4. Learn How to Say No

Many worriers are so conscientious that they can't say no to an-other request or opportunity to do something. Patrick was no ex-ception to this. Because he was so hardworking, he would get more work to do. He worried that his colleagues might think he wasn't perfect, so he always said yes. We examined the costs and benefits to him of occasionally saying no to new requests. One cost, Patrick believed, was that he would disappoint his boss. We examined all of the effective work that he was doing, and the likelihood that he would be more likely to get things done on time if he had less to do. Patrick decided to take a chance and start saying no to new requests that were not really essential and to things that others could do. This helped immensely.

5. Use Someone Else's Time

Another way that Patrick could say no was to delegate work to other people. This was initially quite difficult because he be-lieved he could do a better job at almost anything compared with his colleagues and employees. However, he recognized the bene-fits of delegating. For example, he could concentrate on activities that drew on his *special* talents. After a couple of months, this began to reduce his stress even more, since he was learning to say no to additional work for himself and yes to allowing other peo-ple to do their job and help out.

Summing Up

Worry is almost always about something that is going to happen in the future. Therefore, your perception of time is an essential part of your worry. If you believe that there is not enough time, then you will worry you won't be able to handle things that could happen. This seventh step in handling worry is an important part of taking control of your life. If you feel that time controls you, then you will continually feel pressured to handle everything in the future that could happen, and to get it done right now. As a result of this demand for immediate solutions, you will feel overwhelmed.

But what if you stand back from time and put time in perspective? You can slow down the experience of approaching events by stepping away from time, focusing on the present moment, improving the moment, and mindfully detaching to become aware of your current experience. Once you step back and experience the present moment, your worries about the rapidly approaching future will dissipate.

Stretching time allows you to see things in the perspective of thousands of events, not simply the single worry about a single point in time. Stretching time allows you to step away from the worry to place a point in time in the context of your entire past and future life experience.

Finally, planning future time will help you feel more in control, especially if you prioritize what needs to be done and if you stay on task and avoid procrastinating. It also means learning how to say no and learning how to be realistic about your limitations. Nothing will run efficiently, so plan on it.

You can put time on your side if you are able to step back and view time along an extending time line that stretches before and after your worry. The idea is not to get trapped by a point in time (your worry) that is only one brief moment in an endless series of moments of time.

KEEP IN MIND

- Turn the urgency off.
- Accept impermanence.
- Appreciate each moment.
- Improve the moment.
- Stretch time.
- Plan time.

PART 3

SPECIAL WORRIES AND HOW TO CHALLENGE THEM

11

Social Worries: What if Nobody Likes Me?

IF YOU FEAR NEGATIVE EVALUATION, then you worry about what others might think of you. You worry that you made a bad impression, said the wrong thing, and will be criticized and rejected. Your fears affect friendships and work relationships and can lead to a number of problems—the inability to approach people you want to meet, lack of assertion, anxiety about taking tests or otherwise being evaluated, sexual anxieties resulting in the inability to maintain an erection or reach orgasm, lack of career advancement, inability to get your basic needs met at work or in relationships, increased reliance on alcohol or drugs in order to feel comfortable when you are with other people, unexpressed anger because your needs are not met, and depression.

What Is Fear of Negative Evaluation?

If you fear negative evaluation, you will answer yes to the following statements on the Fear of Negative Evaluation Scale:[1]

• I become tense and jittery if I know someone is sizing me up.

- I feel very upset when I commit some social error.
- If someone is evaluating me I tend to expect the worst.
- I often worry that I will say or do the wrong thing.

You believe that other people are likely to be critical, you feel that people are watching what you are doing, and you base your self-esteem on how you think other people see you. As a result, you are self-conscious about your performance, and you worry that you will make mistakes that others will criticize.

Perfectionistic Standards and Self-Focus

You may have perfectionistic standards for yourself when you are with other people—concern about making mistakes and the belief that you will generally do poorly.[2] You may engage in more self-focused thinking when you are around other people—you focus your thoughts and attention on your own internal sensations (for example, your anxiety, heartbeat, racing thoughts). You may even exaggerate the extent to which others are looking or thinking about you, and you may think other people are critical. As a result, you will have lower self-esteem, and you are less likely to take credit when you do well.[3] In fact, you might think you are an imposter who will be exposed when people get to know you better.[4]

The Different Parts of Who You Are

You may not distinguish or differentiate various parts of your self. You don't recognize that there are many different components to who you are. If you are overly concerned about approval, you may feel that your self-worth is determined by a specific interaction. Psychologist Kenneth Gergen claims that we have "multiple selves," where our sense of self varies across different situations and social roles.[5] As it turns out, the best predictor of how you feel about yourself is how you rate your physical attractiveness.[6] Perhaps because of this pervasive concern about appearance, concern about approval from other people is a major factor in our worries—although few people are truly objective about their looks.

Children who grow up with secure attachments to their parents are more likely to see themselves from different perspectives and are more likely to accept themselves.[7] Psychologist Susan Harter has found that the child's peer group determines how the child feels about his or her appearance, likability with peers, and athletic competence, whereas parents influence how children feel about their scholastic ability or behavioral conduct (e.g., "doing the right thing").[8] If we have different selves, then approval for one behavior in one situation can be seen as "compartmentalized"—it's not the entire picture of who we are.

Unrealistic and Inflexible Self-esteem

Your fear of negative evaluation may also stem from the fact that your self-esteem is inflexible and unrealistic. One of the hallmarks of emotional stability is to maintain realistic self-esteem even within the context of some disapproval. I emphasize *realistic* self-esteem since you need to recognize where your liabilities or problems reside. Simply telling yourself that you are wonderful and successful will not work, since you may miss the opportunity to use feedback to improve your ability to get along with people and to accomplish your goals.

Unrealistically high self-esteem may be as problematic as unrealistically low self-esteem. The person with unrealistically high self-esteem does not recognize that he continues to make the same mistakes—he does not learn from his experiences. Moreover, unrealistically high self-esteem may result in the inability to recognize and accept your limitations, leading you to take on tasks that are beyond your capability. This increases the chances that you will be overburdened or that you will fail. For example, a young man who continued to alienate others was surprised when I pointed out to him that his behavior was failing and that he was not processing the information about his failure. Because his parents had been so focused on telling him how wonderful he was and then excusing his antisocial behavior, he managed to alienate almost everyone else around him. Correcting his unwarranted high self-esteem about his social behavior was actually quite beneficial to him, since it allowed him to modify behavior that was dysfunctional.

Flexibility in your self-concept and being able to use corrective feedback allows you to be more adaptive. By having a more flexible self-concept you will be able to use disapproval as *information*. This means that if someone does not like something that you have said or done, then you can use this as information about something that may be changed. Also, by recognizing the various contexts and dimensions of yourself, you can learn to discount negative feedback if it is not consistent with other positive information about yourself. Indeed, this is what people are able to do when they have high self-worth.[9] They recognize that some of their negative behavior can be seen in the context of a variety of their positive behaviors.

Maladaptive Ways of Coping with Fears of Negative Evaluation

You may be using safety behaviors to make you feel less anxious around other people. These safety behaviors are motivated by superstitious thinking: "I can keep myself from showing others that I am anxious by using these behaviors." Examples of safety behaviors include holding your hands rigidly (so people won't see them shaking), looking away from people (to avoid eye contact), talking softly (so you don't call attention to yourself), and over-preparing (so your mind won't go blank). You might avoid initiating conversations or expressing your own opinion, look for signs of rejection so you can leave early, agree with people you don't agree with, not speak up, or drink before you meet people.

Some people have a general personality trait called avoidant personality, which includes low self-esteem, sensitivity to rejection or evaluation by others, and fear of interacting with people unless there is some guarantee that they will not meet with disapproval. People with this personality style may have one or two friends, but they often complain of loneliness. They escape into their fantasy lives and are drawn toward solitary activities where they will not get rejected. Men with avoidant personality may focus most of their sex life on pornography or in some cases prostitutes, where the chance of rejection is minimal. Women with avoidant personality are likely to avoid intimate relationships since they fear rejection. Or when they get into an intimate relationship and it is not working for them, they are reluctant to assert themselves, fearing criti-cism and rejection and fearing that they will have difficulty finding another relationship.

Seven Steps to Overcoming Fear of Negative Evaluation

Wendy is continually worried that she will appear boring and awkward at a party. She thinks that she doesn't look as attractive as some of the other women because she has noticed some wrinkles. As a result, she often sits in the darker part of a room and seldom initiates conversations. Before she goes to a party, she worries about her makeup, her hair, what she will say, whom she will meet, and how other people will react to her. She tries to rehearse a little speech—"Hi, my name is Wendy. What's your name?"—but she thinks it will come across as stiff and phony. She is afraid that her hands will shake when she holds a glass, so she tries to hold the glass even tighter—but her hands still shake. She worries people will see her hands shaking and conclude that she is a nervous wreck. What can Wendy do about these fears of negative evaluation?

Let's look at our seven-step program.

Step One: Identify Productive and Unproductive Worry

WHAT ARE THE COSTS AND BENEFITS TO THESE WORRIES?

Wendy thinks that worrying about these things will prepare her for the worst—she can quickly catch other people frowning at her and can leave the party. She also believes that her worry will motivate her to try hard to be interesting and attractive. The disadvantages are that she dreads going to parties, she feels she doesn't act like herself, and she ends up doing a postmortem on herself after the party. Wendy concludes that she might be better off with fewer worries, but she is still concerned about letting her guard down.

IS THERE ANY EVIDENCE THAT YOUR WORRIES HAVE REALLY HELPED?

Wendy has been doing this for years. But she can't see any evidence that she is better off—that she has been able to act better at a party or that people respond better when she does this. However, because she never has tried not worrying, she doesn't really know.

WHAT ARE YOUR PRODUCTIVE AND UNPRODUCTIVE WORRIES?

Her productive worries are things that she can do *right now*, such as put her makeup on, go to the party, and talk to people. Her unproductive worries are all the what-ifs that she can't control, such as how other people will feel about her. She is also worried about questions that can't be answered ("What will someone think?") and a chain reaction of unlikely events ("If someone doesn't like me, then they'll tell their friends and everyone will think I'm a loser"). Wendy decided she might be better off if she worried less. So we moved on to the second step.

Step Two: Accept and Commit

Think of all the things that Wendy does not accept—her appearance, her anxiety, how other people may think, the uncertainty of the situation, and the limits of her ability to affect other people. We decided that she needed to practice both acceptance and commitment.

GAIN DISTANCE

I asked Wendy to simply observe her thoughts and feelings: "I notice that I am simply having the thought that I don't look as good as I would like" and "I notice that my heart is beating rapidly." I suggested that her thoughts were simply internal sensations that did not predict reality. Thoughts are thoughts—they are not the same thing as the party.

DESCRIBE WHAT IS IN FRONT OF YOU

I asked her to focus on what is in front of her when she is at a party. When she got to the party, she practiced looking around and described to herself what she saw. I wanted her to notice and describe the men in the room—what they were wearing, their hair and eye color, and where they were in the room: "I am noticing that there is a man near the window who is talking. He is wearing a blue shirt and he has dark brown hair." This directed her attention away from herself and onto seeing other people.

SUSPEND JUDGMENT

Wendy needed to eliminate her judgments about herself and how she should look and act at a party. We decided to focus on accepting and describing what is, rather than label herself as unattractive or awkward or to think that she should be less anxious at a party. Suspending judgment was hard for her, but she was able to focus on observing the people around her and observing her thoughts without feeling she needed to make herself less anxious or more charming.

TAKE YOURSELF OUT OF IT

I suggested that each of the people at a party had his or her own "reality"—their own story and their own perspective. People were not there because of or in spite of her. If someone looked at her a certain way or said something, it was more about that other person than Wendy. I asked her to see the party from the point of view of five other people who were there: "How will the man at the window see what is going on? What is his story?" As she refocused to other people and how they saw things, she began to feel less like the center of attention—and less worried.

DISAPPEAR TO SEE REALITY

I suggested that she imagine that she is not even at the party—that she is watching the party on a closed-circuit television. She has disappeared. Because she has disappeared, no one can see her or judge her. As she watched the party from a detached perspective, she was less self-conscious.

ACCEPT UNSOLVABLE PROBLEMS

We decided that she could not solve the problem of always being attractive to everyone or the problem of being liked by everyone. I suggested that she experiment with surrendering to defeat with these problems, since everything about them was "hopeless." I proposed that if these problems were "hopeless," perhaps we could think of them as no longer problems—perhaps they were simply reality as we *cannot* know it.

KNOW WHAT YOU CAN NEVER KNOW

We examined what she could not know—which was how attracted someone would be to her, or what someone thought, or whether rumors would spread about her anxiety. I suggested giving up on the unknowable so that she could focus on observing and listening to what other people said. You can know what you hear—but you cannot know what someone thinks or feels unless you hear it.

PRACTICE THE EMOTIONAL IMAGE

Since Wendy continually worried about all the things she needed to do to keep herself from being rejected, I asked her to develop a clear and detailed set of visual images that told the story of being completely rejected. This turned out to be a story—with visual images—of people laughing at her and telling her she sounded foolish and that she looked old and unattractive. I asked Wendy to repeat these images for twenty minutes each day. As she did this, the images became boring—even hard to keep in her mind. She said, "I realized that this would never happen. So, I've really been worrying about something that is hard to imagine could ever come true."

FLOOD YOURSELF WITH UNCERTAINTY

I suggested that even if the image seemed implausible, still anything is possible—and that she was worrying in order to eliminate possibility. Therefore, I asked her to flood herself for twenty minutes each day with the following statement: "It's always possible that I could look like a complete idiot and that people will humiliate and reject me." This too became boring and helped decrease her worries.

STAY IN THE PRESENT

Since her worries were all projections of bad things that have never happened, I suggested that Wendy spend as much time as possible in the present while at the party. If she noticed that she was worried, she was to return her attention to something going on that she could see with her eyes or hear with her ears.

COMMIT TO CHANGE

In order to change her worries, Wendy had to commit to doing the opposite of what she had been doing. I asked her to make the choice—what did she want, what needed to be done to get it, and was she willing to make the commitment? She decided that she wanted to go to parties, meet people, and learn how to be more at ease. In order to do this, she would have to do things she did not want to do—at a time she didn't feel ready.

USE SUCCESSFUL IMPERFECTIONISM

As part of her commitment to change, Wendy would have to accept imperfectionism—which included not looking perfect, not sounding interesting, feeling anxious, and even appearing boring. She realized that if she waited to do it when everything was just right, then she would never do it. Imperfectionism was the road to recovery.

PRACTICE CONSTRUCTIVE DISCOMFORT

Finally, Wendy recognized that commitment to change meant accept-ing the discomfort of confronting her fears. Discomfort would be a kind of investment—a means to an end. She was willing to tolerate the dis-comfort of not knowing for sure what would happen if she went to the party and actually initiated conversations with people without following her script.

Step Three: Challenge Your Worried Thinking

KEEP TRACK OF YOUR WORRIES

Wendy kept a record of her various worries and predictions. Her worry record included the following: "I will look old and unattractive. All the other women will be more attractive. No one will talk to me. I'll feel anxious and awkward. What if my hands shake? What if my face turns red or my mind goes blank? What if I have nothing to say?"

SET ASIDE WORRY TIME

I asked Wendy to set aside twenty minutes each day for the first two weeks of our work together and simply write out her worries. She chose to do this when she got home from work each day, and she found that she was repeating herself over and over. But she also recognized that her worries were almost entirely about her appearance, how she sounded, and her inability to impress other people.

TEST YOUR PREDICTIONS

I asked Wendy to come up with a set of specific predictions so we could test her worries. Her predictions were: "I won't have anything to say. No one will want to talk to me. My hands will shake. I will look like an idiot." After she came back from the party, she examined these predictions and found that none of them had come true. She actually did have several conversations where she had plenty to say, and several people talked to her. Her hands began to shake just a little, but she realized this was because she was holding the glass too tightly, which she thought would keep her hands from shaking. I had anticipated this and told her that if she noticed this, she should relax her hand and put the glass down.

DEFEAT YOUR WORRIES

- *What thinking distortion are you using?* Wendy was using mind reading ("They think I'm an idiot"), personalizing ("He's looking away because he doesn't like me"), fortune-telling ("I will look like a fool"), and mislabeling ("I'm an awkward idiot"). She also used discounting the positive

("The only reason my friends like me is that I'm nice to them") and overgeneralizing ("This is typical of me—always screwing up when I meet people").

- *How likely is it that this will actually happen?* Wendy realized that her predictions of looking like a complete fool and having nothing to say had very low probabilities. She thought it was about 10 percent probable (although I thought it was close to 0 percent possible).

- *What is the worst outcome? The most likely outcome? The best outcome?* The worst outcome was her feared fantasy—being humiliated and rejected by everyone. The best outcome was that everyone would tell her how great she was. The most likely outcome, she said, is that she would go to the party, feel a little nervous, and nothing bad would really happen.

- *Tell yourself a story about better outcomes.* Wendy developed a story of going to the party and practicing the ideas we were discussing. Her story included the following: "I am at the party and feel unusually calm and self-confident. I start talking to a few people. I meet a guy who is really nice and kind and intelligent and funny, and we end up going out together."

- *What is the evidence that something really bad is going to happen?* Wendy's evidence was based almost entirely on her emotional reasoning: "I feel nervous, so it probably won't be good."

- *How many times have you been wrong in the past about your worries?* As Wendy looked back at her past worries about being rejected when she met people, she realized that this had never really happened. No one had been rude or critical. Some conversations just tailed off—but this was normal, she realized, and in some cases it was because *she* had lost interest.

Step Four: Focus on the Deeper Threat

Core beliefs about yourself include the view that you are help-less, defective, glamorous, superior, responsible, unlovable, or controlled by others. As a result of these core beliefs, your re-sponse to negative evaluation may be very different from some-one else's response. The person who believes that she is helpless and cannot take care of herself will see negative evaluation as ev-idence she can't do anything right. Another person may view this in terms of how defective (for example, stupid, boring, or ugly) he is. Still another person, who believes that she needs to be glamorous, may believe that if someone does not like her, then this means that she has lost her edge in terms of looks and that no one will want her. Other people—with inflated views of themselves as superior people—will be upset if they are not seen as better than everyone else. They need to feel that all of the at-tention is on them, feeling easily shunned or insulted. Let's turn to how Wendy's core beliefs played themselves out in her worries.

IDENTIFY YOUR CORE BELIEFS ABOUT YOURSELF AND OTHER PEOPLE

Wendy's core beliefs were that she was unlovable, boring, and defec-tive, and her core beliefs about others were that they were superior and rejecting.

HOW HAS YOUR CORE BELIEF AFFECTED YOU IN THE PAST?

Since she feared that her underlying defectiveness would be-come apparent, she tended to avoid opening up to people, even after she had known them for a while. This also made it difficult for her to form deeper relationships with men, since she believed they would find out she was really boring and they would lose interest in her quickly. Because of her anxiety in meeting people, Wendy often left a party early or just simply stood there and said nothing. This meant that people had very little opportunity to get to know her. It also made her look boring—her worst fear come true.

ARE YOU VIEWING YOURSELF IN ALL-OR-NOTHING TERMS?

Wendy saw herself in all-or-nothing terms, as a totally boring person who was incredibly unattractive. In fact, she also saw other people in all-or-nothing terms—they were "interesting," "funny," and "the center of attention." We examined different situations in which she was more interesting and the fact that even interesting people can sometimes sound boring. This led to less black-and-white thinking about herself and other people.

WHAT IS THE EVIDENCE AGAINST YOUR CORE BELIEF?

Wendy was able to recognize that once she felt more comfortable with people, she could be interesting. She had a few close friends who relied on her because she was a good listener, nonjudgmental, and loyal. I asked her how this was consistent with her negative view of herself: "Why is it that the people who know you best like you the most?"

WOULD YOU BE AS CRITICAL OF OTHER PEOPLE?

Wendy said she wouldn't be critical of someone who was shy and worried about going to a party: "Not everyone is outgoing. So what if someone is reserved at a party? It doesn't mean that they don't have something to offer once they feel comfortable." I asked Wendy why she was so tough on herself, but she couldn't figure out why she should be.

MAYBE THERE'S SOME TRUTH IN YOUR CORE BELIEF

Actually, Wendy *was* somewhat boring at times. Because she was so afraid of sounding boring, she would not really talk very much, nor would she show much emotion at a party. She was afraid of sounding "stupid," so she responded with only a few words, which might lead people to think she either had nothing to say or was a snob. In other words, because she was so worried about making mistakes, she actually related in a rather boring way. She also recognized that all of us are boring at times, so there's some truth in that for everyone.

ACT AGAINST YOUR CORE BELIEF

I asked Wendy to consider doing the opposite of her core belief—that is, to try to initiate conversations, ask questions, and identify with what other people are saying. Since she was worried that initiating conversations would call attention to herself and that this would be humiliating, I thought it would be a good exercise for her to find out that she could act against her beliefs about herself. After all, how else could she prove that her core belief was wrong unless she acted against it? She did initiate a few conversations, asking people about themselves and introducing herself to people. This was surprising to her, since the people at the party she spoke with were polite and asked her about herself.

CHALLENGE YOUR NEGATIVE CORE BELIEF

I asked Wendy to imagine the thoughts that she would have if she were going to a party. Wendy said she would think she had nothing to say, that everyone would be sitting there confidently, and that she would look like a fool who didn't fit in. Because Wendy thought she would sound boring, she was reluctant to talk to people at the party. But when we looked at the evidence, she was able to see that she had a lot of the qualities of a good friend, such as loyalty, humor, understanding, compassion, intelligence—in fact, the very qualities that she would want in a man. Since Wendy was so self-conscious about meeting people, I suggested she turn the tables and focus on getting to know other people—ask them about their work, where they grew up and lived, what interests they had. This might make Wendy the most interesting person, since she would make someone else feel interesting.

But I suggested that she challenge her idea that it would be terrible if someone was not interested in what she had to say. What would she still be able to do if someone found her discussion of her work uninteresting? She'd be able to do everything she has always done—in other words, nothing would change.

Step Five: Turn "Failure" into Opportunity

Wendy's main problem in meeting people was that she had perfectionistic standards, and she always evaluated herself as a failure: "If I go to the party and I don't sound interesting, then I failed. I'm a loser." The fifth step—learning how to confront failure—was an essential component in dealing with her worries, since she viewed almost all her interactions as total failures. I suggested that we could handle her worries by using some of the techniques to challenge her fear of failure. To do this, we had to focus on a goal larger than avoiding failure, and that was to be able to meet new people and form new relationships.

Let's take Wendy's worry "I'll make a fool of myself if I go to a party and I don't sound interesting." Consider the following ways to challenge this fear of failure:

1. *Maybe it wasn't a failure.* She is looking at her behavior as something to be judged, rather than an experience with other people. Rather than view it as a failure, we could view it as simply an interaction where she met some people.

2. *I can focus on other behaviors that will succeed.* Simply going to the party and facing her anxieties is a step in the right direction. She did succeed in facing her fears by going to the party, she did initiate a conversation, and she did observe and listen to other people.

3. *It wasn't essential to succeed at that.* It's not crucial to have a great experience at a party. Nothing is necessary about it—it's only an option at one point in time.

4. *There were some behaviors that did pay off.* She did face her fear, so she learned that she could go to a party and speak with people, even if she felt anxious. She also learned that nothing really bad happened. Her worst fears were not confirmed.

5. *Everyone fails at something.* Even though we don't see this as a failure, everyone has an experience when they don't feel comfortable at a party. Everyone is boring at times.

6. *Maybe no one noticed.* Wendy continually thinks everyone is noticing how badly she is doing. How could that be? How could anyone except Wendy really notice she felt anxious and shy? I asked Wendy to recall the last five shy people she met at a party. She couldn't recall a single one.

7. *Were my standards too high?* Yes—Wendy hoped she would go and not feel nervous and that she would meet the man of her dreams. Expecting to be comfortable doing things that you are anxious about is really a contradiction. In fact, why even bother having standards? Why not simply go to the party?

8. *Did I do better than before?* Yes, she did do better than before. She was able to practice staying in the present, being an observer, and noticing what other people said and how they appeared, and she also initiated some conversations. What's so bad about that? She really was showing progress.

9. *I can still do everything I always did, even though this failed.* Again, she didn't fail—but even if she did not feel satisfied with her experience, she can still do everything she has always done. In fact, she will probably be even more likely to go to parties.

10. *Failing at something means I tried. Not trying is worse.* Wendy is trying and will try again. Doing what she felt uncomfortable doing is the way she is overcoming these worries. Not going to the party would just maintain her fear of meeting people.

Step Six: Use Your Emotions Rather than Worry About Them

A central part of Wendy's worry was that people might see that she felt anxious and shy and that they might humiliate her. She was afraid of meeting people while she felt anxious, because she believed she shouldn't feel anxious and that her anxiety was transparent and distasteful to other people. We used some of the ideas on focusing on the meaning and importance of her emotions, rather than continue avoiding her emotions either by worrying or by remaining silent at parties.

WHAT IS THE MEANING OF YOUR EMOTION?

Wendy thought that her shyness and her worries "don't make sense," "they're out of control," and "they'll just go on forever." She believed that no one could understand what it's like, and she felt ashamed about her shyness. When Wendy looked more carefully at these negative views of her feelings, she could see that her worries and anxieties made a lot of sense. She was shy—of course she would worry. Furthermore, she had never "lost control" or fell apart—it was simply her worry that this would happen that made her believe she had to catch herself when she felt anxious. Her anxiety was not going to go on forever, because it was almost entirely situational—it was focused on meeting people. Once she got to know them, her anxieties were a lot less. In order to test her belief that she should feel ashamed of her shyness, I asked her what her friends thought of this. She said, "They tell me I have nothing to worry about because I'm really a terrific person." Moreover, a few of her friends were also shy, which helped her normalize her feelings of shyness.

LEARN HOW TO ACCEPT YOUR FEELINGS

Accepting that she felt anxious when she met people could help Wendy spend less effort focusing on getting rid of her anxiety—it would help make her less self-conscious. I suggested to Wendy that she simply agree to feel anxious and to do nothing about it, not even try to relax. Accepting her feelings rather than struggling against them would help her do things while she felt anxious: "Why not simply accept that you will feel uncomfortable for a while and do these uncomfortable things anyway?"

FEEL LESS GUILTY AND ASHAMED

Like many shy people who worry about looking anxious, Wendy felt ashamed of her anxiety when around other people. We looked at the fact that there is nothing malicious or immoral about feeling shy and worrying. No one is hurt, no one is worse off—except Wendy. To test this out, I asked Wendy to tell her friends that she felt shy and worried when she met people. No one was critical of her—everyone was supportive. In fact, one of the goals that we had was for her to meet someone new, get to know them, and then tell that person that she felt shy when she met new people. She eventually did this and was relieved to hear that the man she talked to also felt anxious at parties.

ALMOST EVERYONE HAS THESE FEELINGS

Like many people who are shy and who worry about being evaluated, Wendy thought she was very unusual. I encouraged her to ask other people if they ever felt shy or worried before meeting new people or talking in front of a group. Her friends poured out stories about fears of public speaking, shyness when meeting new people, anxieties about sexual performance, shame over their bodies, and fears of sounding foolish. If almost everyone has anxieties of various kinds, then what's so bad about hers?

GO THROUGH YOUR FEELINGS TO GET PAST THEM

Finally, Wendy had to decide to make a commitment to go *through* her anxieties—to do the things that made her anxious—in order to get over these feelings. Practicing what makes her anxious became a goal. I suggested that the signal to try something was noticing that she felt anxious thinking about it: "If you feel anxious about walking over to someone, do it immediately." At first, she wasn't able to do this, but after practicing doing what made her anxious, she learned that her worries decreased. This is because by doing the things that made her anxious, her feelings no longer were a guide for withdrawal. Rather than think, "I feel anxious, therefore withdraw," she now thought, "I feel anxious, so do it now."

Step Seven: Take Control of Time

Like many worriers, Wendy was focused on her predictions of how badly she would do at the party. There was a sense of urgency that something terrible would happen (she would make a fool of herself) and that she needed the answer immediately that everything would be OK. We decided to work on her sense of time so that she could view things in perspective and at the same time stay in the moment.

TURN THE URGENCY OFF

Wendy said, "I need to know that I won't look foolish." When she was at the party, she would think, "I need to feel less anxious *right now*!" Because she demanded all the answers immediately and needed to change her feelings on the spot, she became more and more anxious. I suggested we turn off the urgency. There was no crisis or life-threatening emergency. There was no train coming down the track. I asked Wendy what would happen if she didn't know for sure right now that everything would be OK. She said, "I guess if I don't know for sure, then it won't work out." But what if needing to know right now was exactly the problem? Since she could never know for sure right now, then she was trapped by her urgency.

The same thing is true about her need to get rid of her anxiety right now. But what would happen if she didn't? What if she looked at her anxiety as something that is present for the moment? Or if she thought, "I will have to tolerate and experience some discomfort for a short while"? Accepting that she cannot control the moment, accepting her feelings in the moment, and normalizing feeling anxious at that moment could help her turn off the urgency.

NOTICE HOW YOUR FEELINGS PASS BY

Stepping back and noticing that her feelings are real and present but temporary allowed Wendy to let go of controlling her feelings and thoughts: "I notice that I have a worry right now" and—a few seconds later—"I notice that I am thinking of something else right now." Wendy was able to visualize her worries as small particles on leaves that floated away from her. Feelings, thoughts, and discomfort are not permanent, just like the weather.

STAY IN THE PRESENT MOMENT

Wendy's worries were entirely about the future, and the future is not the present moment. Staying in the moment—being mindful of what is going on right now—was a strong antidote to the worries. "In the present moment I notice that there are four people standing over by the window. In the present moment I can hear the music—it's a song I have never heard before. In the present moment I notice that I am thirsty." Staying in the present moment makes it impossible to worry about what will happen in a possible future that may never come.

IMPROVE THE MOMENT

Wendy was staying in the moment, but the moment was also uncomfortable. I asked Wendy to notice what in the present moment could feel good. She said, "I wonder—if I listened more carefully to the music, I might enjoy it." I asked her to think of improving the moment by tasting some food at the party—in fact, to very, very slowly take some food in her mouth and notice the texture and the taste of the food. This helped her feel more comfortable, more at ease, more in touch with the moment.

STRETCH TIME

Wendy often thought that her feelings of anxiety would go on forever. Although rationally she knew this wasn't the case, she felt the anxiety was endless. I asked her to imagine a very long line—a line that was a hundred yards long—and then to place a point on this line. The point represented the moments at this party. I asked her to imagine all the pleasurable things that she would do in the future after this party, and all the fun things she had done in the past before this party. Stretching time helped Wendy worry less about a single point in time.

Summing Up

What did Wendy learn about her worries about negative evaluation? First, she learned that her worries did not protect or prepare her—they made her worry more. *What she thought was the "solution" was actually the problem:* "I will worry so I won't be surprised." Second, she learned that she could accept her limitations—she would be anxious, worried, uncomfortable, unsure that things would work out, and unable to control what people thought of her. She would also commit to successful imperfectionism and constructive discomfort in order to confront her worries. It would not be easy, but it would be helpful.

Third, she learned that she was thinking in a biased and distorted way and that these negative behaviors, such as mind reading and fortune-telling, could be effectively challenged. Fourth, she learned that her core belief that she was boring and unlovable did not hold up to the facts. In fact, a number of people who knew her well thought she was a great friend. Fifth, she learned that her catastrophic view of failure (and her tendency to label herself as a failure simply because she was shy) was also distorted and untrue. In fact, there were many areas of her life in which she had success, and she was making more progress with her worries. Sixth, Wendy learned that her emotions are transitory. She also was not alone in feeling anxious or being concerned about evaluation. And seventh, she could take control of time by staying in the moment, and she could improve the moment by concentrating on sensations and observations. As she stepped back from the moment she could stretch time beyond these anxious moments and recognize that there was a future beyond her discomfort.

Wendy began to initiate more conversations, meet more people, and find that she could do things she did not want to do. Her worries became less upsetting to her because she could recognize that they were simply thoughts about evaluation and predictions about the future and that they seldom, if ever, were valid. Eventually, she met a man whom she began dating. In getting to know him, she started to realize that there were other people who had problems, and that she could actually like someone who has problems—just as she could begin to like herself.

12

Relationship Worries: What if My Lover Leaves Me?

VALERIE HAS BEEN INVOLVED with Brad for the past three years, but she continually worries that he is getting bored with her and that he will leave her. She tries to look as attractive as she can "for him" and won't tell him that she disagrees with him—which she does. She doesn't want him to get angry, because she fears that he might break up with her. "Do you still find me attractive?" she asks Brad. "Do you still love me?" Initially, Brad thought this showed that Valerie was very caring, but eventually he began to feel that every thought and feeling was being placed under a microscope and analyzed. Brad said, "Let me have my own feelings. Stop trying to control me." Valerie tended to personalize Brad's moods and then thought it was her duty to change them.

Valerie is intensely jealous of other women. She notices that Brad is looking at Fran, who is attractive and friendly, and she worries that Brad might decide that Fran is better for him. Later that night, Valerie tells Brad that she thinks that Fran is an "airhead" and a "gold digger" and that she never liked Fran. When they watch movies Valerie glances over to see if Brad finds the young attractive women in the movies sexy. She begins to think about her own body and thinks she is losing her shape. When Brad is away on a business trip she worries he will cheat on her. She vacillates between complaining that he doesn't call enough and telling him she's too busy to take his calls. She feels like breaking off with Brad before he decides to break off with her.

If you're like Valerie and you worry about abandonment, then you become quite anxious when you are in a relationship. You worry that conflicts will result in a breakup or that your partner will find someone more appealing than you. You can fluctuate between intense jealousy and apprehension about being left alone. You might demand reassurance, criticize your partner unnecessarily for not giving you enough attention, or create dramatic conflicts that jeopardize the very relationship you fear losing. You may act as if everything is a test for your partner: "If you really loved me you would . . ." These continual tests of affection and loyalty wear the relationship down, creating a real threat of the relationship ending.

Furthermore, fears of abandonment and being on your own can result in staying in bad relationships or even lead you to choose someone inappropriate in order to have a relationship. Your fear of loneliness can trap you in a bad relationship: you can't leave because you believe you can't live on your own. In some cases, the fear of abandonment may lead you to pursue extramarital relationships in order to "protect" against abandonment. Finally, some people are so frightened that they will be rejected or abandoned that they will not even enter into a relationship: "If I am not attached, I can't get rejected."

See if any of these statements apply to you:

- I worry that arguments will lead to a breakup in our relationship.
- I am continually looking for reassurance that I am attractive or interesting.

- I am very jealous that my partner finds other people attractive.
- I worry about being alone if this relationship doesn't work out.
- It bothers me if I don't hear from my partner often enough.
- I would find it traumatic if our relationship ended.
- I worry about being alone forever.
- I have gotten into relationships simply to avoid being alone.

The Worst Ways to Cope with Worries About Abandonment

You may try to cope with these fears by looking for any signs that your partner is losing interest. One woman would check her partner's answering machine to see if there were any messages from other women and would search through his papers to see if there were any notes about dates. Another woman focused on her appearance to the extent that she would turn down dates with the man she was involved with if she felt she was not looking her best. A man who was jealous of other men would tell his girlfriend that other men were stupid and less successful. He hoped that by belittling other people, he would seem more attractive in comparison.

You may try to be overly pleasing to avoid getting rejected. One woman told me she almost never disagreed with her partner: "It wouldn't do any good. He won't change." However, as we discussed this more, her real worry came out: "If I disagree, he might leave me." One man generally chose women he considered less intelligent than he was, or women who were needy and desperate—especially women who were financially dependent on him. He reasoned that these women would be less likely to break up with him since they would desperately cling to the relationship. Much to his surprise, each of these women left him for another man.

A man who had been married for many years told me that he always had an ongoing affair—but that he would never leave his wife for the other women. He told me that these affairs began soon after he got married, when he began to panic about the thought that his wife might leave him—just as his mother had abandoned the family when he was a child. One woman told me that when she and her partner had an argument she would think that this meant they would have to break up, leading her to tell him, "Well, we shouldn't stay together." Her thought was, "I may as well get the inevitable out of the way." In fact, although she initially feared her husband would leave her for another younger woman, it was she who was pursuing other men "in order to make sure I have someone if he dumps me."

Another problematic style of coping is not to get too deeply involved. This avoidant and distancing strategy is generally an unconscious one, but it is often reflected in people who pursue shallow and meaningless relationships. These people may often say, "I haven't met the right one" or "I don't really know if I am in love." But what is often going on is that the person fears intimate rejection so much that he or she avoids getting close to anyone. One woman told me that she intentionally acts in a superficial and provocative way, since this will attract men that she knows she could never fall in love with. By assuring herself that the relationship will always be superficial, she has already discounted a breakup: "It wouldn't mean much anyway, since I knew from the start that he was only in it for the sex." Alternatively, some people choose relationships with built-in limitations—choosing partners through chat rooms on the Internet, long-distance relationships, or people married to other people.

TABLE 12.1

WORST WAYS TO COPE WITH FEARS OF ABANDONMENT

- Look for evidence that your partner is losing interest.
- Look for signs your partner is interested in someone else.
- Check for infidelity.
- Focus on looking and acting perfect.
- Devalue the competition.
- Never disagree.
- Give up your own needs so you will not antagonize your partner.
- Choose partners who are less desirable and more needy.
- Escalate arguments in order to break things off before you are dumped.
- Hedge by having other relationships on the side.
- Avoid the inevitability of loss by choosing dead-end relationships.

People with a dependent personality style fear they will be abandoned in a relationship, so will sacrifice their needs in order to keep a relationship going. Because they fear that they cannot take care of themselves on their own, and because they believe that being on their own is equivalent to depression, they often develop the ability to charm and entice a partner whom they view as more powerful or competent, hoping that this "rescuer" partner will protect them and never leave them.

Let's look at how these various factors contribute to worries about abandonment. If you feel insecure about being abandoned, you will engage in a lot of mind reading ("He's upset with me"), fortune-telling ("He's going to leave"), personalizing your partner's behavior ("I must have upset him"), and catastrophic thinking ("It would be awful if I ended up on my own"). As a result of these insecurities, you might continually seek reassurance, check on how he feels and what he is doing and where he is going, become overly pleasing, and never assert yourself. Or if you feel that you cannot handle rejection, then you might even precipitate a breakup to "get it over with."

The good news about your worries about abandonment is that you can learn to overcome these worries so that you don't find yourself repeating old mistakes. Let's look at our seven-step program.

Seven Steps to Overcoming Fear of Abandonment

Let's return to Valerie, who was continually worried that Brad was losing interest. We will use the seven-step program and see how she learned to handle these worries about abandonment.

Step One: Identify Productive and Unproductive Worry

WHAT ARE THE COSTS AND BENEFITS TO THESE WORRIES?

Valerie believed that worrying about Brad leaving would prepare her for the worst, and also that she might be able to catch something early and make it better so he would not leave. Although she thought this might be a possible benefit for her worry, she realized that the costs were much greater. These included her constant anxiety, anger, jealousy, insecurity, reassurance seeking, and demands on Brad.

IS THERE ANY EVIDENCE THAT YOUR WORRIES HAVE REALLY HELPED?

There was no real evidence that her worries were helpful. In fact, her jealousy and reassurance seeking often led to more arguments with Brad that made her more insecure.

WHAT ARE YOUR PRODUCTIVE AND UNPRODUCTIVE WORRIES?

Valerie could not identify any productive worries about abandonment. The only thing that she was able to see was that working at having a better relationship meant trying to eliminate the worries and the maladaptive coping—such as her checking, nagging, demanding, and reassurance seeking. This meant that she would first have to work on the second step: accept and commit.

Step Two: Accept and Commit

Valerie was so caught up in her worries about whether Brad would leave her that she had difficulty accepting the relationship as it was and living in the present. We worked intensely on this second step—especially on acceptance.

DESCRIBE WHAT IS IN FRONT OF YOU

Valerie was continually guessing what Brad thought and felt, and she continually jumped to conclusions about the future. I suggested that she simply *describe* the behavior that she saw, without any inferences about motives and thoughts: "Brad is sitting watching TV with his feet up. The dishwasher is making some noise in the kitchen." These innocuous descriptions helped her step back for a moment so that she could move to the next point. She had to momentarily drop her interpretations of his motives and focus only on what she could see and hear—his behavior.

SUSPEND JUDGMENT

I asked Valerie to suspend any judgments about Brad's behavior—or her own behavior—and simply stay with descriptions and observations, without labeling him as "self-centered" or "insensitive." This was important for Valerie, since almost all her worries were judgments about how Brad "should act." She had a catalogue of "shoulds"—he should call more frequently, compliment her more, pay more attention, and be less interested in work and more interested in her.

TAKE YOURSELF OUT OF IT

Valerie continually personalized almost everything that Brad did. If he breathed deeply, it meant he was bored with her. I asked her to imagine how someone else would describe Brad's behavior with minimal reference to Valerie. This helped her realize that Brad had an existence separate from her, and that his behavior was not always directed at her. It also helped her reduce her reassurance seeking.

GIVE UP REASSURANCE

When we are overly dependent in relationships we turn to the other person to reassure us that he or she still cares, isn't angry, and isn't bored with us. Of course, this reassurance seeking becomes annoying and boring. Imagine if I called you every hour for a month and asked you if you were annoyed or bored with me. You probably would finally admit that you were angry at me—but I would have provoked this by nagging you about reassurance.

Valerie was always checking with Brad about what he thought and felt, where she fit in, where they were going, what the future was, how she compared with other women, whether he would still find her attractive when she got old, and if he ever thought about other women. Valerie worried that if Brad thought about other women or found other women attractive, this would mean he would leave her. I told her that it was likely—and probably quite healthy—that men are always finding other women attractive. This is a sign that they are heterosexual and alive. I asked her if she found other men attractive—and, of course, she did. Did this mean that she did not prefer Brad?

But Valerie believed that this checking would keep her worries from spiraling out of control. We examined her beliefs about checking and decided that she would try to go a week without asking Brad how he felt, what he thought, or if he found her attractive. This was hard for Valerie, as she found not knowing for sure terrifying. Ironically, as she checked for reassurance less, Brad became more attentive. Why would this be? It turned out that Brad was a typical male—he didn't like people forcing things on him. The more she checked on Brad, the more Brad felt he needed to demonstrate his independence by not calling and not asking her about herself.

KNOW WHAT YOU CAN NEVER KNOW

Valerie needed to work at accepting that she could not know in the present moment whether the relationship would work out. She had to accept uncertainty and the limitations of what she could know. Valerie practiced repeating for twenty minutes each day, "I can never know if he will leave me." This helped reduce her obsessions about abandonment, since the thought became boring.

PRACTICE THE EMOTIONAL IMAGE—BEING ON YOUR OWN

Like many worriers, Valerie could not face the idea of being on her own. She worried and checked and asked for reassurance in order to avoid thinking about what life would be like without Brad. She kept saying, "It's too painful to think about life without him." We tested this out. First, we made up a plan for the "post-Brad" Valerie. I asked her to make a list of goals that she would like to accomplish if she were not with Brad. As it turned out, Valerie had wanted to take a business course, but because she was afraid of not always being available for Brad, she hadn't taken one. She made a list of other things that she would like to do—see her friends more often, exercise, work at getting promoted at work, meet some new men, go dancing (Brad didn't like to dance), travel, walk through the park, go out to dinner. We then looked at her daily schedule—what she was doing from the time that she woke to the time she went to bed—and noticed that she seemed to be living a lot of her life waiting for the phone to ring.

As Valerie planned her own activities independently of Brad and started to call him less frequently, Brad began showing more initiative. He had been expecting her to call: "Valerie, I didn't hear from you today—what's up?" Valerie responded that she was busy with her friends and her activities. This led Brad to show more initiative in calling her. However, because of Valerie's obsessive qualities in regard to Brad and with other men before this, we decided to initiate a more comprehensive program to deal with her fears of abandonment.

Valerie's fears of being alone and abandoned fed her daily worries. I had her come up with a detailed story with images of exactly what this looked like. She pictured Brad walking out the door and the door closing, and she saw herself alone in the house. Valerie practiced this image along with its details repeatedly for twenty minutes each day until it became boring.

PRACTICE CONSTRUCTIVE DISCOMFORT

Valerie tried to eliminate her discomfort by worrying, mind reading, demanding reassurance, and demanding that Brad tell her he loved her. This never worked. We decided to focus on practicing discomfort on a daily basis—specifically, learning how to tolerate her anxiety when she did not feel secure. Initially, Valerie thought this would be impossible—"I feel like I'm sitting on my hands"—but eventually she was able to tolerate more discomfort as she learned some other techniques, such as improving the moment.

Step Three: Challenge Your Worried Thinking

IDENTIFY YOUR DISTORTIONS ABOUT ABANDONMENT

Valerie had a long list of distorted thoughts that fed her fear of abandonment. We identified and categorized these thoughts as the following:

- Mind reading: "He is angry, therefore he will leave me."
- Personalizing: "He's working hard, and this is a sign that he is losing interest and will leave me."
- Fortune-telling: "If this continues, we will wind up breaking up."
- Catastrophizing: "How would I live without him? I wouldn't survive."
- Labeling: "I'm a complete idiot in this relationship."
- Discounting the positive: "Nothing I do seems to matter."
- Overgeneralizing: "It seems we are always arguing—that means we will break up."

I asked Valerie if she had any evidence that totally supported her mind reading and personalizing. For example, Brad had been angry before, as she had, and they still were together. He had worked hard before and brought work home with him, but he hadn't left. Valerie began to challenge these negative, distorted beliefs about abandonment and discovered that it came down to a core belief: "If Brad isn't paying attention to me the way I demand it, then he will leave me." Valerie began to recognize that these demands for attention on her terms were not a sign of imminent abandonment—they were more a sign of her insecurity.

We then turned to a more detailed analysis of her central dysfunctional beliefs—beliefs that fueled her worry every day. Let's examine each of these beliefs.

IT'S ALWAYS ABOUT ME

If Brad is not in the best mood, she thinks it's because he doesn't like something about her. Valerie was upset when Brad came over, made himself a drink, and sat down to read the paper. Her thought was, "He is rejecting me." However, Brad told her he was stressed out from work and just needed to space out for a while. She examined the consequences of having this bias: exaggerating the extent to which other people's behavior is related to her, feeling as though her moods were on a roller coaster, and annoying Brad because he felt he had to walk on eggshells.

I'VE GOT TO FIGURE OUT WHAT HE'S THINKING

She couldn't stand the uncertainty of not knowing what Brad was thinking or feeling. If she didn't know, she concluded he didn't care or that something was wrong with the relationship. "I'll bet that he has lost interest in me. I've got to find out what's really going on—so I won't be caught by surprise."[1] She is constantly trying to read his mind, examining every expression or intonation for clues. Accepting that people have thoughts and feelings that she doesn't know and may never know can free her to focus on having more rewarding experiences in the present, with or without Brad. We developed a "self-instructional" plan for Valerie: (1) "I can never know what other people think and feel"; (2) "Most of the time it is not relevant"; (3) "I can focus on positive behaviors with or without that person." By refocusing her goal toward activities rather than trying to read Brad's mind, she became less sensitized to Brad's moods, whatever they were. As a consequence, she was less likely to grill Brad about his thoughts and feelings and more likely to plan things with and without him. This shifted her attention away from the uncertainty of what others might think to the control over what she could do.

I NEED REASSURANCE THAT HE LIKES ME

Since she can't stand uncertainty, she thinks that she can make herself feel better by getting Brad to reassure her that things are OK. She can call him up and see if he still cares for her, or ask him if he still finds her attractive. "Are you getting bored with me? Do you still think I'm pretty?" As we have seen in our discussions about worry and about obsessions, these attempts to get reassurance will backfire. Seeking reassurance signals that she cannot tolerate the uncertainty of not knowing for sure. By getting reassurance she reinforces her obsessive-compulsive tendencies. Accepting that she cannot know for sure—and doesn't *need* to know for sure—should really be the goal. I asked Valerie to experiment with giving up on reassurance. Valerie examined the costs of requiring reassurance, examining the negative impact on her relationship of demanding reassurance, experimenting with going first a day and then a week without getting reassurance, asking Brad not to give reassurance, challenging her negative thoughts on her own without relying on other people, and focusing on what she could do in the present time that is rewarding, rather than trying to get certainty about what Brad might think or feel in the present or future.

I CAN'T STAND CONFLICT

Valerie thinks that conflicts are terrible and might escalate out of control. So either she doesn't assert herself or she gives in to Brad. "I can't stand conflicts. I don't like it when people are angry with me." As a result of this fear of conflict, she will not assert her needs, allowing her resentments and frustrations to build up—sometimes to the point where she explodes over something rather trivial. I asked Valerie to tell me exactly what would happen if she had a conflict. Could she imagine conflicts along a continuum, from slight to moderate to severe? Are there certain ways of expressing a difference without the conflict escalating to being severe? If simply stating her needs and talking about change is always going to lead to severe conflict, then perhaps she needs to reevaluate the relationship.

Conflicts are inevitable in relationships, especially intimate relationships, but it is the manner in which partners handle these conflicts that will determine if things get better or worse. John Gottman, a leading expert on marital relationships, has found that certain styles of dealing with conflict are predictive of divorce. These include the use of stonewalling (withdrawing, refusing to talk), contempt, labeling the partner, and threats of leaving. More effective ways of dealing with conflict include what psychologists call "mutual problem solving": (1) state the problem as "our problem," (2) acknowledge your role in the problem, (3) ask your partner for help with "our problem," (4) generate possible solutions, (5) mutually rate the solutions, and (6) set up a plan to carry out a solution.[2] Valerie began to use this mutual problem-solving approach rather than completely avoid conflicts or escalate them to catastrophes. Much to her surprise, Brad was actually somewhat relieved to be able to talk constructively about improving the relationship.

I AM NOTHING WITHOUT THIS RELATIONSHIP

Of course, this was the very foundation of her fears—because she couldn't imagine life without the relationship. She didn't see any value in herself independently of being an appendage to a relationship. If she broke up, it meant that she was a loser that no one could ever love: "I know he's not good for me. But I don't know what I would do without him" or "Life is meaningless if I am alone." I asked her to examine what her life had been like before she met Brad, whose approval and whose companionship she thinks she *absolutely needs*. She realized there were a lot of things that she enjoyed—her work, friends, family, leisure activities, learning, and traveling. I asked her to test out her belief that her relationship with Brad was essential by asking her to list all of the things that she could think about that she did without him. As she went through this list, she realized that there were some things that she did do with Brad, but many of the things that she liked were things that she did on her own. We also examined the opportunities that she could pursue if the relationship did end— other relationships, a possible change in career, possibly going back to school, and seeing her friends more.

No one is "nothing" without a relationship. Think of the irony of this belief that she is nothing without a relationship. It would mean that every person that you know who is not currently in a relationship has no redeeming qualities and no pleasure. It would mean that people who find each other are actually finding another person who has nothing going for him or her. Being in or out of a relationship really reflects different options in behavior. It is a matter of trade-offs—not a matter of what is *essential*.

Step Four: Focus on the Deeper Threat

IDENTIFY YOUR CORE BELIEFS ABOUT YOURSELF

Valerie worried that the loss of the relationship would "reveal" central "truths" about her that were upsetting: "I am unlovable," "defective," "a failure," "ugly," "no longer special (ordinary)," and "inferior." Valerie's ultimate worry was that she was unattractive and would never find a partner. Although Brad professed that he loved her, her worries about abandonment focused on his absorption in work as a "sign" that he "no longer loved her."

These core issues underlying fear of abandonment include the belief that you will not be able to take care of your basic needs on your own, that you could never be happy by yourself, or that if you are alone now, then you will always be alone. For example, one woman worried that if her marriage ended, she would not be able to support herself financially—a fear that was completely irrational given her financial assets. Another man worried that if his partner left him, then he would never find another woman to love. Some people worry that if they are not in a relationship, then they can never be happy—being single is equated with being miserable. Valerie's core belief was that she could never make herself happy without a partner—she could not imagine functioning independently. She equated being single with being unlovable.

WHAT IS THE EVIDENCE AGAINST YOUR CORE BELIEF?

In order to challenge her negative core belief about herself, I asked Valerie to think about who she had been before she met Brad. Valerie had become so focused on Brad over the past few years that she had forgotten that she'd had twenty-five years before she ever met him. We listed the relationships with men and friendships that she'd had before Brad. We looked at her résumé to see what kinds of work she'd done before she met Brad. We talked about trips she'd taken before she ever heard of Brad. We found that there had been a pre-Brad Valerie that was fairly happy and resilient. I asked Valerie to bring in photographs from her childhood and young adulthood. We looked at Valerie's baby pictures, snapshots of her mother and father, a picture of Valerie as a six-year-old on a pony, pictures of her in high school and college, photos of her first boyfriend, images of her girlfriends at different ages, portraits of her grandmother, pictures of England (where she'd traveled to study) . . . lots of pictures that had nothing to do with Brad. Valerie looked at these pictures, took a deep breath, and said, "I really have been having a life."

CHALLENGE YOUR NEGATIVE CORE BELIEF

When we examined these core fears—the fear that she would not be able to take care of herself, that she could never be happy on her own, or that being alone for now meant that she would always be alone—we developed ways to challenge them. For example, the fear that she would not be able to support herself or take care of herself was challenged by looking at the resources that she had, her future earnings, and her support group. She examined the evidence that single people she knew were actually liv-ing rather decent—if imperfect—lives. She also began thinking of other women she knew who were divorced or single and how they were doing fairly well. As she began to fear a breakup less, she worried less about abandonment. This actually was one of several reasons why her relationship eventually improved and the threat of a breakup subsided. As she "needed" Brad less, there was less pressure in their interactions—and less anger on her part.

Step Five: Turn "Failure" into Opportunity

Although Valerie's relationship had not failed, I thought it might be helpful for her to face her fear of failing in the relationship. We turned to how she could be resilient in the face of disappointment—and how she could turn "failure" into perspective.

I DIDN'T FAIL, MY BEHAVIOR FAILED

When relationships break up there is a tendency to cast all the blame on one person. This can make people think of how they will be blamed by other people—or how others will see them as a failure or as a pathetic person. After treating hundreds of patients over a long period of time, I do not recall a single case where a relationship ended because one person was defective, unlovable, ugly, or inferior. Relationships end generally because people do not find them rewarding and because the costs are too high.

Consider the logic of "He left me because I am unlovable." In the first place, he must have gotten involved because he thought you were lovable (attractive, interesting, worthwhile, etc.). Second, being "lovable" is generally in the (loving) eyes of the beholder: what is lovable to you may not be lovable to someone else. And third, being lovable is not something about a person but rather something about a person's behavior—there are lovable behaviors. These behaviors include acting kindly, listening with warmth and understanding, rewarding your partner, showing generosity, and accepting someone with their flaws. These are behaviors that almost anyone can engage in if they decide to. There are no unlovable people—there are only unlovable behaviors.

I CAN FOCUS ON OTHER BEHAVIORS THAT CAN SUCCEED

Valerie feared that one mistake or one conflict would lead to a breakup. Indeed, if someone broke up with you because of one mistake, you might think, "Better sooner than later," because someone with that degree of intolerance is not likely to last. But the fact is that most people tolerate a lot of mistakes—possibly because they make many mistakes themselves. Generally, we weigh the costs and benefits in a relationship, and it's the ratio of the positives to negatives that matters. I asked Valerie to list all of the positives and negatives that each of them had demonstrated in the course of the relationship. Valerie was able to realize that the perspective could change when she saw a few negatives in the context of many more positives. Moreover, she also recognized that she had been willing to accept a lot of Brad's negatives, suggesting that people can accept imperfection and still maintain a relationship.

I CAN FOCUS ON WHAT I CAN CONTROL

Valerie needed to find a self that was not dependent on Brad. I asked her to list all the things that she did that had nothing to do with Brad. And I asked her to list all the roles that she played in life that had nothing to do with Brad: daughter, sister, cousin, friend, manager, employee, volunteer. She then made a list of her activities and interests and qualities that had nothing to do with Brad: "Intelligent, funny, honest, caring, reliable, curious, well-read, artistic, accepting. I am interested in reading, music, art, talking, dancing, nature, animals . . ."

TURN YOURSELF INTO A FRIEND

We are generally a lot nicer to other people than we are to ourselves. Valerie had lots of friends who often called her up and talked to her about their problems. They thought she was understanding and accepting, but they also thought she had great practical advice. What would it be like if Valerie began to talk to herself the way she did with her friends? What if she gave advice and understanding to herself the same way she would to a friend who was worried about losing a lover? I asked Valerie to make believe that I was her and that she was my best friend. Playing the role of Valerie being negative, I said, "I won't be able to exist without Brad." Valerie was able to argue against this negative thought that she was nothing without Brad: "You had a great life before you met him. You had friends, dates, relationships, work, all kinds of things. Why would that disappear if you and Brad broke up? Your life had meaning before Brad. He can't give you meaning. You already have it."

This role-play was helpful for Valerie because it allowed her to stand outside her worries and see herself the way a good friend might see her. What she saw was an intelligent, attractive, understanding woman with friends and work that counted. Even if Brad were to leave, she still had all of the things that really counted. She had herself and her life.

Step Six: Use Your Emotions Rather than Worry About Them

Valerie's style of coping with her emotions was to try to get rid of any feelings of anxiety and insecurity as quickly as she could. She relied on reassurance seeking, checking, and worrying—and sometimes she binged on cake and bread. Needless to say, her coping style wasn't working. I suggested that we examine some new ways of handling her emotions.

WHAT IS THE MEANING OF YOUR EMOTION?

Valerie's view of her emotions—her anxiety and insecurity—was that these feelings would overwhelm her and last "forever," that no one could understand them, and that Brad was to blame for her feelings. She had a hard time accepting these feelings and wanted to get rid of them completely and immediately. She also could not tolerate having mixed feelings about Brad—she loved him, but she also didn't like certain things about him. I asked Valerie if she noticed that her feelings always went away after a period of time and that she was never really overwhelmed by them. Also, I told her that having mixed feelings about someone might be a sign that you know the person better and do not idealize him or her. Everyone has mixed qualities, so "mixed feelings" is a sign of being realistic.

LEARN HOW TO ACCEPT YOUR FEELINGS

She seemed to panic about her insecurity. I suggested that she consider accepting being insecure for now, and examine how her lack of acceptance of her feelings made her more desperate. For example, because she could not accept a feeling of insecurity for a moment—or even feeling angry at Brad for a moment—she then bombarded him with demands for reassurance and accusations about his feelings, because she wanted to get rid of her feelings. What if she just allowed herself to feel uncomfortable for right now and not try to eliminate the feeling? Her initial thought was that these feelings would escalate, but it was precisely by acting on the feeling—by seeking reassurance—that the feelings of desperation escalated.

ALMOST EVERYONE HAS THESE FEELINGS

Because Valerie's insecurity kept her anxious and desperate and because Brad was critical of these feelings, she began to feel that she was rather odd. I asked her if other people sometimes felt insecure in their relationships. Were there other friends who were jealous, needed reassurance, or felt lonely when their partner was away? As she reflected on this she realized that a number of her friends had felt this way at times—in fact, Brad had, on occasion, told her he felt insecure in their relationship. Perhaps feelings of insecurity are quite common. Perhaps people could still have a relationship with occasional feelings of insecurity and jealousy.

Step Seven: Take Control of Time

TURN THE URGENCY OFF

Valerie seemed to always feel that she needed an answer right now. No matter what she thought or felt, she wanted to feel more secure immediately. The second she doubted Brad's feelings, she had to ask for reassurance. The moment she felt upset, she had to tell him immediately, no matter what he was doing. This made Brad feel that he was continually being bombarded with demands for reassurance and that his feelings were always questioned and criticized. Consequently, he backed off and stonewalled. What would happen if she didn't get reassurance immediately? Her thought was, "He'll pull away." Ironically, Brad was pulling away because of her intrusiveness and repetitive reassurance seeking. I suggested that she practice delaying getting reassurance: "Try to wait an hour after you notice that you feel insecure. Do something else during that hour to take your mind off Brad." Her feelings began to level off as she delayed her demands on Brad.

NOTICE HOW YOUR FEELINGS CHANGE

Valerie was so intent on getting an answer immediately that she never stood back to watch her feelings pass by on their own. I told Valerie that feelings are impermanent—they don't last. She could test this out by observing her feelings—rating them, describing them, comparing them to other feelings, and learning that they would go away on their own. Initially, Valerie was skeptical about this, as she felt her feelings would "go through the roof" if she didn't get reassurance right away. But she was willing to experiment with impermanence. I also asked her to describe positive and neutral feelings during this time, to see if other, more pleasurable feelings arose. As she tracked these feelings and her thoughts about Brad, she noticed that her feelings of desperation were not permanent and, therefore, not "overwhelming."

IMPROVE THE MOMENT

Valerie continually jumped to conclusions about the future, which she really did not know. When she would wait for Brad to call, she felt helpless, desperate, and entirely focused on him. I suggested that she develop a plan for the present moment—a plan that she could use at any time to make the here-and-now a better moment for her. Valerie liked to play the piano, and she realized that she seldom did this when she felt insecure. So I suggested that she think of this as an alternative to worrying about Brad. She made a list of other behaviors that she could engage in—taking a bath, listening to classical music, reading poetry, renting a film, taking a walk, and doing her exercise. Once she had more control over improving the moment, she worried less about Brad.

STRETCH TIME

Valerie was focused on her worries right now and on her predictions about the future with or without Brad. I suggested that we expand time beyond these worries to include the past and the future—a future without worries. In order to expand the past, I asked Valerie to review her photographs of her life before Brad and her many experiences with Brad during the prior three years. I also asked Valerie to stretch time beyond her current worries to list all the activities that she and Brad were likely to engage in within the next three months. She also identified a number of activities in the past and in the future that did not involve Brad. She looked at photographs of her family, her friends from childhood and college, her pictures of trips she took before she met Brad, and photographs of prior boyfriends. This put Brad in perspective—she'd had a long and important life before Brad. She also listed activities that she would engage in without Brad—work she was going to do, friends she was going to see, hobbies she pursued, and books she wanted to read. These exercises in stretching time were liberating for Valerie because she realized that she could expand her perspective beyond the present worries to include meaningful options in the past and future—some with and some without Brad.

Summing Up

We have examined some of the specific worries and maladaptive ways of coping with worry in relationships. These are common worries for many of us, and they are not always irrational or inaccurate. Sometimes relationships do end. However, worrying about these things—and ruminating for hours while demanding reassurance—will not help your relationship or your worry. Of course, you should utilize all of the techniques listed in the seven steps to overcoming your worry. You can make distinctions between productive and unproductive worry in relationships, practice flooding yourself with uncertainty, accept what you cannot change, commit to making your relationship better, set up worry time, write down your predictions and test them out, identify and challenge your distorted thinking (such as mind reading, fortune-telling, and personalizing) and examine how your worries in relationships reflect your core beliefs. Furthermore, as we have seen in our discussion about fostering independence, failure in a relationship—the relationship ending—does not necessarily have to be catastrophic. Developing a view of yourself that reflects your multiple selves—different roles and different ways of relating to different people—can free you up from the limited fixation that you are nothing without a particular relationship.

In the table opposite I have summarized a number of techniques and concepts that you can use to help you worry less about your relationships. Go through each one and use these techniques until you are able to put your worries in perspective.

TABLE 12.2	
Techniques	*Your Response*
What situations trigger your relationship worries?	
What are your typical worries? What are you concerned will happen?	
How many times have you made these predictions?	
Why haven't they come true?	
What are your typical thinking distortions in relationships?	Mind reading: Fortune-telling: Personalizing: Discounting the positives: Catastrophizing: Negative filter: Labeling:
Are your expectations unrealistic? Why or why not?	
What maladaptive coping styles do you use? Do you use reassurance, checking, giving in, threatening, withdrawing, challenging, etc.?	
Practice giving up your maladaptive coping—for example, give up checking, seeking reassurance, threatening, etc. What do you predict will happen? What actually does happen?	
What is the cost and benefit to you of your worries?	Cost: Benefit:

Techniques	Your Response
Which of your worries are productive and which are unproductive?	Productive worry: Unproductive worry:
Take your productive worry— what specific action can you take in the next forty-eight hours to help yourself?	
Practice flooding yourself with your feared fantasy or your worries about things that are uncertain.	
What would be the advantage of accepting some uncertainty about your relationship?	
What are the worst, best, and most likely outcomes?	
What if your thoughts and worries are true? What are you worried will happen?	
If your relationship ends, what will this mean about you or your future?	
Identify your core belief or personality style (e.g., helpless, abandoned, defective, unlovable, special, out of control, controlled by others, etc.). How are your current worries related to your personality?	
Do you think that the entire relationship is your responsibility? Why or why not?	
What is the evidence for and against your worries?	Evidence for: Evidence against:

Techniques	Your Response
How will you feel about this in a month? A year? Five years? Why would you feel differently?	
Besides your worry, what other emotions are you having in your relationship (anger, boredom, desire to get out, happiness, contentment, etc.)?	
What do you like to do that does not depend on this relationship?	
If the relationship ended, what would be some advantages to you of moving on?	
If the relationship ended, what would be the relative contributions that each of you made to it not working out?	
What advice would you give a friend with these worries?	

13

Health Worries:
What if I Really Am Sick?

Do you scan your body for blemishes, lumps, aches, and pains and then jump to the conclusion that these are signs of impending doom? Do you seek out reassurance from your friends, family, and doctors, check yourself in the mirror, collect medical information—and then conclude that you are sick with a dreaded disease? You may be one of millions of people who have health anxiety, sometimes called "hypochondriasis."[1] About 16.5 percent of us fear some illness, and 5.5 percent of us have health anxiety. People with health anxiety use twice as many health care dollars.[2] They make 80 percent more doctor visits compared to individuals without health anxiety.[3]

How Does Health Anxiety Affect You?

Your health anxiety takes the form of constant dread of finding out that you will get sick from a disease that you think you could have prevented. You check for lumps, live in dread of your next medical examination, scour medical texts and Web sites for information about different symptoms, reject all the reassurance that you get, and continually live in fear that you will not follow up in time about your possible illnesses. You go for examinations, undergo extra medical tests, and even get unnecessary biopsies and procedures, simply to rule out any possibility. You feel depressed and hopeless at times that nothing will bring you peace of mind. You may have gone through numerous doctors who have lost patience with you or who have not been able to make you feel secure.

Or your health anxieties have gotten so bad that you no longer go to the doctor. You are so afraid to find out that you have a dreaded disease that you do not schedule annual examinations, you avoid reading anything about illnesses, and you will not see a doctor even when you are sick. The people around you may view you as stoic because you never complain about medical problems, but you know that deep down you are so terrified about finding out that you are sick that you cannot face thinking about it, talking about it, or ever seeing a doctor.

Eighty-eight percent of people with health anxiety also have a history of another psychological problem—usually depression, generalized anxiety, or physical complaints.[4] In fact, some researchers believe that health anxiety and depression overlap so often that health anxiety may be a part of depression, although others believe that health anxiety is simply another manifestation of obsessive-compulsive disorder. People with health anxiety are also higher on "anxiety sensitivity," the tendency to focus on their anxious sensations and to misinterpret them. Health anxiety, with the constant preoccupation with one's symptoms and the refusal to accept reassurance (while demanding it), often interferes with marital relationships.

Ironically, even though people with health anxiety worry about hav-ing a dreaded disease, they are just as likely as other people to smoke or to eat less-than-healthful foods. Adults who have health anxiety are more likely as children to have experienced serious illness or child abuse.[5] Perhaps because of this

earlier exposure to illness, these individuals become more focused on illness as a problem. Moreover, early experiences of
child abuse may foster the belief that terrible things are beyond
your control, leading to an attempt to adapt to this vulnerability
by anticipating how you can notice problems early and control
them before they get out of hand.

Sylvia's Search for Certainty

Sylvia sat in my office wringing her hands and looking like she
was about to have a panic attack. She told me that she saw a doctor for a checkup about every three weeks, but they couldn't find
anything wrong with her. She told me that she surfs the Internet
for medical Web sites, looking up all kinds of cancers and odd
diseases. She can read through a list of symptoms—nausea,
aches, pains, fatigue, dizziness—and then think that her physical
complaints are a sign of cancer, brain tumors, and other deadly
diseases. She regularly saw her internist, her gynecologist, and
various specialists and had numerous exams and tests, none of
which revealed anything. But Sylvia wasn't about to give up. She
would go home, muse about what could be overlooked, and then
think, "But what if they missed something? The doctor didn't do
every test. What if I have cancer and they could have detected it
but they didn't?"

She was focusing more and more on her aches and pains. She
lost sleep, sat in her apartment dwelling on her fate, and worried
that she might be overlooking something. She even called her
mother: "Mom, didn't Dad's father die from cancer?" "Yes, but he
was seventy-eight." "But doesn't cancer run in the family?"

Every time Sylvia picked up the morning paper she would
turn to the science section. There she'd see another story about
a new drug for cancer that could improve patients' chances, but
only if they took the drug in time. Sylvia began to think, "If I

have cancer, I can catch it now, take the drug, and be one of the lucky ones." If only she could be one of the lucky ones—someone who was diligent, responsible, someone who got all the information, someone who caught the signs of the disease before it killed her. Not like her neighbor, the one who didn't go to a doctor for fifteen years. They found out she had breast cancer. She was dead in three months. "I'm not going to be like her."

She would call her friend Isabel. "I have these pains in my back. I don't know, maybe I'm crazy. Do you think it could be something?" Isabel tried to be a good friend, but she was getting a little tired of this and said, "Look, Sylvia, you've seen ten doctors in the last four months. They all tell you the same thing. You're not sick." "You really think so? I need to hear that I'm OK." "Oh, look, you're just nervous. You'll be OK." Sylvia felt a little relieved. If Isabel thought it was OK, probably it was. Isabel's mother had died from cancer, so Isabel wouldn't be indifferent about that. It was good to hear that someone could give her reassurance.

But then Sylvia heard that a famous actor died from cancer—he was only fifty-five. What if he had caught it early? A lot of cancers can be eliminated if you catch it early. How many of those little warning signs go unnoticed? Then Sylvia began to notice a pain in her lower back and thought, "That's a *symptom,* isn't it?" It was like having a death sentence—just not knowing when or how.

One therapist told Sylvia that she had this problem because of her "survivor guilt"—because her grandparents were in a concentration camp in 1943. It sounded crazy to Sylvia—because it was. Another therapist told her that she has unconscious and unacceptable hostile feelings, so she takes it out on herself. Her mother told her, "Just stop worrying." As we have already learned, this never works for very long. And knowing this just made Sylvia feel more alone and more depressed. How could she stop thinking that she might have cancer? Or that she might overlook something? Or that she might regret it? Or that the doctors might be wrong? And she might die and it all could have been prevented?

The Seven-Step Program for Health Anxiety

Step One: Identify Productive and Unproductive Worry

You have mixed feelings about getting rid of your health anxiety. You may believe that your worries may help you catch things early and avoid things getting out of hand, and that worrying about your health is a sign of your responsibility. So examine the costs and benefits of your worry. Let's take Sylvia's worry about the pain in her back.

TABLE 13.1	
EXAMINE THE COSTS AND BENEFITS OF HEALTH WORRIES	
Costs	Benefits
Dread, fear, depression	I might catch a problem early
Constant worry	If I catch it early, I can get treated
Can't enjoy my life	I'll feel I'm doing the responsible thing

Do the costs—constant anxiety, dread, checking, needing reassurance—outweigh the benefits? Is there any real evidence that Sylvia is catching dreaded diseases early? Let's also look at whether her worry is productive or unproductive. Productive worry is something that you can take action on today and that seems plausible, but unproductive worry is just constant what-iffing about very implausible problems.

TABLE 13.2

IS THIS WORRY PRODUCTIVE OR UNPRODUCTIVE?

Worry	Productive—I can do something useful about it today	Unproductive—this is just a what-if and I can't do anything about it today
Maybe it's cancer	No	Anything is possible
It can get out of hand	No	That hasn't happened—it's just a "what-if"
Maybe the doctor missed something	No	I can't get complete certainty

Now, if her worry is productive—for example, if she has excessive headaches that she usually doesn't have—the productive thing to do is to call a doctor and make an appointment. Being productive means doing something now that could possibly be helpful. Worrying beyond the productive behavior is useless.

YOU FEEL EXCESSIVELY RESPONSIBLE

Part of believing that your worry is productive or meaningful is the belief that you have a responsibility to worry about certain things. In fact, one of the core beliefs in health anxiety is the belief in the responsibility to worry.[6] The question is, "What is your real responsibility?" Sylvia believed that "I am responsible for checking out anything once I have the thought it could be something bad." This is *excessive responsibility*.[7] Let's think about the logic here: "I have the thought that it could be a disease. I should always be responsible. Being responsible means that you do everything to cover all the bases. Being responsible means that I should eliminate any doubts. If I have a thought that it could be bad, I should do everything to eliminate any doubt. Therefore, for me to be responsible I have to do everything to completely rule out that it is a dreaded disease." Since this is impossible, Sylvia could use the "reasonable person" criterion—a reasonable person would accept her limitations.

Sylvia believed that simply having a thought about a negative possibility automatically created a responsibility about that thought. The responsibility is that "I have to do everything to prove that the thought is wrong." This is really saying, then, "I have to prove a negative—I have to prove that something does not exist." Think of the implications of this demand: any negative thought becomes a campaign for certainty. I could have the negative thought, "Perhaps I have HIV." Now, I doubt very much that I have HIV, but it is *possible*. So perhaps I have HIV. OK. From the obsessive point of view, that makes me responsible for checking until I have absolute certainty.

Having thoughts about negative possibilities means nothing about being responsible. One way of testing this out is to ask if every single person in the world is responsible for checking out—to the ends of certainty—every single negative thought. What would the reasonable person do with a negative thought such as the ones that you have? The reasonable person would wave it away as nonsense.

YOU THINK CHECKING WILL HELP

You cannot be responsible for behavior that is impossible. When you assume that you need to check in order to be responsible, then you are really assuming that checking will help in some way. You think that checking will be *productive*—that it will help you with your feelings of responsibility. But think back about the hundreds or thousands of times you're engaged in obsessive and worried checking. Has it really helped? An assumption behind the checking is that it helps you catch things early. Of course, prudent and reasonable checking for breast lumps is helpful, as is going for regular exams. These are things that your doctor would expect you to do. This is productive worry. But the compulsive checking for symptoms and irregularities, as well as checking all the information on diseases, has probably been useless for you.

Sylvia asked herself, "What would be the sacrifices I would have to make?" and "What is the probability of this disease?" Was she willing to sacrifice the quality of her life by continuing compulsive checking and worry in order to eliminate a remote possibility? Or was she willing to accept a very small risk—it's not zero—in order to improve her life? "But what if I am that one person in 280 million who dies a horrible death from this rare disease? I would regret not having done something to prevent it." What trade-offs make sense? What risk is acceptable? I asked her to think about what she is giving up in quality of life in order to eliminate that one chance it could be something bad. How useful is it?

YOU THINK CHECKING WILL FREE YOU FROM REGRET

Another way in which you think that checking will be productive is that it will keep you from ever regretting things. I asked Sylvia, "Do you regret having health anxiety? And worry?" Of course she did. I said, "Checking is something that you might actually regret. It takes up time, makes you anxious, causes you to worry about not checking enough, and makes you believe you are doomed. Are you glad you've been doing this? Think about this: no matter what you do, you'll probably have some regrets. For example, I regret not having bought Microsoft stock when it was really low and selling it when it was really high. I'm sorry I wasn't all-knowing. I wish I had a crystal ball. But I don't think I was irresponsible and stupid for not knowing. You believe that you must check out everything because if you ever did get something and you had not checked it out, then you would regret it. I am sure you would. But what would be the nature of your regret?"

There are two kinds of regret: "I must be a total idiot for not check-ing out everything" and "It's too bad I didn't know everything. But I did what any reasonable person would have done." I asked, "Do you regret not knowing everything? Does not knowing everything mean that you are stupid? Are reasonable people—who don't know everything—stupid and irresponsible?"

CHECKING MAINTAINS YOUR WORRY

Since Sylvia wanted to get rid of any uncertainty, she constantly checked herself for symptoms. I told her, "Checking reduces your anxiety for a very short period of time—but that's all you need to develop a bad habit of checking." But, of course, checking for symptoms or getting reassurance doesn't work for very long. That's because you are trying to eliminate any possible doubt. Soon you are right back where you started—you haven't gotten that 100 percent certainty that you think you need. This convinces you that you need to check some more.

HOW TO GET RID OF CHECKING AND REASSURANCE SEEKING

Let's look at some things to think about and do when you think it will be productive to check and seek reassurance.

TABLE 13.3

HOW TO GET RID OF CHECKING AND REASSURANCE SEEKING

- Recognize that checking hasn't worked—if it had, you wouldn't still be checking.
- Examine the negative consequences to you of checking. It makes you anxious and obsessive.
- Do not ask people for reassurance. This is just another form of checking, and it only works for a few minutes.
- Tell your partner and friends not to give you reassurance. Tell them that they are well-meaning in offering reassurance, but that the fact that you are seeking out reassurance and getting it only adds to your worry. It adds to your worry because it means that you cannot live with the idea that there is uncertainty, mortality, and a degree of helplessness at times.

- Delay checking and reassurance seeking. When you notice your desire to check or seek reassurance, put it off for one hour. Most of the time when you delay a compulsion, the desire to do it decreases or goes away.
- Distract yourself with something that is totally unrelated to your worry.
- Practice uncertainty training: Repeat for fifteen minutes, "I could always get sick and die from something that I could have checked." Keep repeating your fear of uncertainty until you are completely bored with it.

Step Two: Accept and Commit

WHAT ARE THE COSTS AND BENEFITS OF ACCEPTING UNCERTAINTY?

There is no certainty about health. Accepting uncertainty—accepting the possibility that you could have an undetected, even an undetectable disease—is accepting reality. What are the advantages and disadvantages of accepting this as a possibility?

TABLE 13.4

ACCEPTING UNCERTAINTY ABOUT DISEASE

Advantages	Disadvantages
I can relax and not worry.	I can overlook something.
I can give up checking.	I can be caught by surprise.
I can enjoy my life in the present.	I can end up regretting not doing something.

Sylvia looked at whether her life would be better or worse if she accepted her limitations when it came to disease. Accepting that she cannot control the unknown and the uncontrollable would free her from checking and continual worry.

ACCEPT YOUR LIMITATIONS

Like many worries, health worries put you literally in the center of things, making you feel that *you* can do something to take control and make things work out perfectly well. Sylvia recognized that realistic limitations included being mortal, getting sick, not knowing everything, understanding that reassurance seeking cannot change reality, and acknowledging that she can never control everything. Accepting limitations about your health doesn't mean that you don't ever go to doctors, examine your breasts, or watch what you eat or drink, but it did mean for Sylvia that she had to accept the limitation of what she could know for sure.

PRACTICE YOUR FEAR

She feared having the thought "I could have a dreaded disease" or "I could have a dreaded disease and fail to do something about it." Each time she had one of those thoughts, her worry process was activated. This included focusing on her body, getting information, seeking reassurance, and worrying about the future. But what would happen if she just practiced the thought "I could have a dreaded disease and fail to do something about it"? Sylvia said that having the thought made her feel like she would get cancer *unless she did something about it.* This is thought-reality fusion—the belief that having a thought actually will make something real happen. So having the thought about cancer and doing nothing about it meant she would be at a higher risk for cancer.

Sylvia's homework assignment was to do the following each day: (1) Repeat her feared thought for twenty minutes: "I am thinking about having this disease and I am doing nothing to catch it and prevent it." (2) If she had the thought "This could be a symptom of cancer" (or something like this), she would have to repeat two hundred times, right then and there, "It's possible that this is cancer."

Sylvia came back the next week surprised that she was feeling so much less anxious about her fears of disease. She had practiced her feared thoughts over and over, and she said that she found her mind drifting elsewhere when she would repeat the cancer thoughts. The thoughts had become boring.

Boredom was a sign of getting better, so I told her to do this every day for the next month. Sylvia improved very rapidly—so much so that she was able to cut back on her therapy sessions. A couple of months later she wrote to me that she was feeling immensely better. She was getting on with her life. The cancer fears—fears that she had for years—were gone.

LIVE WITH MORTALITY

The fear of death and of regrets about not having done everything to avoid death are central to health anxiety. Psychologists Abigail James and Adrian Wells found that superstitious and negative views of death were associated with health anxiety.[8] For example, a woman who had fears of cancer also feared that her death would lead to eternal punishment in hell. What happens after you die is anyone's guess as far as I can determine. But if you have a belief that death is a continuation or increase in suffering, then you will have greater anxiety about your health. Moreover, if you fear that the process of dying is filled with pain and suffering, then you will be even more cautious about your health.

One way to deal with our mortality is to deny that it exists. In a fascinating book, *The Denial of Death*, Ernest Becker describes how American culture seems to operate in denial of the fact that everyone dies. We attempt to maintain an illusion of permanent youth and health with plastic surgery, weight control, cosmetics, hair dyes, an active lifestyle, and hopes to extend our life expectancy indefinitely. Although a healthy lifestyle is important, no lifestyle will keep you from dying. *Death can be delayed, never denied.*

So how does one come to terms with death? One question that arises is what death means to you. Does it mean punishment and suffering—and is it punishment and suffering for your human mistakes? Does death mean that life has had no meaning? Does death make you regret all of the things that you did not do or the mistakes that you made?

I would suggest a different, perhaps unusual view of death. Death implies that life has more meaning than you ever thought it did. Let me give you an example of one such image. A secular Jewish man who thought of converting to Orthodoxy spoke with his rabbi, who was paralyzed and sitting in a wheelchair. He told the rabbi his worries about business, and the rabbi responded, "I am sitting in a wheelchair and I do not worry about the meaning of life. I am not depressed. How can this be?" The man responded, "I don't know how you do it." The rabbi said, "If I offered you ten million dollars and then the next day said I can only give you nine million, how would you feel?" "Nine million would be a lot," my patient said. The rabbi answered, "God has given me ten million and taken back one. I have everything else left." This caused a profound shift in the man's perspective. It touched him (and me, listening) at a very deep and emotionally meaningful level. His worries gradually shifted from his business concerns to appreciating the importance of things in his life.

Step Three: Challenge Your Worried Thinking

YOUR WORRY RECORD

I had Sylvia keep track of when and where her health worries were worst. She kept a worry record for two weeks to see what the triggers were and what she did after she worried. She found she was more likely to worry about health when standing in front of a mirror or when she was alone. For example, she noticed herself looking in the mirror, checking her skin, pinching the skin (which will increase the redness), and then going onto the Internet to check diseases.

SET ASIDE WORRY TIME

She set aside thirty minutes a day to record her health worries. The same illnesses kept coming up, as did the same demand for perfectionism. Limiting health worries to a specific time and place allowed her to find out that her worries are limited.

TEST YOUR PREDICTIONS

Sylvia kept a list of her health predictions—"I have cancer," "I have a brain tumor," "The doctor will tell me that I will die"—and then checked them out against reality. She had made similar predictions in the past and none of them had come true.

CHALLENGE YOUR THINKING DISTORTIONS

We went through Sylvia's different automatic thoughts about health to test them out.

1. *What thinking distortion was she using?* Emotional reasoning: "I feel anxious, therefore I must have a disease." Fortune-telling: "I'll find out I have leukemia." Negative filter: "This spot looks like cancer." Discounting the positive: "The exam isn't 100 percent perfect. They may have missed something." Mislabeling: "This is melanoma." Catastrophizing: "I'm going to die." What-iffing: "What if it really is AIDS?"

2. *How likely is it that this will actually happen?* Susan realized that the likelihood that she had cancer was almost zero. Another way to challenge her fortune-telling was to ask how sure she was that her prediction was accurate. Would she be willing to bet all of her money on this? She said, "I'm really saying, 'I *might* have cancer' "—something that is true for everyone.

Of course she *might* have cancer. It's always true that she might have anything, no matter how much she checked. In fact, "I might have cancer" (or anything else) is not really a prediction. It is reality. Anything *might* happen. By thinking "I might have cancer," Sylvia was really trying to *change the nature of reality*. She was trying to make absolutely sure that she *didn't* have cancer. This can't be done—no one can eliminate uncertainty. All anyone can do is think in terms of probabilities. Was it probable that Sylvia had these diseases?

3. *What is the worst outcome? The most likely outcome? The best outcome?* The worst outcome was a dreaded disease, but the most likely reality or outcome was that there was nothing really wrong. Sylvia recognized that the best outcome (being healthy) was the most likely.

4. *Tell yourself a story about better outcomes.* Write out a short description of how this current problem could have a good outcome—for example, you find out that all you have is indigestion and anxiety. Sylvia wrote out a story of a better outcome that was actually a description of what she always found to be true—she saw the doctor and she was fine.

5. *What is the evidence that something really bad is going to happen?* Are you relying on poor evidence? Your emotions? Sylvia used her emotions and her supposed "symptoms" (that is, her imperfection) as evidence. We often overestimate probabilities because we can imagine ourselves having the disease. You might get a picture of yourself in a hospital bed (what I call "imagery probabilities") or you tell yourself a detailed story about how you got this disease and then use this story as evidence that the disease is likely (what I call "narrative probabilities"). Realistically, we don't know what percentage of people with headaches actually have brain tumors (although we could reasonably assume it's

very small, we don't carry these figures around with us). Sylvia estimated probabilities by getting pictures in her head of diseases. These pictures increased in intensity as she surfed the Internet for stories of people dying from dreaded diseases. But a picture in your head is not the same thing as a fact about illness. It's your imagination at work. The same thing is true with those fascinating stories about how you got the disease. They're stories, not facts—and certainly not diseases.

I said to Sylvia, "You never come up with detailed images or stories about how you did *not* get the disease. Imagine a picture in your head of being healthy. What do you look like *without* a brain tumor or *without* AIDS? I'm willing to bet you never conjure up these images." Images and stories of disease are not information about disease—they are information about how imaginative and creative and worried you are. Would your doctor ask you to imagine having AIDS in order to test you for HIV? No, she would order a blood test. Your imagination and stories are not in the same league as blood tests or X-rays. In fact, even though you can imagine things, you should remind yourself that no matter how intense your imagination, it is completely irrelevant to medicine.

6. *Are you paying attention to the wrong thing?* We are predisposed to attend to and remember information that confirms our beliefs—this is called "attentional bias" or "confirmation bias." We ignore information that disconfirms our thoughts. Sylvia selectively attended to anything that was a symptom of a disease, looked for information on the Internet about diseases, and thought that anything she read was especially relevant to her "disease." I asked Sylvia to avoid searching the Internet, to ask her doctor what would be a good guideline for regular checkups rather than rely on worry as a guideline for calling the doctor, and to try to delay checking herself for symptoms. I also

suggested that she list all the things that were normal about her health, to help her put her attention in the right place.

7. *How many times have you been wrong in the past about your worries?* Are you almost always predicting the worst about your health? Could this simply be another false prediction? Sylvia was always wrong about her predictions.

8. *Examine unrealistic estimates of probabilities.* You can ask yourself if you do any of the following, which will make you overestimate probabilities:

- *Category errors.* Sylvia viewed irregularities or unpleasant sensations as if they were symptoms.
- *Mislabeling.* She believed "If I have a symptom, then it's probably a terrible disease."
- *Uncertainty.* She equated uncertainty with the idea that it was risky.
- *Imagery.* She thought that if she could imagine a disease, getting it was more likely.
- *Stories.* She thought her ability to tell a story about a disease meant that it was more likely.
- *Need to prove a negative.* She thought that if she couldn't prove she didn't have a dreaded disease, then it was likely she *did* have a dreaded disease. She thought that if she doesn't know something for certain, then it was more probable: "I don't know that it's not HIV, so maybe it is." But what you mean by "maybe" is "probably" or "worth worrying about." In fact, if you had more evidence that you did not have HIV or cancer, this doesn't really reduce the probability. The probabilities are out there in reality—not in your head. *You are not at greater risk if you have less knowledge.* Your body cells are not abnormally multiplying based on the degree of knowledge you have of your CAT scan. Ignorance of facts does not change the facts.

Sylvia was doing all of these things—which made her worry even more—but the realistic probability of cancer was really low.

9. *How could you cope if the bad outcome actually happens?* What if you really did have a dreaded disease? How could you cope? What treatments are available? Do people get better? Sylvia realized that most cancers caught early are highly treatable.

10. *Are you demanding perfection in your health?* The blemish on her face became her sole focus. She noticed that the longer she looked at a blemish or other symptom, then the more obvious it seemed that she had a dreaded disease. She thought that because she could locate an imperfection, this proved she had a disease. I asked her to test this out by looking at someone else's face and noticing any imperfections. Of course she saw some, because we all have slight imperfections—they're signs of being slightly imperfect—or just of being alive.

Step Four: Focus on the Deeper Threat

ILLNESS AND YOUR CORE ISSUES

Your worries about health may be related to your personal core beliefs. So if you were to get ill you might worry that you won't be able to take care of yourself (helplessness, autonomy, and control), you may become "inferior" or weak (need to be special and unique), people will leave you because you are sick (abandonment), or you could have prevented it all by being responsible. For example, Sylvia worried that if she got sick she would be all alone and no one would take care of her. She would lose her special status as someone who is unique and superior. Mark, on the other hand, worried that if he got sick it would mean that he had overlooked something—reflecting his fear of being irresponsible. Dave worried that if he got sick he wouldn't be able to take care of his family (responsibility and caretaker issues). And Emily worried that if she got sick she would no longer be attractive and appealing to men.

HEALTH PERFECTIONISM

Health perfectionism is the belief that your body and your sensations should be perfect all of the time. Life would be so nice, we think, if we were free from aches and pains, blemishes, discoloration, lumps, moles, lines, pings and stings, tremors, nausea, headaches, dizziness—anything that makes our bodies less than what they could be. If we think that our bodies and sensations should be perfect and should never have any abnormalities, then we are in for a rude awakening. What you consider "abnormal"— the aches, the blemishes, the lumps, the difficulties of various and unpleasant kinds—are the norm! You thought that a healthy person doesn't have a headache, doesn't have back pain, doesn't feel stiffness in the legs, or doesn't feel like throwing up now and again. If you tell yourself that your body and your sensations should be perfect all the time, then you are going to find thousands of imperfections. And if your rule is "If it's imperfect, then it's a symptom of a disease," then you will find "diseases" and "symptoms" every day and live in constant fear.

Normal bodies have lumps, bumps, aches, pains, irregularities, discolorations, and blemishes. Normal internal sensations include feeling dizzy, being tired, having headaches, experiencing heartburn, feeling gas, having a rapid heartbeat, feeling short of breath, and feeling a tingling in your fingertips. It is normal to have what you consider "symptoms."

WHAT YOU CAN DO ABOUT HEALTH PERFECTIONISM

Health perfectionism was a source of many of Sylvia's worries. I suggested she try to develop some "constructive imperfectionism."

Sylvia's belief that any irregular sensation or appearence was a sign of cancer came from the standard that healthy people have perfect sensations and perfect physical features—no blemishes, bumps, or aches and pains. I asked Sylvia to do a survey of her friends and family and ask each of them the following: "Have you ever had any blemishes, bumps, aches, pains, or physical sensations that you noticed?" Everyone she asked said yes. And then I instructed her to ask them, "Why didn't you think this was a sign of a dreaded disease?" They all commented that aches and pains, blemishes, and bumps are normal.

TABLE 13.5
WHAT YOU CAN DO ABOUT HEALTH PERFECTIONISM

- Consider the costs and benefits of demanding health perfectionism. The costs are that you will continue to jump to conclusions and mislabel yourself as having dreaded diseases. The benefits? You might think that this keeps you on your toes—but it really keeps you worried.
- Recognize that no one has a perfect body or perfect sensations inside his or her body.
- Sensations in your body—or aches and pains—may be signs of being alive, not of a dreaded disease.
- Consider all the ways that your body is normal and that your sensations are not out of the ordinary.
- When you notice an "imperfection," look for the worst interpretation and the best interpretation. Then ask yourself what most people would think is the most likely interpretation.

Step Five: Turn "Failure" into Opportunity

IMPERFECTION IS NOT FAILURE

Your constant checking may be related to your belief that you would be a failure or irresponsible if you did not catch a disease early. You need to make a distinction between being a reasonable versus being a perfect person. Since you have no chance of ever being perfect, we can only hope that you can be reasonable. Failing to catch everything is inevitable—and beyond your control.

Another way of looking at health is to ask, "What would the reasonable person do?" Sylvia recognized that her expectations about protecting herself were excessive and that she was trying to be perfect in order to avoid regret. However, she could ask herself, "How would other people deal with aches, pains, or symptoms?" Of course, following the guideline of what reasonable people might do was not a guarantee that her vigilance would be enough. It could fail. But in the event it failed and she really ended up with a dreaded disease that she did not spot early enough, she would know that she had done what everyone else would have done.

The real question comes down to the trade-off between trying to be perfect and choosing to live a normal life. Her health anxiety was driving her mad, she said, so risking a failure was worth it if it meant she could have a normal life free from obsessions.

PROTECTION AND PREVENTION CAN WORK

I told Sylvia it might be important to have a plan for how she would deal with health care crises if they should arise. For example, you can turn your worries about health into practical questions that you can address:

- Do I have adequate health care insurance?
- Am I getting regular checkups?
- Am I keeping my weight down? Do I smoke or drink too much?
- Do I get adequate exercise?
- Do I have a will?

Some of these questions may seem a bit morbid. Ironically, though, I have found that some people who worry about their health are not adequately following proper health care guidelines—they drink, smoke, get into cars with drunk drivers, and don't see the doctor often enough. Sylvia herself smoked—something that is a risk-related behavior. We developed a plan for her to stop smoking.

Step Six: Use Your Emotions Rather than Worry About Them

Your worries about your health may indicate that you are not allowing yourself to feel anxious or sad when it might make sense to have those emotions. I asked Sylvia if there were some legitimate fears, sadness, or even anger that she was not expressing. Sylvia was feeling angry about her relationship with the man she was involved with, and angry toward her mother, who criticized her. Many people who have health anxiety have difficulty asking for support for their feelings, so they turn to talking about physical symptoms to get love and attention. It's like saying, "It's OK to have a physical illness but not OK to have an emotional problem." As Sylvia expressed some of her frustrations with her partner, she focused less on her physical complaints and worries.

FACE THE WORST CASE

You can try to carry your fears to the worst-case scenario. What is the worst possible outcome that you can imagine? Is it lying in a hospital bed, with no one around? Is it feeling physically helpless? Is it regretting that you could have avoided everything? Is the emotion anger, sadness, or helplessness? I asked Sylvia to repeatedly imagine the worst-case scenario with as strong an emotion as she could have. The emotional intensity of the image of lying in bed with cancer decreased with repetitions of the image.

KEEP AN EMOTION AND SYMPTOM DIARY

Keep track of your physical sensations along with the feelings and situations associated with them. Sylvia's physical preoccupations were greatest when she was alone in her apartment, and they were associated with feelings of loneliness and anger.

DEVELOP EMOTIONAL STRATEGIES

When you feel angry, sad, or anxious, you may view your emotions in the most negative light. For example, Sylvia believed she should always be rational and in control, so she thought that she could find a perfect solution to fears of illness by worrying about symptoms. She actually had very negative beliefs about her emotions—that she should get rid of her anxiety immediately, that she should focus on how bad things felt, that she needed a simple and clear answer to everything, and that if she allowed herself to feel sad or anxious, her feelings would go on forever. Most importantly, Sylvia thought that complaining about being sad or anxious about her personal life—her feelings of loneliness—was a sign of being "childish." We developed new emotional beliefs: that it was very human to feel lonely, that sharing your feelings was a way that people could get close to you and know you, and that feelings do not have to be controlled and eliminated.

Step Seven: Take Control of Time

FOCUS ON CURRENT ACTIVITIES

Your worries about health pull you away from everyday life. Consider replacing your current worries about your symptoms with an activity list of pleasurable and productive things to do today. For example, Sylvia was able to schedule going to the health club, seeing her friends, watching a video, and reading a book. As she did these things, she would concentrate on the pleasure and sensations in the moment. This reduced her worries about possible future catastrophes.

VISIT THE PAST WORRIES

Think back to the many health worries that you had in the past. Are you still worried about them? Did these predictions prove false? What was distorted in your thinking back then?

Sylvia could readily see that her past worries about health always turned out to be false. I suggested that this might be the very reason she continued to worry—she believed that her worry had kept these bad things from actually happening!

STRETCH TIME

Your current worries about health are not likely to be your future realities or worries about anything. Ask yourself, "How will I feel about these worries a week from now? Or a month from now? What are some other interesting things that I could be doing tomorrow or next week?" Sylvia recognized that her current worry would subside and that she would later look back on it as wasted energy.

Summing Up

Sylvia's health worries were substantially reduced, and her personal life improved dramatically. We can see that she was able to recognize that she had a preoccupation with illness and control. She had selective attention, focusing on symptoms, collecting information about illnesses, and imagining all kinds of dreaded diseases. She had health perfectionism that led her to discount the actual probability of any given disease. For example, even though almost everyone has had a headache, she ignored this informa-tion and concluded that *her* headache was a sign of a brain tumor. She demanded certainty and sought out reassurance and medical exams to achieve that certainty, always leading to a need for more reassurance later. Underlying her health anxiety was her fear of regret, which made it hard to accept uncertainty.

Sylvia recognized that her reassurance seeking and checking not only were useless but actually made things worse. As she delayed and eventually abandoned her checking, her anxiety about health was reduced. She found that practicing images of disease and regret over and over eventually led her to become bored with her fears. Sylvia's health anxiety had plagued her for many years, even making her feel at times that life was not worth living. Now that she was freed from these worries, she was better able to focus on what was meaningful in her life rather than dread getting a diagnosis.

14

Money Worries:
What if I Start Losing Money?

MOST OF US HAVE WORRIED about money at some time—especially when the news tells us that the economy is slowing down, unemployment is high, interest rates might climb, the stock market is shaky, and your job could be on the line. These money worries may make you feel inadequate or ashamed about your financial condition, or create conflicts with your partner. In fact, you may be so worried about money that you can't even look at how much money you have or how much you spend.

Identify Your Money Worries

Look at the list of forty-three statements below and see to what extent each describes how you generally have felt over the past month. Then write *T* (true) or *F* (false) next to each statement.

TABLE 14.1

1. I won't have enough money to make me feel secure.

2. If I don't make enough money, then I won't be successful.

3. People will be less impressed with me if I don't have enough money.

4. I often feel I won't have enough money.

5. I am fearful that I will lose my money.

6. I worry that I will lose my job and not keep up with my bills.

7. I deserve more than I get paid.

8. I feel guilty when I spend money.

9. I think that I spend too much money.

10. Others think I spend too much money.

11. I often spend money just to feel good.

12. I have more debt than I feel comfortable with.

13. The most important part of my job is how much money I make.

14. I would be willing to work more hours for more money even if I had to spend less time on things that I like to do.

15. People will take advantage of me and try to get my money.

16. People rely on me to provide money.

17. I rely on others to take care of me financially.

18. I get anxious when I spend money on myself.

19. People think I'm stingy and cheap.

20. I think I spend too much money on other people.

21. I feel embarrassed if people know how much I have.

22. If you spend money on someone, they should feel that they owe you something.

23. People are ungrateful about the things that I've done for them.

24. People would respect me less if I made less money.

25. I generally compare myself with others who have or make more money.

26. I feel envious of how well others are doing.

27. I feel it's important to me that I make more money or have more money than others do.

28. I want others to know that I'm doing well.

29. I don't like socializing with people who make more money than I do.

30. I often save and hoard things that I don't really need.

31. I frequently check to see how much money I have.

32. I'm so anxious about money I am afraid to check to see how much money I really have.

33. I have to watch my investments all of the time to make sure that everything is OK.

34. If I make an investment or a large purchase (like a car or house), I worry afterward whether it was the right decision.

35. I worry that I won't be able to make enough money in the future.

36. I am concerned that I will not live up to the financial expectations that others have of me.

37. There are a lot of things that I appreciate that cost nothing. (R)

38. The most important thing for me is to enjoy my work—not necessarily make a lot of money. (R)

39. The most important thing for me is to have time for relationships, family, or relaxation. (R)

40. Religion or spiritual values are very important to me. (R)

41. I am making more money than I had expected to make. (R)

42. I have very specific goals for myself about how much I want to make. (R)

43. I am living up to my expectations about money. (R)

Scoring: Note that items marked (R) are reverse scored. Add up your total of items that you scored as true.

Key:

0–5	Very few money worries
6–10	Some money worries
11–15	Significant money worries
16–20	Extreme worries about money
21 or more	Obsessed with money worries

Look at your responses and examine what your thoughts are about what money means to you, your feelings about how much you are entitled to, how you want to use money, how you spend money, how money is reflected in the meaning of your work, how money plays itself out in your relationships, who you compare yourself with, how attached you get to hoarding money, what you worry about, the things that you appreciate, and how you view yourself living up to expectations. You may see a pattern of how money has become overly important in your life, how your money is tied to your self-esteem, or how money is important in impressing other people. Money may have become your primary focus at times, rather than a means to an end.

The Consequences of Money Worries

Partners often have different theories about how money should be viewed. For example, one partner may be relatively protective and want to establish a budget, set up a savings plan, and review the necessity of major purchases. The other partner may view money in a more risk-tolerant fashion, believing that current expenses can be covered by hoped-for future earnings. When the second partner spends money, the first partner may begin worrying, and this is likely to lead to an argument. However, it may be that the worries have some legitimacy.

In America, we say that someone who works a lot works like a dog. In Europe, with their generous vacation plans, they say, "He works like an American." Money worries about unnecessary expenses may decrease the quality of your life simply because you are working extra hard to cover these recurring debts. Another consequence of money worries is that your self-esteem may suffer. If you begin thinking, "I am not going to have enough money," you may link this to "I am a failure" and "I am inferior to other people." These depressive thoughts add to your anxiety and lead to a sense of shame: "I can't hang out with those people anymore because I don't have the kind of money I used to."

How You Learn to Be Dissatisfied

There are seven factors that determine your financial worries.[1]

1. *Earlier economic deprivation may make you vulnerable to financial worries* regardless of how much better off you are financially now. The old saying "Once poor, never rich" has some validity. For example, one man who had been impoverished as a child became a remarkably successful businessman, but told me he always worried that it could all be taken away.

2. *You worry about money if you have perfectionistic standards of what your life must look like materially.* Some people have arbitrary goals—"I need X in order to feel financially secure." Others will have an image of a lifestyle that they feel they need. One man told me that he grew up looking at the *New Yorker* (a magazine that reflects an affluent urban lifestyle) and this became his template of what he believed he needed. You might think, "I need the very best," "Without the best, I am ordinary," or "Life is only worth living if you stand out."

3. *You exaggerate how useful money will be.* Significant increases in wealth only temporarily increase general happiness. Exaggerating how important money will be in buying happiness will lead you to worry about not having enough money. You might think, "The more money I have, the better I will feel" or "Money will bring me happiness and security."

4. *You use "upward comparisons,"* comparing yourself with people who have more, and then you exaggerate how happy they are.

5. *You overvalue effort in obtaining money.* We often think that the only reason we do not have more is that we did not try hard enough or that we are not paying attention to these terrific opportunities in front of us. Professional investors worry they may

be missing something—which makes some of them obsessively watch their screens as stock prices fluctuate. This leads to decision making based on emotions rather than reasoning and information, and to blaming yourself. You think, "If I work harder, I will get what I want," "I need to keep checking my stocks," or "Work and money will bring me fulfillment."

6. *Money has symbolic value for you,* symbolizing security, success, effort, pride, and how morally worthy you are. Losing money or not having enough reflects your lack of personal worth. You feel the need to make a public display of the items that you have purchased—making sure other people know about the expensive car you drive, the stylish designer clothing you wear, and the expensive restaurants and vacations you enjoy. Your thoughts are "Money reflects your personal success" or "People who have less money are failures." The need for these public displays of success becomes the "conspicuous consumption" that social historian Thorstein Veblen described over a century ago. It also drives you deeper into debt.[2]

7. *You are always raising your standards.* Once you achieve a standard, you raise the bar so that you are no longer satisfied. You never feel satisfied for very long. You think, "The more I make, the more I need to make" or "Too much is never enough."

Are you more worried about money because of financial setbacks your parents experienced? If so, in what way is your current financial plan or strategy different from your parents? Ken's father's business failed when Ken was a young man, and although Ken had accumulated some financial assets, he continually worried about money. However, when he examined how his finances were different from those of his father (who was a risk taker, unlike Ken), he realized that he had been overgeneralizing his father's risky attitude to his own conservative attitude.

Financial perfectionism make you vulnerable to worries about not living up to unrealistic expectations. Andy had a perfectionistic idea of how much money he needed. I asked him to list the activities that he had enjoyed most in the past two years—including mundane or simple activities. The experiences he enjoyed most were either free or nearly so. Ironically, because he had been focusing so much time and effort on making more money, he had forgone the activities with his wife and children that were more meaningful. As a consequence, he decided to spend less time at work (and, therefore, make less money) and more time with his family.

If you believe that increased effort and vigilance will yield correspondingly increased benefits, you will become obsessed with work and watching your investments bounce up and down. For one investor who diligently and compulsively tracked his portfolio, we experimented with him refraining from watching the screen for several hours each day, instead spending this time on actually collecting useful information about the fundamentals of different companies. Another antidote to overvaluing effort or work is to schedule pleasure breaks that give you perspective. At first, the compulsive investor will find this difficult, predicting that she will "miss something." After experimenting with gaining distance and relinquishing useless effort, you can then make a better decision as to which information and decisions are prudent. Simply working harder and longer is no guarantee of a better outcome. Indeed, this is likely to lead to foolish, emotion-based trading—thereby incurring increased transaction costs for buying and selling stocks.

Consider your upward comparisons. This is destined to make you feel poorer and contribute to worries about money. Useful exercises for you to do are to compare yourself now with when you had less. You may actually find that you enjoyed yourself more when you had less. Consider people who have less than you do. Are they all miserable? What are they doing that brings them some happiness and meaning? If people with less can enjoy themselves, then why worry about money?

Examine your belief that money has *symbolic value*. Perhaps you think that it is a way of keeping score of who is more successful. Many Wall Street investors say to me, "I want to make enough money so that I don't have to work anymore." This is like putting off sex until you retire. Rather than using money as a symbol of how successful, important, or good you are, you might focus on having more successful and important *experiences* in your life. This might include better relationships, learning how to see things in perspective, and developing a better set of values. I can't imagine wanting to have someone as a friend who would value me because of my money. I would want someone who could value me even if I were poor.

In contrast to money as a goal in itself, psychologists have found that developing gratitude can have significant effects on psychological and mental health. Robert Emmons and Michael McCullough found that providing college students with a simple instruction to pay attention to what they could be grateful to significantly enhanced their sense of psychological and physical well-being—a finding consistent with other research that relationships, meaningful work, and a sense of purpose are more important than increased wealth for a positive psychological outlook.[3]

Finally, consider the paradox of the *receding reference point*. No matter how much you make, it's never enough. What if you used your reference point as "less than what I make now?" The consequence of this is that you could become immediately appreciative of having more than you expected. Or what if your reference point was a set of different goals and experiences that had nothing to do with money? You could use as reference points being a better friend or family member, living a healthier life, learning more, developing values that you could be proud of, and getting perspective on things. The consequence of eliminating your financial receding reference point is not that you would lose your ambition to succeed—rather, you would be able to focus on succeeding in many other areas of your life.

Kathy and the Bubble That Burst

Kathy was a middle-class woman who made a decent salary. She had gotten a rather large credit card bill that was out of proportion to what she was used to seeing. She had not taken into account that she had recently taken a trip to the Virgin Islands, where she had a terrific time—her first real vacation in two years. When she picked up the bill, she thought, "I'll never be able to pay this off," and then she thought, "I'm going to run out of money." The fact was that she has savings and future earnings. But Kathy was thinking that this bill was a harbinger of bills to come, even though she hadn't had a bill like this in the past.

Kathy had been worrying a lot over the past year about her finances. Although she had been working at the same company for three years, there had been layoffs. A few of her friends had been out of work for some time, and Kathy worried frequently that she would lose her job and fall behind in her payments. When I asked Kathy to tell me what she saw happening if she lost her job, she said that she imagined not being able to get another job, losing her apartment, and ending up on the street. When I asked her how much she had in her different savings and investments, she told me that it had become too upsetting to look at her financial position—it just reminded her of how far she was falling behind. Kathy would sometimes let her bills pile up because she didn't want to be reminded of how tight her money situation was.

Kathy was also worrying about her big losses in the stock market. Like millions of people, during the stock bubble in the 1990s she saw her small portfolio of savings balloon into something much bigger. Now she was worried about money. "Will I have enough to retire? What will happen if I keep losing money? Why was I so stupid to hold on to those tech stocks?" Kathy was waking up at three-thirty in the morning worried about money, wondering if she could ever get a handle on it.

Let's look at how Kathy was able to use the seven steps to deal with her money worries.

The Seven-Step Program for Money Worries

Step One: Identify Productive and Unproductive Worry

COSTS AND BENEFITS OF MONEY WORRIES

Kathy believed that worrying about money could help her catch her losses quickly, take control over her spending, and prevent any surprises. In fact, she thought that worrying about money showed she was responsible. The disadvantages were that she was anxious, afraid, regretful, and unable to enjoy her life. Her money worries kept her up at night.

PRODUCTIVE AND UNPRODUCTIVE MONEY WORRIES

I asked Kathy if she could do anything productive in the next day about her finances. She decided that she could get her financial statements together, look at how she was spending money, begin to keep a budget, and think before she spent. Her unproductive worries were the what-ifs and catastrophic stories she told herself.

CHALLENGE YOUR UNPRODUCTIVE WORRIES

Look at the table opposite and see if you can identify some of your own unproductive worries about money and how you can challenge them.

		TABLE 14.2	
Unproductive worry	*Example*	*How to challenge your thoughts*	*Productive action*
1. I worry about unanswerable questions.	Will I lose money in the market?	I can't know what the future will be in terms of income and investments.	Diversify my investments and develop a savings plan and budget.
2. I worry about a chain reaction of events.	One loss will lead to more losses—that will continue until I have next to nothing.	I have no evidence that this will happen. Stocks go up and down. I should take a longer-term perspective.	Same as above.
3. I worry about unsolvable problems in the future	What if I am unable to pay my bills when I get old?	I am not that old. There are safety nets, like Medicare.	Same as above.
4. I worry about what I can never know.	Will I be able to take care of myself if all my money runs out and I need to go to a nursing home?	There is no sense in worrying about something that hasn't happened and isn't likely to happen. I can focus now on saving money and getting a budget.	Same as above.
5. I reject a solution because it is not perfect.	No one can tell me for sure that the market won't crash and I won't get fired.	There is no certainty or perfection in any solution. I have no evidence that any of these things will happen. I can always get another job.	Same as above.

Unproductive worry	Example	How to challenge your thoughts	Productive action
6. I think I should worry until I feel less anxious.	I keep worrying because I am still anxious about this.	Just because I am anxious, it doesn't mean that my finances will be wiped out.	Same as above. Focus on current rewarding activities.
7. I think I should worry until I control everything.	I have to find a solution that I know I can carry out.	I can't control everything—and I don't need to. Just because I don't control something doesn't mean it will be bad.	Same as above. Focus on current rewarding activities.

Step Two: Accept and Commit

DON'T TAKE IT PERSONALLY

You think that what is happening is exclusive to you. You don't realize that millions of other people are in the same boat. In fact, people who worry about their financial losses tell me that they like going to parties where other people talk about *their* losses. This helps normalize the experience and helps them not take the loss personally. The reality is that stocks go up and down for reasons that you and every financial analyst will never know. When Ted lost some money in his stock portfolio, he began thinking, "What's wrong with me?" It's as if he made the company stock decline in value. He had nothing to do with the value of the stock, and he could never have known what direction it was going. Keep in mind that for every buyer there's a seller, which means that every time you sold a stock, there was someone else who thought it was a good deal at the price that you were willing to sell at. One of you had to be wrong.

ACCEPT THAT MONEY IS FLEXIBLE

You may believe that your net assets and your earnings should always increase in value. Nothing could be further from the historical truth. Markets go up and down, real estate rises and falls, and people are often unemployed. Kathy had an illusion that her stocks and her income would continue to rise every year, and this made her worry that any decrease was a sign of bad things to come. Accepting that money and markets are up and down can help you normalize the unexpected.

ACCEPT LIMITATIONS

Similar to not taking it personally is recognizing that there are limi-tations in your earning capacity and your ability to predict the value of stocks. These limitations do not mean that you are a failure or that you are powerless—they only represent the fact that you can't know everything or control everything. But what can you control? You can control how you spend your time, how you respond in your relationships, and whether you are willing to put money in perspective. If you work too much or obsess about your stocks, you should consider cutting back on work, eliminating checking, and focusing on things that you can control that produce a benefit, such as exercising, learning, and building your relationships. Accept-ing limitations in one area may open opportunities in other areas—if you choose to pursue them.

DO THE UNCOMFORTABLE: KEEP A BUDGET

Ironically, one of the hardest things for people with money worries to do is to keep a budget and stay within it. If you are worried about money, it seems obvious that you should find out how much you're spending and what you are spending money on. But you might resist doing this, because you think, "If I write down what I spend, I'll find out I can't spend money on anything," "I'll see that I have no money left," or "I'll feel poor." In fact, you might try this out as a homework assignment: write down *every* expense for one month. If you were to decrease your spending by 10 percent, what would you still be able to do with the other 90 percent?

Step Three: Challenge Your Worried Thinking

KEEP TRACK OF YOUR WORRIES

Record your money worries, noting the events that trigger these worries—for example, getting bills in the mail, making a purchase, hearing that someone else has more, or looking at your stock portfolio. For Kathy, the trigger was getting a bill. She blamed herself, then she checked her stocks and thought of all the ways that she could go broke.

SET ASIDE WORRY TIME

Kathy listed all of her money worries each day for a week. The pattern that emerged was continually predicting she would go broke and not be able to take care of herself.

TEST YOUR PREDICTIONS

Exactly what do you predict will happen? Will you lose all your money, have your house foreclosed on, lose your job, feel humiliated by your friends? When will these terrible events occur? Her recurrent predictions were that her money would run out and she would not be able to pay her bills.

EIGHT WAYS TO DEFEAT YOUR WORRIES

1. *What thinking distortion are you using?* Kathy was fortune-telling ("I'll keep losing money"), catastrophizing ("I'll end up homeless"), discounting the positives ("My equity in my apartment doesn't count since I can't spend it"), and labeling ("I must be an idiot for buying that stock").

2. *How likely is it that this will actually happen?* She was jumping to conclusions that something terrible would happen that in fact has a low probability—for example, "I'll lose all my money." She had only lost a small percentage of her wealth.

3. *What is the worst outcome? The most likely outcome? The best outcome?* The worst outcome was losing all her money, but the most likely outcome was that she would have a cash-flow problem.

4. *Tell yourself a story about better outcomes.* She came up with a detailed story about future earning potential, using a budget, and developing a savings plan. We then put this into an action plan, making it "productive worry."

5. *What is the evidence that something really bad is going to happen?* She was taking a single piece of information—such as stock losses or spending more—and jumping to the conclusion that there would be a terrible financial catastrophe. But she had other resources and other ways of making and saving money in the future.

6. *How many times have you been wrong in the past about your worries?* Her past money worries had been going on for years—and they all had proven false.

7. *Put predictions in perspective.* She could see her current financial concerns as an inconvenience by examining all the things that she could still do even with the current financial problem. In fact, there was nothing she could not do that she had been doing.

She also thought that one loss in her stocks would trigger a chain reaction of other losses. But you might not be able to tell until you are able to stand back and see what the real trend is over a long period of time. Mathematician and investor Nassim

Taleb, in his fascinating book *Fooled by Randomness,* notes that investors often mistake random (and unpredictable) variations in prices of stocks as an indication of trends that they can foresee.[4] If you sit and watch closely the daily fluctuations in prices, you are more inclined to make foolish, emotionally driven trades, absorbing increased trading costs that can wipe out any investment profits you might achieve. I asked her to avoid looking at her stocks for two weeks. This reduced her obsessions.

Finally, she assumed that all her earning potential and financial assets might suddenly disappear. I suggested that she keep in mind her earning potential and her current assets, which were scattered in different investments—stocks, real estate, and pensions.

8. *Show yourself why this is not really a problem.* Let's take Kathy's loss of $25,000 from her portfolio. It seems like a lot of money. But the real question is "What problem has been created by this?" What would she be *unable to do*? Her first thought was, "I won't be able to retire when I expected to retire." Now, for someone who is thirty-nine years old, it's hard to know exactly when you are going to retire. People generally retire in their sixties. But I asked her exactly when she was going to retire and how much she would need. She didn't know—she had some vague idea that it would be sometime "before I'm sixty." Where did this come from? Why not sixty-one? Or fifty-nine? Perhaps Kathy would be in a better position to answer this question in another fifteen years. But was there any *current* problem that she would have? She thought perhaps not having as much in the bank was a problem. But when she had had less in the bank— say, four years ago—had she viewed that as a problem? No— she'd actually thought she was right on track. So when she made more money by luck and then lost it, suddenly the money she'd made by a lucky investment became something she "needed." But needed for what?

I asked her, "What would you do differently if you had not lost that money?" Kathy said, "I'd just let it sit in the bank and gain interest." I asked her to make a list of all the things that she could still do even though she'd lost this money—all the relationships that would continue, work, exercise, learning, entertainment. Kathy realized that everything remained the same.

PUT IT IN PERSPECTIVE

You may focus on a loss in one area and ignore your wealth portfolio. What is a "wealth portfolio?"[5] It includes your stocks, bonds, CDs, cash, real estate, pension plans, objects of value (jewelry, art, cars, boats, furs), and—most importantly for most people—your *future earning potential*. Then calculate all of your debt—the outstanding balance on your mortgage, credit cards, loans, and leases. When Kathy worried about her loss in stocks, she focused on only one part of her wealth portfolio. But when we looked at her entire wealth portfolio, we found that a lot of her portfolio was actually still quite good. In fact, her apartment had increased in value over the past two years, and her earnings were increasing. When we examined her future earning potential, it amazed Kathy to realize that the loss in her stocks was really only a small amount compared to her future earnings.

DON'T CONFUSE PREFERENCE WITH NECESSITY

We think that we absolutely *need* certain things rather than *prefer* them. People have told me that they *need* an expensive apartment, designer clothing, a vacation home, expensive restaurants, and vacations, and that their kids *need* to go to expensive schools. What you think of as needs are simply things that you *prefer* having—and then you tell yourself that *you must have them.* This, of course, fuels your worry—especially when you see your stocks decline in value.

It's nice to be able to buy whatever you want without having to think about it. Still, probably many of the things that you buy that cost more than $50 are completely unnecessary. You could live without them. If you need a Hermès tie to make you feel attractive, then there's something wrong with your self-image, not your tie. If you need your partner to buy you expensive jewelry to prove he loves you, you're probably not getting the more important things that make a relationship work well. No one needs an expensive car. I wear a watch that costs $60; I could afford a more expensive watch, but what is the utility to me of a more expensive watch? I am less interested in spending money on things that will impress other people and more interested in buying books.

If you think something is necessary, then think back to the time before you had it. Let's take the car that you think you need. Did you always have as nice a car? Was there a time you didn't even have a car? Or the clothing, restaurants, travel, house—whatever. I doubt that you were born with all of these things. These things became objects that you possessed or used for a period of time. But if they were really necessary, you would never have been able to live without them. Examples of true necessities are things such as air, water, and food. Designer clothes, dinners in restaurants, and the latest personal computer are *preferences* for some but never a necessity for anyone. When we worry about money, we often think about the things we would prefer having. Some of these things may cost a good deal of money. But if you think of them as alternatives rather than necessities, then you will worry less.

Step Four: Focus on the Deeper Threat

MONEY WORRIES AND YOUR CORE ISSUES

Your money worries reflect your personal core beliefs or your personality style. For example, if you have an overly conscientious personality, you will fear losing control, regretting mistakes, and not taking care of your responsibilities. You will likely hoard your money, criticize your partner for spending too much, and be reluctant to make purchases. In contrast, if you are dependent in your relationships and believe you would be helpless without someone to rely on, you worry you could end up destitute and alone, and you will need someone to take care of you. If you believe that you should be special and superior, then your worries will focus on the possibility that you cannot have the unique and superior lifestyle that others will envy, leading you to fear becoming inferior to everyone because you are not superior to everyone. Examples of these personality styles, money worries, coping strategies, and the problems that they create in your relationships are shown in the table below. Kathy's issue was the need to be conscientious and special.

TABLE 14.3

PERSONALITY AND MONEY WORRIES

Personality	Perception of debt	Adaptation	Money and relationships
Conscientious	Small debts will lead to total losses. Debt is a sign of being irresponsible and out of control. Debt means failure.	Hoard Compulsive work Inhibited spending Overinsure Criticize spending Indecisive over large purchases	Withholds from partner Worries that partner will be irresponsible—creating vulnerability Criticizes partner for spending too much money

Personality	Perception of debt	Adaptation	Money and relationships
Dependent	Someone else will rescue me and take care of the debt. I could end up with nothing. I can't take care of this on my own.	Try to please others Seek reassurance from partner Avoid thinking about unpleasant financial issues Idealize partner Self-deny	Expects partner to take care of him/her Hides information from partner about expenses Does not develop self-reliance, expecting partner will protect him/her Defers to partner on investments, expenses, taxes, etc. Feels obligated to partner because of financial dependence.
Special and unique	I can handle anything. I'm entitled to have whatever I want. My schemes will work out.	Purchase prestigious and expensive items Overextend credit Look for get-rich-quick schemes Use alcohol or drugs to escape from financial problems	Tries to impress partner with great success and wealth Expects partner to lavish expensive gifts and tribute Uses money to create obligations in partner Extravagant spending makes partner fear financial instability

Personality	Perception of debt	Adaptation	Money and relationships
Dramatic	I won't think of it now. It's too disturbing. It'll make me feel great to have what I want right now.	Avoid financial information Impulsive spending Overextend credit Seduce to get others to buy	Viewed by partner as frivolous and irresponsible in purchases Does not cooperate with partner in financial planning or budgeting, viewing it as too constraining and depriving
Antisocial	The others (e.g., creditors) can afford it. They have more than I do. They'll never catch me. I should get what I want right now.	Steal and lie Evade taxes Illegal activities— illicit drug sales, small and large theft, embezzlement Trick others Borrow Use alcohol or drugs to seek excitement and comfort	Steals from partner Hides information from partner Creates credit risks that partner fears Takes investment risks that jeopardize financial stability

ARE YOU TAKING IT PERSONALLY?

Kathy then turned to her feelings about regret. "I'm not only worried about my finances in the future—I regret having bought that stock that crashed. I shouldn't have been such an idiot." Kathy was experiencing *hindsight bias*. This means that she believed after the fact that she had known all of the important information before her decision. In other words, her hindsight is

20-20—she thinks she knew it was a bad decision when she made the decision. But did she know?

Kathy had been relying on information that millions of people rely on—the financial news, brokers, and analysts. And she wasn't alone in buying stocks that crashed. In fact, in 2002 professional investors could actually take credit for *not losing as much* as the market lost. People would have been happy to break even. Of course, almost no one broke even. Why should Kathy think she should have a crystal ball that no one else has?

Step Five: Turn "Failure" into Opportunity

MONEY LOSSES DON'T MEAN YOU FAILED

If you lose money, it doesn't mean that you failed—it may mean that your company is changing, the market is unpredictable, or investments are out of your hands. Think of all of the things that you have succeeded at. Kathy tended to blame herself for her financial loss—but she could also take credit for her positive experiences on the job, her friendships, her decent values, and her other successes in investing and savings.

EXAMINE YOUR STANDARDS FOR FAILURE

We have already seen how we often compare ourselves to people who have more, and we may use a receding reference point—always more and more, no matter how much we have. What are your standards for financial failure? I have known people who make $25,000 per year who do not worry about money and who don't think of themselves as failures, and I have known people who make $500,000 per year who think they are failures because someone else makes a million. The average American family income is about $40,000—are half the country's people failures? Kathy was making more money than 90 percent of people.

LOSSES CAN HELP YOU APPRECIATE MORE

We tend to view our income and assets as a sign of success, but they are simply material possessions. One man who had been unemployed for a year recognized that his wife, children, and health were far more important than the slave-driving atmosphere at work. He told me that his loss of his job was one of the best things that had ever happened to him. I asked Kathy to think of the things she could now appreciate more—such as her friends, her intelligence, the culture that was available to her, and the music that she loved. Appreciating more makes money less valuable and essential.

SOMETHING FOR NOTHING: WHAT YOU CAN GET FOR FREE

I asked Kathy to recall images of the most wonderful times in her life. She remembered walking on the beach at sunset, feeling the water running over her toes, holding her boyfriend's hand. I asked her if there were some things that she could do for free this week. She said, "I can tell my boyfriend I love him. I can watch the sunset from the roof of my building. I can cook dinner with my boyfriend. I can hold him and love him."

I asked Kathy to imagine that everything—all of her possessions, her body, her family, friends, memory—has been taken away. "So now God looks down and says to you, 'You can have one thing back at a time, but I'm not going to tell you how many things I will give you. It's up to you to convince me that each thing is important to you. If you don't, you don't get it back. You decide. Try to convince me. Where do you want to start?'" Kathy started with her senses. "I would need my ability to see and hear and understand, or nothing else would matter." "But what is it you would want to see?" "I want to see my boyfriend. I want to see the sky. I want to see everything around me." "What else?" "My memory, because I would want to remember all the things that mattered to me—like when my boyfriend first told me he loved me and the first time he kissed me."

We laboriously went through each thing and why they mattered. And then I said, "You have all these things right now. You just have to see that they are here for you."

Money wasn't on the list.

If the most important things on the list were things that she already had, then what could failure in money really mean?

MAYBE NO ONE NOTICED

We often think that everyone will notice our financial losses. How could they? Who has access to your accounts? This is something that almost all worriers are bewildered about—they are the only ones concerned about these losses or worries. The only people who knew of Kathy's financial loss were the people she told, and they weren't worried about it in the least. Think about all the people that you know. How many of these people have you been concerned about in terms of their finances? Probably next to none—because you don't consider it particularly relevant to your own life.

TAKE CREDIT FOR PAST SUCCESS

One opportunity that you can take is to view your money losses in the context of all of the past successes that you have had in all areas of your life. Kathy was able to list the following as past successes: her performance on the job, her friendships, her savings, her family relationships, and her health.

Step Six: Use Your Emotions Rather than Worry About Them

NOTICE YOUR FEARS AND EMOTIONS

You may have a range of feelings when you worry about money. Do you feel angry that someone let you down or that you are dependent on someone for money? Do you feel afraid because you don't know what is going to happen? Sad, because you feel a loss or because you feel like a failure? Do you feel helpless? Try to notice what you are feeling and toward whom you have this feeling. Kathy felt self-critical, anxious, and ashamed.

FACE THE WORST CASE

Kathy's worst image was being unemployed, unable to pay her bills, and running down the last dollars in her bank account. We did three things with this. First, I asked her to make a tape about what her life would look like in this worst-case scenario. I then asked her to play the tape for thirty minutes each day and focus on how bad it seemed. As Kathy became more exposed to her worst fear, it seemed more and more implausible. Third, I asked her to tell me what she could do with her time if she were unemployed and had very little money. She thought for a short time and then somewhat happily said, "I'd have more time to read, watch films, and go to museums." Facing the worst case and feeling the fear decreased her worries, since she could imagine even coping with the worst.

KEEP AN EMOTION DIARY

Kathy was so focused on her money worries that she was ignoring her feelings about other things. She kept an emotion diary that recorded her feelings about money (fear), friends (shame and loneliness), and her mother (fear that her mother might be sick). She also noted her positive emotions with her friends (gratitude), mother (happiness and peace), and listening to music (joy). This helped Kathy realize that her emotions were not entirely related to money.

MAKE SENSE OF YOUR EMOTIONS

If you feel sad because you are having financial difficulties, think of how you can validate that your emotions make sense, that your feelings are probably shared by millions of people, that these feelings have come and gone in the past, and that you need not feel ashamed of feeling afraid or sad. You can accept that you are upset right now—and that you can also have other emotions that are positive. Even if you are upset about financial troubles, can you also find other things that you enjoy or laugh at or find interesting? Right before you start worrying, can you notice what feelings you are having? For example, Kathy noticed that she was afraid and sad—and then she started to worry about her money. I asked Kathy to stay with her sad and fearful feeling and validate that she had every right to have these feelings right now.

CLIMB A LADDER TO HIGHER MEANING

She then said, "I don't have any right to be sad or anxious—I have a good job and I have savings." I told Kathy that having feelings is everyone's right, and that feelings contain information about what your values are. Kathy's sadness and anxiety were linked to her *values* of being self-sufficient and successful—she took pride in being a woman who supported herself and was respected. I suggested that these were terrific values for her to embrace and respect and that it made sense that she would feel sad when she thought she was not living up to her values. The ladder that Kathy climbed was: "I want to make enough to support myself, so I don't have to rely on someone else, so I can be independent and strong, so that I can respect myself as a working woman." These were admirable values that she could be proud of.

Step Seven: Take Control of Time

REDUCE URGENCY

Kathy had an unrelenting sense of urgency about money. She needed an answer *right now*. She thought, "I need to make back what I lost . . . I can't stand it." Why this sense of urgency? Why did the money have to be made back right now? What was the disadvantage of demanding an urgent immediate solution? What would actually happen if she did not make the money back right now? This sense of urgency just simply drove her anxiety through the roof. It fed her negative predictions, because then she said, "If I don't get an answer right now, then I think I'll never get an answer!"

THINK OF FUTURE EARNINGS

Think about your losses in terms of your future earnings. Take your current earnings, multiply that figure by the number of years that you are going to work before you retire, include inflation to adjust your income upward, and think about how small your current losses are compared to your future earnings. Let's think of Kathy's loss of $25,000 in terms of her future earnings. If we round her current income to $100,000 (taking into consideration minuscule raises adjusted for inflation) and multiply by 25, then her future earnings are $2.5 million. Now, she will have expenses along the way, but she has already saved a significant amount on her past income, which was lower. Just take the $25,000 and compare it to the $2.5 million. It represents just 1 percent of her future earnings. This doesn't even include her current and future savings. One percent!!!

GET INTO A TIME MACHINE

I asked Kathy to imagine traveling in a time machine five years into the future. What did she see? She saw herself in a more advanced position in her job. She could see herself married to Roger, her current boyfriend, since they had been talking about getting married a lot in the past four months. She saw herself going for walks in the woods. Maybe they'd have a dog—probably one from the shelter. I asked her to describe her typical day five years from now. She would get up at about 7 a.m., she and her husband would have breakfast, she'd take the dog out, and she'd walk to her office—it would be a beautiful September day in New York. Maybe she'd stop at Starbucks for a decaf special blend. She'd go up to her office, which had a nice view. And then she would get to work on an account for the company in Cleveland. Since I had Kathy in a mental time machine, I asked her to go back into the past and look at some of her worries ten years ago. What had she been worried about then? She'd worried she'd never get a job in public relations—but she had in fact gotten a good job. She'd worried she'd never be able to afford an apartment in New York—but she'd gotten lucky and found an affordable one. She'd worried she wouldn't find a partner—and now she was happily involved.

WHAT MADE YOU HAPPIER WHEN YOU HAD LESS?

Kathy is like a lot of people who believe that once they have a certain amount of money, they can't live without it. What they never had before has become essential today. I asked Kathy to tell me what she'd done for fun when she had less. Kathy made a list of things she'd enjoyed when she had less: conversations with friends, working, sex with her partner, seeing puppies, laughing, reading, listening to music, cooking delicious food, movies, looking at old photographs, fall foliage, sleeping, seeing the sunset, walking on the beach, trying to tell a joke, traveling, the smell of rain on the leaves, walking in the woods, the feel of the water when she swam, looking at moss on the side of a rock . . . the list seemed to be endless. Most importantly, almost none of these experiences cost her anything.

STRETCH TIME

Most worries have an element of nearsightedness in that we often believe that what is happening right in front of us at this moment is an indication of a lasting and progressive (or regressive) trend. Like many other worries, we have a difficult time standing back and gaining a longer perspective. Being nearsighted could give you a very unrealistic perspective. Standing back, seeing all the data, and taking a longer time horizon that includes past and the future can completely change your sense of what is happening. When Kathy drew a chart of her earnings and savings, she realized that she was gradually accumulating more—especially compared to the time when she had no savings.

When we worry about money, we often feel that the game is almost over—but, in fact, it may only be the third inning in a nine-inning game. When you lose money, you might want to consider how many more innings there are. This is called your "time horizon."[6] How many more times can you collect a paycheck or save money? How many more years do you have? Kathy had another twenty-five years of earnings and savings.

Summing Up

The demands on consumer spending, the extension of credit, the insecurity of the labor force, the volatility of the stock market, and upward comparisons make us vulnerable to worrying about money. However, there are numerous techniques and concepts that you can use to understand your money worries and transform them. We have seen that worrying about money is seldom productive—in fact, it may be more productive and enjoyable to do things that don't cost you anything. Worries about money that you may or may not use in the future deprives you of enjoying and appreciating the present moment.

We have seen that money comes to symbolize things to you—success, security, acceptance, status, or freedom. But it may be overvalued. In fact, the research on money shows that when people earn more, their happiness increases only slightly for a short period of time. In fact, some people spend so much time either worrying about money or trying to earn more that their quality of life decreases.

The real security lies in developing a "life portfolio" that includes relationships, intimacy, work, personal growth, and a sense of community. Your sense of urgency when you are faced with worries about money can be tempered by a sense of appreciation for the present moment. The question to ask yourself when you worry about possible financial losses or pressures is "What can I still do that has meaning for me?"

Maybe it will be free.

15

___

Work Worries:
What if I Really Mess Up?

ANXIETY ABOUT WORK is increasingly more common as we read about people being "downsized," companies going out of business, skills becoming obsolete, and our reliance on dual-career incomes to make ends meet. Recent social trends indicate the following sources of worry:

- We are more worried about losing our jobs—and that we won't get an equivalent job, or even any job.
- Rapid changes in technology add to the probability that our skills will become obsolete.
- Staying with a company for many years is now the exception to the rule—unlike our parents, who could count on job security.
- We spend more time at work than our parents did—making us the "overworked Americans."

We worry about what our boss might think, promotions, getting the project done, and getting evaluated. We worry that, should we lose our jobs, we will experience a downward drift in the job market, ending up with an "inferior" job, one that will make us feel like a failure. We worry because things aren't fair—and then we dwell on the unfairness for hours. We worry that our work will be criticized—and then we either procrastinate about doing it or we exhaust ourselves doing the perfect job. We view criticism as a certain sign of our incompetence, revealing that we are really "impostors," undeserving of any job at all. Our worries result from perfectionism, our desire for fairness and appreciation on our jobs, increased work hours (and the tendency to take more work home), loss of community outside of work, and social trends that make jobs less secure. While we procrastinate we think, "I need to do a perfect job or I will be criticized." As we wait to feel ready to do the perfect job, putting things off longer and longer, we then worry about getting it in late. This makes us feel more anxious—leading to more procrastination and more fears of antagonizing the boss.

Our worries about work are compounded by five factors—the "impostor syndrome," the need for fairness and appreciation, perfectionism, overworked Americans, and the decline in community. Let's look at each of these factors.

The Impostor Syndrome

You may believe that people view you in a way that is inconsistent with your underlying self-doubts. Psychologists Harvey and Katz found that some people have the "impostor syndrome"—they think they have fooled others into overestimating their abilities, they fear being exposed as a fraud, and they attribute their success to luck or easy work rather than ability or effort.[1] This underlying self-doubt adds to your worries that your performance will eventually collapse and you will be exposed.

The Need for Fairness and Appreciation

You may view work as the place where you should be appreciated, treated fairly, or cared about. If you view work in terms of these personal need gratifications, then you see criticism as a sign that you are a victim. You become resentful that your boss and colleagues don't express their gratitude that you are doing your job—or that you are exerting yourself to the limits of your endurance. You may view this, along with any criticism, as evidence that you are not being treated fairly, further fueling your resentments about the work environment and your worries that there may be other hidden factors that can come back to hurt you. These hidden factors can become, in your mind, the signs that you are not part of the group, that you have fallen out of favor with the boss, or that promotion will be blocked or you will be terminated.

You may begin to feel that there is no equity—no fairness—at work, leading you to reduce your input—you work less, care less about quality, and delay getting things done.[2] As this passive-aggressive style unfolds, this triggers your worry that your withholding behavior will be noticed and that you will be reprimanded and fired.

Perfectionism

The fear that our work is not good enough may cause us to become work-absorbed, leading us to spend inordinate amounts of time at work, sacrificing time with our families, and forgoing sleep, recreation, and exercise. People whose work absorption conflicts with family life are twenty-nine times more likely to have physical and mental health problems.[3] As work becomes the sole focus of our entire lives, any rewards that we may gain—and any perspective that we could have—are lost as our contacts with friends evaporate, our partners are no longer a major source of support, and we are no longer available to our children. Ironically, as the balance is lost in our personal lives, we may be more likely to become even more obsessed with work, leading to greater absorption. This narrowed focus enhances our worries, since everything is now staked on the workplace. Work worries can persist and result in burnout, characterized by exhaustion, cynicism, indifference, withdrawal, and reduced productivity.[4] This can eventually lead some people to leave the workforce.[5]

Overworked Americans

Harvard economist Juliet Schor indicates that over the last twenty years there has been an increase in the number of hours per year we spend at work—a trend that reverses earlier historical trends of working fewer hours.[6] As we demand more and more from ourselves at work, our time for family, sleep, and leisure declines. Although we earn more and consume more than we did in previous decades, we have less free time. This is further compounded by the rise of dual-career families, where women are trying to perform the role of mother and worker simultaneously. Ironically, though, the corporate entities that we may work for have less commitment to providing employees with the security of a career within the firm, due to frequent merging, downsizing, and changes that lead to rapid turnover. As we focus more on our commitment to work, companies have reduced their commitment to their workers.

Decline in Community

A parallel social trend is the decline in community—a sense that you par-ticipate on a regular basis with other people to pursue common goals, activities, values, or interests. Harvard social historian Robert Putnam captures this in his provocative book *Bowling Alone: The Collapse and Revival of American Community*.[7] Putnam describes a sense of community as "social capital"—that is, the "connections among individuals and the social networks and the norms of reciprocity and trustworthiness that arise from them" (p. 19). The decline in community is reflected in the fact that participation in civil organizations—such as church groups, unions, interest groups, and political groups—has declined, marriages are more likely to end in divorce, people move more frequently, friendships last for shorter periods of time, and jobs are more tenuous. This lack of community is reflected in the fact that people "bowl alone" rather than in the leagues or groups of men and women who bowled together forty years ago.

This lack of community outside of work can make us more vulnerable in terms of our work performance, since we may feel we do not have a community to turn to for perspective and support. Moreover, without a community to connect with, we begin to believe that our personal and private needs can only be met at work. This adds to our risk for worry, since work will seldom meet the needs that a community can provide.

Mia's Worries and Resentments

Mia had been working for the past two years in a small marketing firm, and she noticed that Paula—her boss—favored Laura. Mia couldn't understand why. After all, Mia got to work on time, did all the work she was supposed to do, and never made any trouble. Not only that, but Mia did more work than Laura, and she was better at doing it. Mia went home, had a drink, and then thought, "Why does Paula favor Laura? What am I doing wrong?" When Mia went into the office she looked for signs that Paula was not friendly toward her. Since Mia looked for rejection, she frowned and was aloof toward Paula. Mia vacillated between resenting the fact that she was not appreciated and doubting her own abilities. The economy had been on a downturn for months, and her industry was being hit hard. Mia worried she would lose her job if Paula was forced to choose between her and Laura. As Mia worried about losing her job, she engaged in mind reading ("Paula doesn't like my work"), personalization ("I must be the only one that is doing badly here"), fortune-telling ("I will probably be let go soon"), catastrophizing ("If I lose my job I will never get another job"), and labeling ("This proves what a loser I really am— that I can't seem to do well at work").

Mia believed that worrying about this would lead to an answer, give her reassurance, and reduce any uncertainty that she had. She believed that this worry would be a way to solve the problem, avoid any surprises in the future, and make her feel calmer. Mia could not stand the uncertainty of not knowing whether she would keep or lose her job, so she kept worrying in search of this certainty, never obtaining it.

When Mia thought that she would lose her job, she imagined herself out of work endlessly, and saw other people humiliating her for her failure. Not having a job was equivalent with being a failure as a person, in her mind, and she thought the job market was so terrible she might never get a job. She then recalled a story that she read in a magazine about a computer programmer in California who had drifted into bankruptcy during the dot-com bust in the San Jose area. She thought, "This is what will happen to me."

Mia couldn't sleep because she was worrying about her job, her lack of support in the office—and now about falling asleep. She then thought that after losing more sleep she would be even less effective, less alert, and more debilitated the next day. She worried that her lack of energy—and now her depression— would keep her from performing her job adequately and that she would finally get fired for her incompetence.

Seven Steps to Overcoming Work Worries

Step One: Identify Productive and Unproductive Worry

EXAMINE YOUR THEORY OF WORRY

Mia thought that worry was a way to figure out her problems, avoid surprise, and be prepared for the worst that could happen. She thought her worry would help motivate her to do a better job. But she could find no evidence that she was solving her problems or preparing for the worst. She was simply repeating worries without any workable solutions for her to carry out.

PRODUCTIVE AND UNPRODUCTIVE WORRY

Mia focused on unanswerable questions ("Why am I being treated unfairly?), a chain reaction of events ("Paula will be displeased, I will get fired, and I will never get another job"), unknowable information ("What is my boss thinking?"), a demand for perfect solutions ("I need to have absolute certainty that I will never get fired"), and events beyond her control (such as the downsizing that occurs in a recession). Her worry focused on potential negatives that led her to feel responsible to solve every possible problem that she could imagine. Although nothing really terrible had happened at work, Mia superstitiously believed that her worry had prevented her from getting fired. I asked Mia to look at the difference between worries about the unknown future—"I might never get another job"—and worries about current behavior that could be addressed by taking immediate action. What immediate action could Mia take?

Mia felt that Laura was always "sucking up" to Paula, asking her about her weekend and her trips: "She seems to be friendlier than I am." Mia felt that being overly friendly toward Paula was "not my job." I asked Mia if her goals on the job were to have influence on Paula, to get more responsibility, and to eventually advance. When she said these were her goals, I suggested that developing a better relationship with Paula might be part of the job. I suggested that the productive worry is "I am not getting these accounts done." We decided Mia should try an experiment—act friendlier toward Paula every day for two weeks and complete two assignments she'd been procrastinating on.

Mia carried out these two assignments—being friendlier toward Paula and getting the accounts done. Much to her surprise, Paula was friendly toward her. This actually opened up a conversation with Paula, who told Mia she had had the sense that Mia was unhappy working there, since she seemed to keep to herself. As Paula and Mia exchanged more small talk, Mia felt less anxious. Mia had gotten locked into a self-fulfilling prophecy—she assumed that Paula disliked her, so she withdrew, which made Paula act less friendly toward her. By taking action that was strategic and acted against her worry, Mia was able to disconfirm the negative beliefs that drove her worry.

Step Two: Accept and Commit

There were two things that Mia had difficulty accepting—the uncertainty of her job and the unfairness of how things were working in the office. We started first with learning how to accept uncertainty.

ACCEPT UNCERTAINTY

Mia was intolerant of the uncertainty about losing her job and her uncertainty about how Paula felt about her, and she believed that worrying about this might reduce the uncertainty. Since there was no way of achieving complete certainty about the security of her job, she continued to loop back into more worry: "I need to worry to gain certainty—I don't have certainty—I need to continue to worry." I asked Mia to examine the costs and benefits of accepting uncertainty.

Mia thought that if she accepted uncertainty she would worry less, feel more relaxed at work, and probably get her job done more effectively. But she also said that if she accepted uncertainty she could be caught by surprise and get fired. However, Mia recognized that worrying had not eliminated uncertainty.

ACCEPT UNFAIRNESS AS A REALITY

Mia said, "I want to be assertive and go tell Paula that she isn't being fair with me. She gives all her attention to Laura. I can't believe that Paula spends all that time talking with Laura." Mia kept ruminating about this—"Why doesn't she treat me fairly? Did I do something that offended her? Is she unhappy with my work? Is she going to replace me?" The fact that she wasn't treated fairly made her feel like a loser. But it may be inevitable that you will be treated unfairly at work. I am not suggesting that you should never assert yourself, but an overemphasis on fairness can lead to rumination, worry, and self-defeating confrontations with your boss. Three questions arise when you think that you are not being treated fairly:

1. What does it mean to you that you are not being treated fairly? Does it mean that you are not competent, that your job is on the line, that your boss is a terrible person?
2. What responses are you likely to take when you are treated unfairly? Are you likely to become passive-aggressive, resentful, withholding, or antagonistic?
3. What are your most important goals at work? Are they to be appreciated and treated fairly—or to get your job done, secure your job, and achieve greater rewards and power?

I suggested she take the following approach:

- View unfairness as *part of the job*. It is not unique to you; it is part of being an employee.
- Identify positive work-related goals—get the job done, secure your position, and achieve advancement.
- Do not expect that because you are an expert or good at what you do that this will be *sufficient* for success at work. You may need to learn how to "play the game."
- Develop a *strategic approach* to your boss and your work.

This was radical acceptance—that is, the recognition that *the world is as it is* and that *this is the reality from which you begin*. Radical acceptance does not imply that you like the way things are, and it does not imply that you have not been treated unfairly. However, it does imply that you view things realistically and you do not focus on protesting, complaining, and ruminating. In Mia's case, radical acceptance meant accepting as a reality that she might not be treated fairly, and then developing a strategy of how to deal with this reality. Mia examined one strategy—going into Paula's office and asserting herself. Now, assertion can often be an excellent problem-solving tactic because you can sometimes identify some productive changes that the other person can make that will make things better. However, I also often find that direct confrontational assertion at work can jeopardize your status. Your boss may not care about how you feel and may view your confrontation as insubordination. This could actually jeopardize your position.

An alternative strategy is to become a "gamesman." This is an orientation toward the workplace where you do the following:

- Establish the goal of achieving greater security on the job and getting the work done.
- Determine who controls the rewards on this job and which alliances it would be good to form.
- Figure out how to reward people who have power and who control rewards.

You might consider this approach too manipulative or Machiavellian. I can understand that objection, but I also would argue that this is a *professional* way to look at work. Work entails getting the work done, coordinating your work with others, and developing interpersonal strategies to become more effective. It also means working with people you may not like. That is part of the job.

The first thing to consider is who controls the rewards— whose opinion is worth cultivating? Certainly, your boss's goodwill is important—but it also may be the case that the office administrator or colleagues with equal or lower job status have an influence on who gets rewarded. For example, the boss's administrative assistant may be the most influential person in the office. Cultivating that person as an ally may be essential for you. If that person is your ally, you might end up worrying a lot less.

The key thing is to find out *what the game is*. Who gets rewarded and for what? Mia's mistake was that she thought that the only thing that was rewarded was going to her desk and working hard. When I asked Mia to tell me what Laura was being rewarded for, she said it was asking Paula about herself, talking to her about the news, and getting her coffee. We decided to look at this as the *game* that Mia had to play to get ahead. Mia protested that this wasn't "professional" or "fair." Perhaps it's not fair—if you think that the only game is to reward you for your performance. But this might be the way the real world is set up. In fact, it might actually be what is involved in being a professional—learning what the game is and playing it to win. Mia decided to adapt this strategic approach, rather than feel like a victim who was helpless and forced into a corner of resentment and passivity. We made a list of strategic goals for each week, such as complimenting the office administrator, talking with Paula about Paula's weekend and her interests, and reinforcing her coworkers for their good work. Mia had been thinking, "Hey, I'm doing a great job. Why doesn't she appreciate me?" Mia thought that being an expert was the only thing on the job that would count. In fact, Mia thought that hanging out and joking with her colleagues was a waste of time.

Step Three: Challenge Your Worried Thinking

EXAMINE AND CHALLENGE YOUR DISTORTED THINKING

Mia was engaging in mind reading, personalization, fortune-telling, labeling, catastrophizing, and discounting positives. We examined some of these thoughts, collected evidence, and set up predictions. Mia set up her predictions—Paula would be unfriendly (100 percent) and Mia would lose her job in three months (50 percent). I asked her what could be the best possible outcome, the worst outcome, and the most likely outcome if she started being more friendly toward Paula. She said, "The best outcome is that she is really friendly toward me. The worst outcome is that she fires me when I talk to her. And the most likely outcome is that she is cordial but not really warm." I then asked her to tell me a possible story about a really good outcome at work. Mia said, "Well, let's see. I could start talking with her at work, she could start telling me about her personal life, she could become friendly toward me, and she could begin to appreciate my work." She also came up with a positive story about leaving the job: "I could lose this job, get into the job market, move out of the city, and find a good job in a place I really want to live in. That could happen because I am really competent and I work hard and I am willing to relocate." I asked her, "What advice would you give a friend if she were as worried as you are?" "I'd tell her, 'You are doing a really good job. You could develop some strategies to become disarming and charming toward your boss. Just focus on what you can do right now. Also, you could always get another job if you needed one.'"

Step Four: Focus on the Deeper Threat

EXAMINE THE CORE BELIEFS

Mia's core belief was that she was inadequate and that people would immediately think this if her boss criticized her. Her deeper thought was that the real reason that Paula was so unfair was that she realized how inadequate and inferior Mia was. She thought, "Maybe I'm not as good as Laura" and "If Paula doesn't tell me I'm doing a good job, she must see that I'm really not that smart." She said that she tried to make up for her inadequacy by "trying really hard—I work long hours and I worry about my mistakes. I review things after I do them and think about how it could have been better." This is called a postmortem—you review your work after the fact and then only focus on mistakes. She said, "Maybe I can learn from my mistakes and get better." Mia ignored her positives—since she thought this was expected of her—so there was no way for her to see any evidence of her adequacy. When she looked at her positive performance she said, "Well, other people do better." This led to her core belief, "If I am not the best, then I am inadequate."

CHALLENGE THE SOURCE OF YOUR CORE BELIEF

Where did Mia get this idea that she was inadequate? "My older brother was nearly a genius. He had terrific grades, got into a great college. The teachers were always comparing me to him—I did well, I guess, but not as well as him. And my father really favored him over me." I asked, "Even if your older brother was nearly a genius, does this mean that you are inadequate?" Mia realized this wasn't rational. I asked her to imagine arguing against her father's perfectionism, and she said, "I wish I could tell him that I am good enough and I deserved better treatment. He wasn't fair with me."

DEVELOP YOUR BILL OF RIGHTS

Mia said she always worried about how someone in authority would view her performance, whether it was her teachers or her bosses. We decided to develop a Bill of Rights for Someone Who Is Good Enough: *I have the right to make mistakes, to be less than perfect, to grow through my experiences and mistakes, to have a learning curve, and to be human.* We tested out the Bill of Rights by using the double-standard technique: were these good rules for someone else? Mia said she used these rules for accepting other people, because she felt people should be treated decently. The new challenge, however, was to apply these standards to herself.

Step Five: Turn "Failure" into Opportunity

CHALLENGE THE FEAR OF FAILURE

Mia worried that if her work was ever criticized, this meant that she was a failure. What did "failure" mean—how could someone "be a failure"? "If they don't accomplish what they want to accomplish," Mia said. But wouldn't everyone be a failure, then, since all of us will fall short of some goals? "A person is a failure if they can't have the success that they want," Mia elaborated. I asked her to tell me the names of some failures that she knew, and she replied, "I don't think of people that way. But I think that I could become a failure if I don't watch myself." Mia believed that worrying was keeping her from being a failure. But weren't there some things on the job she was doing well? "Actually almost everything," she admitted. I suggested, "Rather than saying, 'I'm a failure,' you have a lot of other things to think about: 'It's hard for almost everyone, I could learn from this experience, it's a challenge.' "

Mia had thought that failure at work was final—"It's over and I am a failure." I suggested that she think about the thousands of tasks that she will do—this is just one of them. There will be other successes in the future. I said, "It's like walking on a narrow board that is suspended a hundred feet in the air—one mistake is fatal. But what if you were to put the board five inches off the ground?" "I'd be less afraid—less worried," Mia realized. "You can't fall as far."

PUT FAILURE IN PERSPECTIVE

Mia and I examined her other ideas about failure. These included her belief that she should never fail at something, that everyone would notice her mistakes and dwell on them, and that her failure would be a permanent defect for her. I asked Mia to examine the idea that she should never fail, by considering the fact that failure is inevitable—that making mistakes is part of the process of working. We also looked at her belief that everyone would be thinking about her failure, rather than the reality that people may understand that making mistakes is part of the job. Furthermore, she had no evidence that people were spending much time thinking about any of her work—indeed, this was what she complained about. However, if people were not thinking about her work all the time, this might also mean that making mistakes would be relatively unimportant to her colleagues or to her boss. Finally, if failures or mistakes were part of the process—and if they were generally followed by some productive and successful behaviors—then failures could not imply a permanent defect. Since Mia was worried about failing, and since she believed that worry prevented her from failing, taking the importance away from failure was an essential component of changing her worry.

USE CRITICAL FEEDBACK AS A LEARNING EXPERIENCE

She told me that the fact that her work had been criticized meant that she wasn't competent and could get fired. She viewed the critical feedback as devastating and terrible—it meant that she was a failure, and failures generally give up. Critical feedback, however, is inevitable at work—as it is in intimate relationships. Imagine that you want to get better at tennis. Which would be more valuable to you—someone telling you that you are a wonderful person or someone telling you the mistakes that you are making and how to correct them? Critical feedback is a great opportunity to learn how to improve your work so that it can be as good as you can make it.

As we looked at the critical feedback that Paula gave her, Mia saw that it was mixed feedback—some positive and some negative. But the negative feedback was "corrective feedback"—it told Mia what she needed to do to make it better. It turned out that Mia needed to be more concise—more to the point. But because Mia was focused on how bad the feedback felt to her, she overlooked the information that she could use. Critical feedback does not mean that you are incompetent—it means that you are not perfect and that you can improve. Everyone gets critical feedback—if they don't, then they are talking to the wrong people.

I asked Mia to make a list of the positive and negative points that Paula had made about her work. It was initially a lot easier for her to list the negative points—reflecting her biased negative thinking in recalling feedback from Paula. I then asked Mia to list the behaviors and strategies that she could use to address this feedback, and also to list why it was useful to have this kind of feedback. Mia said, "My gut feeling is I would prefer just getting praise, but I know that the way to get better is to make changes and to learn from feedback. I guess it's helpful to me because Paula does have a lot of experience in this area. She has some expertise."

FOCUS ON OTHER BEHAVIORS THAT WILL SUCCEED
Create Alternatives to This Job
I remember a conversation I had with a business executive many years ago about job security. In his current position as a leading executive he could get fired that very day, but he said he never worried about getting fired, because he had skills the market demanded. So why worry about falling or failing or getting fired? For me this was a revolutionary idea. *Security is in the marketplace*—not with any particular job. What skills would the marketplace demand? If your company went out of business, what alternatives for work would you be able to pursue?

Very few people stay in their jobs or with the same company for more than a few years. People are constantly changing jobs. Security might mean knowing that you have a parachute of skills that you can land with. Mia was so worried about criticism, feeling marginalized at work, and not being appreciated that she kept thinking, "I will get fired." She treated this thought as an imminent reality and believed that she would never be able to cope with not having this job. The current job became, in her mind, an essential component of her life. I asked her, "What would happen if they told you the company is going bankrupt and everyone will be let go next month?" "It's interesting. I would feel relieved. I'd feel, 'It's not my fault I am out of work.'" Mia said she would begin to network and look for a job: "I think if I am realistic, I could get a job. In the past year, two companies approached me." But she went on, "It's humiliating to get fired." I said, "Millions of people get fired or lose their jobs. How do they cope?" I suggested that while she was considering alternatives, she could strengthen her position on the current job by creating "added value." Not everyone who has a job will keep their job, and not everyone will get promoted. "If you are worried about your job," I said, "then think about how you can convince your boss that you add special value. What additional work and what additional skills can you develop that will make you seem indispensable?"

Develop a Community Outside of Work

Because Mia had become so focused and worried about work, she had less and less time for friends and other activities, which meant that the only meaning and satisfaction came from how her boss responded to her. Mia decided to change this by contacting friends, seeing her mother and her sister more often, dating more, and getting involved in her church. At her church there was a need for volunteers to work on a housing rehabilitation program. She joined this group on the weekends, working with other volunteers in a poor area of the city: "I realized that there are a lot of people a lot worse off—but I can make a difference. And I found that the people who volunteer are the kind of people I want to be with. It's funny, I used to do volunteer work a few years ago, but I got so career-oriented that I lost touch with that part of myself." Developing a sense of community outside of work helped Mia put work worries in perspective. When she began to worry, she could look forward to seeing friends, helping people, and belonging to something greater than herself.

Step Six: Use Your Emotions Rather than Worry About Them

ACCEPT AND USE EMOTION
I believed that Mia's angry feelings were really covering up

the anxiety, helplessness, and confusion that she felt. As we dug deeper behind her anger Mia said, "I feel confused because I don't know what I should be doing. It makes me feel like I don't know how to change. Sometimes I feel helpless." I said, "Sometimes we worry in order to try to get rid of these difficult feelings. I wonder if you are doing this. And sometimes we can't stand having mixed feelings—like we want to have only one feeling. I sense in your case that feeling is anger." Mia nodded and said, "It's easier for me to feel angry than to feel anxious." As it turned out, she was afraid of her anxiety—she feared that if she felt anxious, then she would break down, start crying, humiliate herself, and appear weak. She tried to cover up the anxiety with worry (looking for solutions), anger, and hard work. I decided to have her use some mindfulness techniques to give her the experience of anxious feelings with detached awareness.[8]

I asked Mia to form an image that she had been fired: "You are now out of a job and you are sitting in your apartment feeling very anxious." Her anxiety began to increase, and I asked her to concentrate on her heartbeat. "Don't try to change it. Breathe slowly—breathe in, out. Hold the breath for seven seconds, breathe out seven seconds. Good. Now, as you are breathing, try to notice your heart beating rapidly. Stand back in your mind and detach from it. Watch it. Don't try to change it. Just let it happen." After she had been focused on her breathing and her heartbeat for a few minutes, I asked her to allow herself to have the thought "I am inadequate." "Let that thought flow into your mind very slowly. Do not try to change this thought. Just let it happen. Watch yourself having the thought. Stand back, allow the thought to flow in and out like the waves on a beach." I asked Mia to practice this for thirty minutes each day. "When you have the thought that you are inadequate—during the day—just practice the breathing along with the detachment. Use the image of the wave on the shore as the thought—and let the wave come in gently and go out gently."

Mia was overly attached to her negative thoughts and feelings, dwelling on them and giving them great importance. The goal of mindfulness was to become more detached and less "moved" by thoughts and sensations that might occur. By becoming more detached and more observant, her worries would decrease. Rather than worry to get rid of thoughts and sensations, she could become mindfully detached and learn that allowing the thoughts to come and go like waves on a beach would detract from their importance for her.

FACE THE WORST FEAR

Mia's worries were an attempt to avoid the image of her worst fear—"I would lose my job and be unemployed indefinitely. I see myself sitting in my apartment in the dark thinking, 'I will never get a job.' It makes me cringe to think of it." I told Mia that she would need to practice that fear. I asked Mia to repeat this thought and this image for fifteen minutes in the session. Then I told her to practice this image every day for twenty minutes, focusing on what she was saying. She repeated this image fifty times whenever it occurred to her during the day so that she could learn to tolerate the image. Her anxiety began to decrease.

CLIMB A LADDER OF MEANING

As psychologist Leslie Greenberg claims, our painful feelings are a window into higher values that we have.[9] I suggested to Mia that when she worried about her performance she was looking for something important—something that pointed to her higher values. Mia replied, "When I worry about not doing well, I believe that if I *did* do well, then I would get recognition for doing a good job." She then climbed a ladder of what recognition would mean—"I am conscientious, responsible, worthwhile— that I can pull my weight."

I could see that Mia felt more positive as we climbed the ladder to higher values. Ironically, she had been using worry, defensiveness, perfectionism, and personalizing to deal with these feelings, so I thought we could examine how these were positive goals—and goals that she was already achieving. "Can you tell me some ways in which you are conscientious at work right now?" Mia said, "I always get into work on time. I get my work done—I work really hard. I try to do my best." Then I asked, "Is it possible that you are already conscientious and you are already pulling your weight?" Mia replied, "I guess I am. But I could be doing more." "Are you saying that the only way to be conscientious is to be perfect?" Mia thought for a moment and then said, "I guess that is a core problem for me . . . never good enough."

Mia decided to keep a "competency record" every day—listing everything that she did at work that was at least somewhat positive. Much to her surprise, she was accomplishing a tremendous amount, but because she had been a perfectionist, she had been focused on the few things that were unfinished or imperfect. The laddering technique revealed her positive values of being conscientious and pulling her weight, but her cognitive distortions and perfectionism led her to discount these positives.

Step Seven: Take Control of Time

IMPROVE THE MOMENT

Mia's obsessive worries about work occupied her when she was alone at home. In order to use time more effectively, she decided to improve her moments at home by scheduling activities that had nothing to do with work. Mia's list for improving the moment included the following: listening to classical music, reading poetry, talking to friends on the phone, renting foreign movies, and drawing. She also decided to take a yoga class, which helped her with her mindfulness and detachment. She learned how to do meditative breathing, slow down her thinking, become less attached to her thoughts and worries, and become more aware of her sensations.

STRETCH TIME

Mia's worries focused on little things that she blew up in her mind as the "future." I asked Mia to recall things at work that she had been worried about in past years. She had worried two years ago about getting criticized at work—only to find out that she got a larger-than-expected raise. She had worried six months ago about what her boss thought of her—only to find out that her boss was merely trying to get information about what work was being done. Along with stretching time by going back to the past, she was able to stretch time by projecting herself in the future. She anticipated that next week she would be less worried about what was going on today, because new things had to be done and projects came and went. Finally, she was able to stretch time by scheduling "Mia goals" in the future—plans to see friends, dates, classes, and a hiking trip. As she escaped from the immediate moment of the worry to the future activities that she would pursue, she became less concerned about things at work.

Summing Up

Many people who worry about work will worry about not getting the job done, getting criticized by their boss or by their colleagues, or getting fired. There are social and economic factors that have contributed to this growing anxiety about work—the rapid changes in the economy lead to some of our skills becoming obsolete, companies merge and downsize their workforce, and there is a reduction of civil community, such as church groups, interest groups, and participation in political organizations. Work has become more insecure, and community support—especially from family—has declined.

As we can see with Mia, there is a tendency to worry in order to motivate ourselves to try harder and to avoid being caught by surprise. However, worry about work can lead you to personalize, mind read, and jump to conclusions that are unwarranted. These anxieties interfere with your performance and, in some cases, result in burnout. We often have tunnel vision—that work is everything and that there is no meaning or possibility in life beyond the current job. Our fear of failing results in our inability to accept constructive feedback as an opportunity to learn and can result in our fear that negative comments from our boss reveals the incompetence that lies beneath our façade of competence.

No amount of hard work or perspective-taking can eliminate the possibility that you could ever lose your job. Excellent and productive employees lose their jobs every day. Worrying about this, however, does not increase your chances of remaining in the current job. You can use acceptance, uncertainty training, and constructing alternatives in the marketplace as strategies for coping with possibilities that may eventually be beyond your control. Indeed, normalizing the fluidity of the job market— where people come and go in different companies—may be the most realistic view.

Creating alternatives to work will help you place your job in perspective. It will also help you step back when you need to and develop strategies for finding even better, more profitable, and meaningful work. Rather than worry because you view yourself as the victim of authority and evaluation, you can begin to develop strategic ideas to take control of your own behavior and thoughts. You can gain alternatives in meaning by balancing work with participation in a larger community—gaining support from friends, family, and civic organizations. Stepping back from work on a regular basis makes the few worries of work seem less essential.

Another source of worry and rumination is our tendency to view conflicts at work or criticism as an indication that we are being treated unfairly. We certainly should value being treated fairly, but this is not always plausible in a work setting.

Moreover, what we view as fairness someone else may view as necessary feedback or simply "the way things are done." It may be necessary at times to leave a job where the environment is oppressive, but this is seldom the case, in my estimation, for people who are worried about work. Rather, intolerance of critical feedback and the demand that one be appreciated and cared for all the time at work adds to rumination and self-doubt.

16

Summing Up

WHEN YOU BEGAN THIS BOOK you may have thought, "Oh, just another person telling me not to worry" or "More advice that I need to believe in myself." If it were that simple, you never would have needed a book on worry—and you wouldn't have plagued yourself with worries for so long. No, believing in yourself and telling yourself to stop worrying are next to useless. In fact, it may even make you depressed to hear advice like that.

We have seen how worry makes sense to you—it makes you think that you are looking for solutions, that you won't be caught by surprise, that you will be motivated and responsible. In fact, some of this is true, but you need to distinguish productive worry from unproductive worry. So the next time you start worrying, the first thing you can do is ask yourself, "Is there some action I need to take *now*?" If there is, then you can turn your worry into problem solving, rather than look for more problems or for the perfect answer.

Rather than plague yourself with what-ifs or worries about the way the world should be, you can learn how to accept reality as the starting point. But the starting point toward what? You need to start with accepting the present situation—along with the uncertainty of things—to begin to commit to taking action where action is needed. Rather than worry about your taxes, you can collect the information and complete the taxes. Rather than worry about being lonely, you can take action to get involved in activities where you might meet some new people. Rather than worry in order to reduce uncertainty, you can accept uncertainty as an interesting and challenging part of reality and commit to take action in an uncertain world.

The next time that you start worrying, you may notice that you are jumping to conclusions, taking things personally, predicting catastrophes, and sliding down a slippery slope. Simply knowing that you distort reality doesn't change the way you feel and think about it. You will need to practice—over and over—the many techniques and strategies outlined here. You can examine the costs and benefits of your thoughts, look at the evidence, put things in perspective, search for different ways of looking at things, or give yourself the advice you would give a friend. Changing your thinking is like getting in shape—it's a lot harder when you are first starting out, but then it gets easier. To stay in shape, though, you have to keep working at it.

You now have an idea about the core themes of your worry. It may be about being ineffective, or about having demanding standards, or about needing to be special. Whatever it is, the good news is that the same problems keep coming up, so the same solutions should work. Your worry actually distracts you from these core issues, because you keep thinking of ways to prevent the "secret" of your core issue from coming out. You worry about doing a perfect job because you don't want the core issue of your laziness or inferiority to show through. But you now have techniques that you can use to cut to the core: are you really inferior, unlovable, inept? How would you challenge these negative beliefs? How would your best friend advise you on this?

Even if you master everything in every self-help book you will ever read, you will still face failure in your life. Failure is inevitable but not fatal. It is normal, not a sign of defectiveness. It is part of a process, not final. Many of your worries have been about the possibility of failing. Although you might want to pump yourself up and tell yourself you will never fail, you know that you are kidding yourself. But now you can look at possible failures as temporary events, learning experiences, challenges, part of the process, and the beginning of the next step. Don't forget that progress is built on failures. Christopher Columbus thought he was discovering a route to the East Indies. He failed and found America.

The next time you start worrying, you can set aside your abstract worry thoughts and ask yourself, "What are my emotions telling me?" Are you anxious because you want to be conscientious? Are you really angry because things are unfair? You have seen how worry suppresses your emotions, so you need to get in contact with your emotions to get rid of this worry. Emotions contain information about your needs and your values. If you are worried about finding the right person, your emotions of loneliness point to your value of love and caring. If you worry about doing well at work or school, then your fear is based on your value of pride in performance. And don't just identify one emotion—you are filled with a range of feelings, some which may seem contradictory. Identify each one, accept it as part of the sensitivity and complexity of who you are, and climb a ladder to the higher meaning of what you value.

All of my worries, like yours, have been about the future—a future that may never occur. How do you handle a future that may never occur? Of course, we have seen that you can determine if there is some productive worry to address—if there is some action to take right now. If not, then living in the present moment is where the action is. Rather than be a captive of your worries about the future, you can become mindful, appreciative, and engulfed in the present moment—you can improve the present moment.

What are you ready to do if you can handle your worries?
Everything—with less anxiety.

Without your worries you can approach new people, speak in public more easily, take on work that is challenging, take risks that you didn't take before, enjoy your relationship for what it is today, focus on your work rather than what other people think of your work, overcome procrastination, and get more out of your life today. After years of feeling controlled by your worry—and feeling that reassurance has gotten you nowhere—you can finally find solutions that can give you your life back and free you from thoughts that have almost never predicted what you thought they would predict.

You can live life in the present moment and see what is in front of you. You can live for now rather than worry about a future that never comes.

NOTES

1: Understanding Worry

1. National surveys indicate that 48 percent of the general population has a history of a psychiatric disorder, with anxiety disorders and depression leading the list. See Kessler, R.C., McGonagle, K.A., Zhao, S., Nelson, C.B., Hughes, M., Eshleman, S., Wittchen, H.-U., & Kendler, K.S. (1994). Lifetime and 12-month prevalence of DSM-II-R psychiatric disorders in the United States. *Archives of General Psychiatry, 51,* 8–19.
2. Cross-national Collaborative Group (1992). The changing rate of major depression. *Journal of the American Medical Association, 268,* 3098–3115.
3. Kessler, R.C., Walters, E.E., & Wittchen, H.-U. (2003). Epidemiology of Generalized Anxiety Disorder. R. Heimberg, C.L. Turk, & D.S. Mennin (Eds.), *Generalized Anxiety Disorder: Advances in Research and Practice.* New York: Guilford.
4. See Heimberg, R., Turk, C.L., & Mennin, D.S. (Eds.) (2003). *Generalized Anxiety Disorder: Advances in Research and Practice.* New York: Guilford. Davey, G.C.L., & Tallis, F. (Eds.) (1994). *Worrying: Perspective on Theory, Assessment, and Treatment.* Chichester, UK: Wiley.
5. Roemer, L., Molina, S., Litz, B.T., & Borkovec, T.D. (1997). Preliminary investigation of the role of previous exposure to potentially traumatizing events in generalized anxiety disorder. *Depression and Anxiety, 4,* 134–138.

6. Borkovec, T.D. (1994). The Nature, Functions, and Origins of Worry. In G.C.L. Davey & F. Tallis (Eds.), *Worrying: Perspectives on Theory, Assessment and Treatment* (pp. 5–33). Chichester, UK: Wiley.

7. Perris, C., Jacobsson, L., Lindstrom, H., von Knorring, L. & Perris, H. (1980). Development of a new inventory for assessing memories of parental rearing behavior. *Acta Psychiatrica Scandinavica, 61*, 265–274.

   Parker, G. (1979). Reported parental characteristics in relation to trait depression and anxiety levels in a non-clinical group. *Australian and New Zealand Journal of Psychiatry, 13*, 260–264.

   Parker, G. (1979). Reported parental characteristics of agoraphobics and social phobics. *British Journal of Psychiatry, 135*, 555–560.

   Parker, G. (1981). Parental representation of patients with anxiety neurosis. *Acta Psychiatrica Scandinavica, 63*, 33–36.

   Parker, G. (1983). *Parental Overprotection: A Risk Factor in Psychosocial Development.* New York: Grune and Stratton.

8. Chorpita, B.F., & Barlow, D. (1998). The development of anxiety: The role of control in the early environment. *Psychological Bulletin, 124*, 3–21.

   Nolen-Hoeksema, S., Wolfson, A., Mumme, D. & Guskin, K. (1995). Helplessness in children of depressed and nondepressed mothers. *Developmental Psychology, 31*, 377–387.

   Rapee, R.M. (1991). Psychological Factors Involved in Generalized Anxiety. In R.M. Rapee & D.H. Barlow (Eds.), *Chronic Anxiety: Generalized Anxiety Disorder and Mixed Anxiety-Depression* (pp. 76–94). New York: Guilford.

9. Roemer, L., Molina, S., Litz, B.T., & Borkovec, T.D. (1997). Preliminary investigation of the role of previous exposure to potentially traumatizing events in generalized anxiety disorder. *Depression and Anxiety, 4*, 134–138.

10. Borkovec, T.D., Shadick, R.N., & Hopkins, M. (1991). The Nature of Normal and Pathological Worry. In R.M. Rapee & D.H. Barlow (Eds.), *Chronic Anxiety: Generalized Anxiety Disorder and Mixed Anxiety-Depression* (pp. 29–51). New York: Guilford.

Borkovec, T.D. (1994). The nature, functions, and origins of worry. In G.C.L. Davey & F. Tallis (Eds.), *Worrying: Perspectives on Theory, Assessment and Treatment* (pp. 5–33). Chichester, UK: Wiley.

Nolen-Hoeksema, S. (2000). The role of rumination in depressive disorders and mixed anxiety/depressive symptoms. *Journal of Abnormal Psychology, 109,* 504–511.

11. MacLeod, C., Mathews, A., & Tata, P. (1986). Attentional bias in emotional disorders. *Journal of Abnormal Psychology, 95*(1), 15–20.

Butler, G., & Mathews, A. (1983). Cognitive processes in anxiety. *Advances in Behaviour Research & Therapy, 5*(1), 51–62.

12. Matthews, G., & Wells, A. (2000). Attention, automaticity, and affective disorder. *Behavior Modification, 24,* 69–93.

13. Borkovec, T.D., Newman, M.G., Pincus, A.L., & Lytle, R. (2002). A component analysis of cognitive-behavioral therapy for generalized anxiety disorder and the role of interpersonal problems. *Journal of Consulting & Clinical Psychology, 70*(2), 288–298.

Mennin, D.S., Turk, C.L., Heimberg, R.G., & Carmin, C.N. (in press). Focusing on the Regulation of Emotion: A New Direction for Conceptualizing and Treating Generalized Anxiety Disorder. In M.A. Reinecke & D.A. Clark (Eds.), *Cognitive Therapy over the Lifespan: Theory, Research and Practice.* New York: Guilford.

14. Matthews, G., & Wells, A. (1999). The Cognitive Science of Attention and Emotion. In T. Dalgleish & M.J. Power (Eds.), *Handbook of Cognition and Emotion* (pp. 171–192). Brisbane, Australia: Wiley.

Wells, A. (1995). Meta-cognition and worry: A cognitive model of generalized anxiety disorder. *Behavioural and Cognitive Psychotherapy, 23,* 301–320.

Borkovec, T.D., & Hu, S. (1990). The effect of worry on cardiovascular response to phobic imagery. *Behaviour Research and Therapy, 28,* 69–73.

Borkovec, T.D., Alcaine, O.M., & Behar, E. (2004). Avoidance Theory of Worry and Generalized Anxiety Disorder. In R.G. Heimberg, C.L. Turk, & D.S. Mennin (Eds.), *Generalized Anxiety Disorder: Advances in Research and Practice.* New York: Guilford.

15. York, D., Borkovec, T., et al. (1987). Effects of worry and somatic anxiety induction on thoughts, emotion and physiological activity. *Behaviour Research & Therapy* 25(6): 523–526.

16. Papageorgiou, C., & Wells, A. (1999). Process and meta-cognitive dimensions of depressive and anxious thoughts and relationships with emotional intensity. *Clinical Psychology and Psychotherapy, 6,* 156–162.

    Wells, A. (1995). Meta-cognition and worry: A cognitive model of generalized anxiety disorder. *Behavioural and Cognitive Psychotherapy, 23,* 301–320.

    Wells, A. (2004). Meta-Cognitive Beliefs in the Maintenance of Worry and Generalized Anxiety Disorder. In R.G. Heimberg, C.L. Turk, & D.S. Mennin (Eds.), *Generalized Anxiety Disorder: Advances in Research and Practice.* New York: Guilford.

17. Salkovskis, P.M., Forrester, E., & Richards, C. (1998). Cognitive-behavioural approach to understanding obsessional thinking. *British Journal of Psychiatry, 173*(Suppl 35), 53–63.

    Purdon, C., & Clark, D.A. (1994). Obsessive intrusive thoughts in nonclinical subjects: II. Cognitive appraisal, emotional response and thought control strategies. *Behaviour Research and Therapy, 32,* 403–410.

    Wells, A. (1997). *Cognitive Therapy of Anxiety Disorders: A Practice Manual and Conceptual Guide.* New York: Wiley.

18. Dugas, M.J., & Ladouceur, R. (1998). Analysis and Treatment of Generalized Anxiety Disorder. In V.E. Caballo (Ed.), *International Handbook of Cognitive-Behavioural Treatments of Psychological Disorders* (pp. 197–225). Oxford: Pergamon Press.

19. Reiss, S. (1999). The Sensitivity Theory of Aberrant Motivation. In S. Taylor (Ed.), *Anxiety Sensitivity: Theory, Research, and Treatment* (pp. 35–58). Mahwah, NJ: Erlbaum.

20. Reiss, S., Silverman, W.K., & Weems, C.F. (2001). *Anxiety Sensitivity.* In Vasey & Dadds, (Eds.), *The Developmental Psychopathology of Anxiety.* (pp. 92–111). New York: Oxford.

21. Leahy, R.L. (2003). Emotional schemas and metacognitive beliefs about worry. Paper presented at the annual meeting of the European Association of Cognitive and Behavioral Psychotherapy, Prague, Czech Republic. September.

22. Norem, J.K., & Cantor, N., (1986). Defensive pessimism: Harnessing anxiety as motivation. *Journal of Personality & Social Psychology.* *51*(6), 1208–1217.

23. Sarason, I.G. (1984). Stress, anxiety, and cognitive interference: Reactions to tests. *Journal of Personality & Social Psychology,* *46*(4), 929–938.

2: The Worst Ways to Handle Worry

1. Wegner, D.M. (1989). *White Bears and Other Unwanted Thoughts: Suppression, Obsession, and the Psychology of Mental Control.* New York: Penguin.

2. Taleb, N.N. (2001). *Fooled by Randomness: The Hidden Role of Chance in the Markets and in Life.* New York: Texere.

3. Gigergenzer, G. (2003). *Calculated Risks.* New York: Simon & Schuster.

4. Slovic, P. (Ed.). (2000). *The Perception of Risk.* Sterling, VA: Earthscan.

5. Tversky, A., & Kahneman, D. (1974). Judgment under uncertainty: Heuristics and biases. *Science, 185*(4157), 1124–1131.

6. Salkovskis, P.M., & Kirk, J. (1997). Obsessive-Compulsive Disorder. In D.M. Clark & C.G. Fairburn (Eds.), *Science and Practice of Cognitive Behaviour Therapy* (pp. 179–208). New York: Oxford University Press.

7. Wells, A. (1997). *Cognitive Therapy of Anxiety Disorders: A Practice Manual and Conceptual Guide.* New York: Wiley.

8. Mennin, D.S., Turk, C.L., Heimberg, R.G., & Carmin, C.N. (in press). Focusing on the Regulation of Emotion: A New Direction for Conceptualizing and Treating Generalized Anxiety Disorder. In M.A. Reinecke & D.A. Clark (Eds.), *Cognitive Therapy over the Lifespan: Theory, Research and Practice.* New York: Guilford.

9. Hinrichsen, H., & Clark, D.M. (2003). Anticipatory processes in social anxiety: Two pilot studies, *Journal of Behavior Therapy & Experimental Psychiatry, 34*(3–4), 205–218.

10. Salkovskis, P.M., Clark, D.M., Hackmann, A., Wells, A., & Gelder, M.G. (1999). An experimental investigation of the role of

safety-seeking behaviours in the maintenance of panic disorder with agoraphobia. *Behaviour Research and Therapy, 37,* 559–574.

Clark, D. M. (1999). Anxiety disorders: Why they persist and how to treat them. *Behaviour Research and Therapy, 37,* S5–S27.

11. Nolen-Hoeksema, S. (2000). The role of rumination in depressive disorders and mixed anxiety/depressive symptoms. *Journal of Abnormal Psychology, 109,* 504–511.

Papageorgiou, C., & Wells, A. (2001). Metacognitive beliefs about rumination in major depression. *Cognitive and Behavioral Practice, 8,* 160–163.

12. Leahy, R.L. (2002). A model of emotional schemas. *Cognitive and Behavioral Practice, 9*(3), 177–190.

13. Purdon, C., & Clark, D.A. (1993). Obsessive intrusive thoughts in nonclinical subjects: I. Content and relation with depressive, anxious and obsessional symptoms. *Behaviour Research & Therapy, 31*(8), 713–720.

Rachman, S. (1998). A cognitive theory of obsessions: Elaborations. *Behaviour Research and Therapy, 36,* 385–401.

14. Rachman, S. (2003). *The Treatment of Obsessions.* New York: Oxford University Press.

15. Rachman, S. (1997). A cognitive theory of obsessions. *Behaviour Research and Therapy 35:* 793–802.

Rachman, S. (1993). Obsessions, responsibility and guilt. *Behaviour Research and Therapy 31,* 149–154.

16. Rachman, S. (2003). *The Treatment of Obsessions.* New York: Oxford University Press.

3: Take Your Worry Profile

1. Meyer, T.J., Miller, M.L., Metzger, R.L., & Borkovec, T.D. (1990). Development and validation of the Penn State Worry Questionnaire. *Behaviour Research and Therapy, 28,* 487–495.

2. Ladouceur, R., Freeston, M.H., Dumont, M., Letarte, H., Rheaume, J., Thibodeau, N., et al. (1992). The Penn State Worry Questionnaire: Psychometric properties of a French translation. Paper presented at the Annual Convention of the Canadian Psychological Association, Quebec City, Canada.

3. Molina, S., & Borkovec, T.D. (1994). The Penn State Worry Questionnaire: Psychometric properties and associated characteristics. In G.C.L. Davey & F. Tallis (Eds.), *Worrying: Perspectives on Theory, Assessment and Treatment* (pp. 265–283). New York: Wiley.

4. See Table 11-2 from Molina & Borkovec, 1994, in note 3.

5. Borkovec, T., Robinson, E., Pruzinsky, T., & DePree, J.A. (1983). Preliminary exploration of worry: Some characteristics and processes. *Behaviour Research & Therapy, 21*(1), 9–16.

6. Tallis, F., Davey, G.C., & Bond, A. (1994). The Worry Domains Questionnaire. In G.C.L. Davey & F. Tallis (Eds.), *Worrying: Perspectives on Theory, Assessment and Treatment* (pp. 285–297). New York: Wiley.

   Tallis, F., Eysenck, M.W., & Mathews, A. (1992). A questionnaire for the measurement of nonpathological worry. *Personality & Individual Differences, 13*(2), 161–168.

7. Tallis, F., Eysenck, M.W., & Mathews, A. (1992). A questionnaire for the measurement of nonpathological worry. *Personality and Individual Differences, 13*(2), 161–168.

8. Items reprinted in Tallis, F., Eysenck, M., & Mathews, A. (1992). A questionnaire for the measurement of nonpathological worry. *Personality and Individual Differences, 13*(2), 161–168. © Elsevier Science. Full measure reprinted in Tallis, F., Davey, G.C.L., & Bond, A. (1994). The Worry Domains Questionnaire. In G.C.L. Davey & F. Tallis (Eds.). *Worrying: Perspectives on Theory, Assessment and Treatment* (pp. 287–292). New York: Wiley. Reprinted with permission of Elsevier Science, John Wiley & Sons, Limited, and Frank Tallis, Ph.D.

9. Tallis, F., Davey, G.C., & Bond, A. (1994). The Worry Domains Questionnaire. In G.C.L. Davey & F. Tallis (Eds.), *Worrying: Perspectives on Theory, Assessment and Treatment* (pp. 285–297). New York: Wiley.

10. Wells, A. (1997). *Cognitive Therapy of Anxiety Disorders: A Practice Manual and Conceptual Guide.* New York: Wiley.

11. Freeston, M.H., Rhéaume, J., Letarte, H., Dugas, M.J., & Ladouceur, R. (1994). Why do people worry? *Personality and Individual Differences, 17*(6), 791–802.

12. Dugas, M., Buhr, K., & Ladouceur, R. (2003) The Role of Intolerance of Uncertainty in the Etiology and Maintenance of Generalized Anxiety Disorder. In R. Heimberg, C.L. Turk, & D. S. Mennin (Eds.), *Generalized Anxiety Disorder: Advances in Research and Practice.* New York: Guilford.

13. Freeston, M.H., Rhéaume, J., Letarte, H., Dugas, M.J., & Ladouceur, R. (1994). Why do people worry? *Personality and Individual Differences, 17*(6), 791–802.

14. Dugas, M., Buhr, K., & Ladouceur, R. (2003). The Role of Intolerance of Uncertainty in the Etiology and Maintenance of Generalized Anxiety Disorder. In R. Heimberg, C.L. Turk, & D.S. Mennin (Eds.), *Generalized Anxiety Disorder: Advances in Research and Practice.* New York: Guilford.

15. Ladouceur, R., Dugas, M.J., Freeston, M.H., Leger, E., Gagnon, F., & Thibodeau, N. (2000). Efficacy of a cognitive-behavioral treatment for generalized anxiety disorder: Evaluation in a controlled clinical trial. *Journal of Consulting & Clinical Psychology, 68*(6), 957–964.

16. Beck, A.T., & Freeman, A.M. (1990). *Cognitive Therapy of Personality Disorders.* New York: Guilford Press.

17. Beck, A.T., Butler, A.C., Brown, G.K., Dahslgaard, K.K., Newman, C.F., & Beck, J.S. (2001). Dysfunctional beliefs discriminate personality disorders. *Behavioral Research and Therapy, 39,* 1213–1225.

18. Ibid.

19. Oldham, John M. & Morris, Lois B. (1995) *The New Personality Self-Portrait: Why You Think, Work, Love and Act the Way You Do.* New York: Bantam. For the sake of brevity I have not included the schizoid, paranoid and borderline personality disorders. However, we can view schizoid style as lacking interest in close relationships, preferring to do things alone, and as showing few emotions. Paranoid style is marked by distrust—and a tendency to look for "clues" that others are threatening or exploitative. Borderline personality is the most complicated style, characterized by fears of being alone, intense and unstable relationships, impulsivity, self-destructive behaviour, intense anger, and significant emotional instability.

4: Step One: Identify Productive and Unproductive Worry

1. Wells, A. (2000). *Emotional Disorders and Metacognition: Innovative Cognitive Therapy*. New York: Wiley.

   Wells, A. (1997). *Cognitive Therapy of Anxiety Disorders: A Practice Manual and Conceptual Guide*. New York: Wiley.

2. Nolen-Hoeksema, S. (2000). The role of rumination in depressive disorders and mixed anxiety/depressive symptoms. *Journal of Abnormal Psychology, 109*, 504–511.

   Papageorgiou, C., & Wells, A. (2001). Positive beliefs about depressive rumination: Development and preliminary validation of a self-report scale. *Behavior Therapy, 32*(1), 13–26.

3. Wells, A. (1995). Meta-cognition and worry: A cognitive model of generalized anxiety disorder. *Behavioural and Cognitive Psychotherapy, 23*, 301–320.

   Wells, A. (1997). *Cognitive Therapy of Anxiety Disorders: A Practice Manual and Conceptual Guide*. New York: J. Wiley & Sons.

4. Dugas, M.J., Buhr, K., & Ladouceur, R. (2003). The Role of Intolerance of Uncertainty in the Etiology and Maintenance of Generalized Anxiety Disorder. In R.G. Heimberg, C.L. Turk, & D.S. Mennin (Eds.), *Generalized Anxiety Disorder: Advances in Research and Practice*. New York: Guilford.

5. Wells, A. (1997). *Cognitive Therapy of Anxiety Disorders: A Practice Manual and Conceptual Guide*. New York: Wiley.

   Wells, A., & Carter, K. (2001). Further tests of a cognitive model of generalized anxiety disorder: Metacognitions and worry in GAD, panic disorder, social phobia, depression, and nonpatients. *Behavior Therapy, 32*(1).

6. Rachman, S. (2003). *The Treatment of Obsessions*. New York: Oxford University Press.

   Shafran, R., & Mansell, W. (2001). Perfectionism and psychopathology: a review of research and treatment. *Clinical Psychology Review, 21*(6), 879–906.

7. Matthews, G., & Wells, A. (2000). Attention, automaticity, and affective disorder. *Behavior Modification, 24*, 69–93.

Wells, A. (1997). *Cognitive Therapy of Anxiety Disorders: A Practice Manual and Conceptual Guide.* New York: Wiley.

5: Step Two: Accept Reality and Commit to Change

1. Hayes, S.C., Jacobson, N.S., & Follette, V.M. (Eds.). (1994). *Acceptance and Change: Content and Context in Psychotherapy.* Reno, NV: Context Press.

   Linehan, M.M. (1993). *Cognitive-Behavioral Treatment of Borderline Personality Disorder.* New York: Guilford.

2. Kabat-Zinn, J. (1990). *Full Catastrophe Living: The Program of the Stress Reduction Clinic at the University of Massachusetts Medical Center.* New York: Delta.

3. Linehan, M.M. (1993). *Cognitive-Behavioral Treatment of Borderline Personality Disorder.* New York: Guilford.

   Kabat-Zinn, J. (1990). *Full Catastrophe Living: The Program of the Stress Reduction Clinic at the University of Massachusetts Medical Center.* New York: Delta.

4. Teasdale, J.D. (1999). Metacognition, mindfulness and the modification of mood disorders. *Clinical Psychology and Psychotherapy, 6,* 146–155.

   Segal, Z.V., Williams, M.J.G., & Teasdale, J.D. (2002). *Mindfulness-Based Cognitive Therapy for Depression: A New Approach to Preventing Relapse.* New York: Guilford.

   Teasdale, J.D., Segal, Z.V., Williams, M.J.G., Ridgeway, V.A., Soulsby, J.M., & Lau, M.A. (2000). Prevention of relapse/recurrence in major depression by mindfulness-based cognitive therapy. *Journal of Consulting and Clinical Psychology, 68,* 615–623.

   Williams, M.J.G., Teasdale, J.D., Segal, Z.V., & Soulsby, J. (2000). Mindfulness-based cognitive therapy reduces overgeneral autobiographical memory in formerly depressed patients. *Journal of Abnormal Psychology, 109,* 150–155.

5. Wells, A. (1995). Meta-cognition and worry: A cognitive model of generalized anxiety disorder. *Behavioural and Cognitive Psychotherapy, 23,* 301–320.

   Wells, A. (2000). *Emotional Disorders and Metacognition: Innovative Cognitive Therapy.* New York: Wiley.

6. Wells, A. (2000). *Emotional Disorders and Metacognition: Innovative Cognitive Therapy*. New York: Wiley.

7. A somewhat similar exercise is described in Hayes, S.C., Jacobson, N.S., & Follette, V.M. (Eds.). (1994). *Acceptance and Change: Content and Context in Psychotherapy*. Reno, NV: Context Press.

8. Dugas, M.J., Buhr, K., et al. (2004). The Role of Intolerance of Uncertainty in the Etiology and Maintenance of Generalized Anxiety Disorder. R.G. Heimberg, C.L. Turk, & D.S. Mennin (Eds.), In *Generalized Anxiety Disorder: Advances in Research and Practice*. New York: Guilford.

9. Dugas, M.J., Buhr, K., & Ladouceur, R. (2003). The Role of Intolerance of Uncertainty in the Etiology and Maintenance of Generalized Anxiety Disorder. In R.G. Heimberg, C.L. Turk & D.S. Mennin (Eds.), *Generalized Anxiety Disorder: Advances in Research and Practice*. New York: Guilford.

   Dugas, M.J., Laouceur, R., Leger, E., Freeston, M.H., et al. (in press). Group cognitive-behavioral thrapy for generalized anxiety disorder: Treatment outcome and long-term followup.

   Dugas, M.J., Freeston, M.H., & Ladouceur, R. (1997). Intolerance of uncertainty and problem orientation in worry. *Cognitive Therapy and Research, 21,* 593–606.

10. Dugas, M.J., Gosselin, P., & Ladouceur, R. (2001). Intolerance of uncertainty and worry: Investigating specificity in a nonclinical sample. *Cognitive Therapy and Research, 25,* 551–558.

    Ladouceur, R., Gosselin, P., & Dugas, M.J. (2000). Experimental manipulation of intolerance of uncertainty: A study of a theoretical model of worry. *Behaviour Research and Therapy, 38,* 933–941.

11. Ladouceur, R., Dugas, M.J., Freeston, M.H., et al. (2000). Efficacy of a cognitive-behavioral treatment for generalized anxiety disorder: Evaluation in a controlled clinical trial. *Journal of Consulting and Clinical Psychology, 68,* 957–964.

12. Davies, M.I., & Clark, D.M. (1998). Thought suppression produces a rebound effect with analogue post-traumatic intrusions. *Behaviour Research and Therapy, 36,* 571–582.

    Purdon, C., & Clark, D.A. (1994). Obsessive intrusive thoughts in nonclinical subjects: II. Cognitive appraisal, emotional response and thought control strategies. *Behaviour Research and Therapy, 32,* 403–410.

6: Step Three: Challenge Your Worried Thinking

1. Wells, A. (1997). *Cognitive Therapy of Anxiety Disorders: A Practice Manual and Conceptual Guide.* New York: Wiley.

    Borkovec, T.D., & Roemer, L. (1994). Generalized Anxiety Disorder. In M. Hersen & R.T. Ammerman (Eds.), *Handbook of Prescriptive Treatments for Adults* (pp. 261–281). New York: Plenum.

    Leahy, R.L., & Holland, S.J. (2000). *Treatment Plans and Interventions for Depression and Anxiety Disorders.* New York: Guilford.

    Burns, D.D. (1990). *The Feeling Good Handbook: Using the New Mood Therapy in Everyday Life.* New York: Plume.

2. Beck, A.T., Rush, A.J., Shaw, B.F., & Emery, G. (1979). *Cognitive Therapy of Depression.* New York: Guilford.

    Beck, A.T., Emery, G., & Greenberg, R.L. (1985). *Anxiety Disorders and Phobias: A Cognitive Perspective.* New York: Basic Books.

    Leahy, R.L., & Holland, S.J. (2000). *Treatment Plans and Interventions for Depression and Anxiety Disorders.* New York: Guilford.

3. Borkovec, T.D., Newman, M.E., Pincus, A.L., & Lytle, R. (2002). A component analysis of cognitive behavioral therapy for generalized anxiety disorder and the role of interpersonal problems. *Journal of Consulting and Clinical Psychology, 70*(2), 288–298.

4. Beck, A.T., Emery, G., & Greenberg, R.L. (1985). *Anxiety Disorders and Phobias: A Cognitive Perspective.* New York: Basic Books.

    Wells, A. (1997). *Cognitive Therapy of Anxiety Disorders: A Practice Manual and Conceptual Guide.* New York: Wiley.

7: Step Four: Focus on the Deeper Threat

1. Beck, A.T., & Freeman, A.M. (1990). *Cognitive Therapy of Personality Disorders.* New York: Guilford.

Young, J.E., Klosko, J.S., & Weishaar, M. (2003). *Schema Therapy: A Practioner's Guide*. New York: Guilford.

2. Beck, A.T., & Freeman, A.M. (1990). *Cognitive Therapy of Personality Disorders*. New York: Guilford.

3. Guidano, V.F., & Liotti, G. (1983). *Cognitive Processes and the Emotional Disorders*. New York: Guilford.

4. Leahy, R.L. (2001). *Overcoming Resistance in Cognitive Therapy*. New York: Guilford.

5. For more examples of modifying core schemas see Leahy, R.L. (2003). *Cognitive Therapy Techniques: The Practitioner's Guide*. New York: Guilford.

6. Oldham, J.M., & Morris, L.B. (1995). *The New Personality Self-portrait: Why You Think, Work, Love and Act the Way You Do*. New York: Bantam. Oldham has reframed the various personality styles as "sensitive," "conscientious," etc. in order to stress both the negative and positive polarities.

7. Leahy, R.L. (2001). *Overcoming Resistance in Cognitive Therapy*. New York: Guilford.

Beck, A.T., & Freeman, A.M. (1990). *Cognitive Therapy of Personality Disorders*. New York: Guilford.

Young, J.E. (1990). *Cognitive Therapy for Personality Disorders: A Schema-Focused Approach*. Sarasota, FL: Professional Resource Exchange.

8: Step Five: Turn "Failure" into Opportunity

1. Abramson, L.Y., Seligman, M.E.P., & Teasdale, J. (1978). Learned helplessness in humans: Critique and reformulation. *Journal of Abnormal Psychology, 87*, 49–74.

2. Dweck, C.S. (1975). The role of expectations and attributions in the alleviation of learned helplessness. *Journal of Personality and Social Psychology, 31*, 674–685.

Dweck, C.S., Davidson, W., Nelson, S., & Enna, B. (1978). Sex differences in learned helplessness: II. The contingencies of evaluative feedback in the classroom and III. An experimental analysis. *Developmental Psychology, 14*, 268–276.

Dweck, C.S. (1986). Motivational processes affecting learning. *American Psychologist, 41,* 1040–1048.

3. Bandura, A. (1995). *Self-efficacy in Changing Societies.* Cambridge: Cambridge University Press.

Bandura, A. (1997). *Self-efficacy: The Exercise of Control.* New York: Freeman.

4. Eisenberger, R. (1992). Learned industriousness. *Psychological Review, 99*(2), 248–267.

Eisenberger, R., Heerdt, W. A., Hamdi, M., Zimet, S., & Bruckmeir, M. (1979). Transfer of persistence across behaviors. *Journal of Experimental Psychology: Human Learning & Memory, 5*(5), 522–530.

5. Quinn, E.P., Brandon, T.H., & Copeland, A.L. (1996). Is task persistence related to smoking and substance abuse? The application of learned industriousness theory to addictive behaviors. *Experimental & Clinical Psycho-pharmacology, 4*(2), 186–190.

6. Abramson, L.Y., Seligman, M.E.P., & Teasdale, J. (1978). Learned helplessness in humans: Critique and reformulation. *Journal of Abnormal Psychology, 87,* 49–74.

Abramson, L.Y., Metalsky, G.I., & Alloy, L.B. (1989). Hopelessness depression: A theory-based subtype of depression. *Psychological Review, 96,* 358–372.

Alloy, L.B., Abramson, L.Y., Metalsky, G.I., & Hartledge, S. (1988). The hopelessness theory of depression. *British Journal of Clinical Psychology, 27,* 5–12.

7. Dweck, C.S. (1975). The role of expectations and attributions in the alleviation of learned helplessness. *Journal of Personality and Social Psychology, 31,* 674–685.

Dweck, C.S., Davidson, W., Nelson, S., & Enna, B. (1978). Sex differences in learned helplessness: II. The contingencies of evaluative feedback in the classroom and III. An experimental analysis. *Developmental Psychology, 14,* 268–276.

Dweck, C.S. (1986). Motivational processes affecting learning. *American Psychologist, 41,* 1040–1048.

8. Alloy, L.B., Abramson, L.Y., Metalsky, G.I., & Hartledge, S.

(1988). The hopelessness theory of depression. *British Journal of Clinical Psychology, 27,* 5–12.

9. Weiner, B., Nierenberg, R., & Goldstein, M. (1976). Social learning (locus of control) versus attributional (causal stability) interpretations of expectancy of success. *Journal of Personality, 44*(1), 52–68.

10. Constructing Alternatives to the Current Goal Is a Major Strategy in Cognitive-Behavioral Therapy. See Kelly, G.A. (1955). *The Psychology of Personal Constructs.* New York: Norton.

    Beck, A.T., Rush, A.J., Shaw, B.F., & Emery, G. (1979). *Cognitive Therapy of Depression.* New York: Guilford.

11. Alloy, L.B., Abramson, L.Y., Metalsky, G.I., & Hartledge, S. (1988). The hopelessness theory of depression. *British Journal of Clinical Psychology, 27,* 5–12.

    Abramson, L.Y., Seligman, M.E.P., & Teasdale, J. (1978). Learned helplessness in humans: Critique and reformulation. *Journal of Abnormal Psychology, 87,* 49–74.

12. Gottman, J.M., & Krokoff, L.J. (1989). Marital interaction and satisfaction: A longitudinal view. *Journal of Consulting & Clinical Psychology, 57*(1), 47–52.

13. Abramson, L.Y., Seligman, M.E.P., & Teasdale, J. (1978). Learned helplessness in humans: Critique and reformulation. *Journal of Abnormal Psychology, 87,* 49–74.

14. For examples of the continuum technique and other ways of putting things in perspective see Leahy, R.L. (2003). *Cognitive Therapy Techniques: A Practitioner's Guide.* New York: Guilford.

15. Basco, M. R. (2000). *Never Good Enough: How to Use Perfectionism to Your Advantage Without Ruining Your Life.* Carmichael, CA: Touchstone.

16. Leahy, R.L. (Ed.). (1985). *The Development of the Self.* San Diego, CA: Academic.

17. Leahy, R.L. (2003). *The Psychology of Economic Thinking.* New York: Springer.

18. Dweck, C.S. (2002). Beliefs that Make Smart People Dumb. In R.J. Sternberg (Ed.) *Why Smart People Do Stupid Things.* New Haven: Yale University Press.

19. Jacobson, N.S., Follette, W.C., Revenstorf, D., Baucom, D.H., Hahlweg, K., & Margolin, G. (1984). Variability in outcome and clinical significance of behavioral marital therapy: A reanalysis of outcome data. *Journal of Consulting and Clinical Psychology, 52,* 497–504.

20. Seligman, M.E. (2003). Positive psychology: Fundamental assumptions. *Psychologist, 16*(3), 126–127.

21. Nolen-Hoeksema, S., & Harrell, Z.A. (2002). Rumination, depression, and alcohol use: Tests of gender differences. *Journal of Cognitive Psychotherapy, 16*(4), 391–403.

9: Step Six: Use Your Emotions Rather than Worry About Them

1. Dugas, M.J., Buhr, K., & Ladouceur, R. (2004). The Role of Intolerance of Uncertainty in the Etiology and Maintenance of Generalized Anxiety Disorder. In R.G. Heimberg, C.L. Turk, & D.S. Mennin (Eds.), *Generalized Anxiety Disorder: Advances in Research and Practice.* New York: Guilford.

   Dugas, M.J., Ladouceur, R., Leger, E., Freeston, M.H., Langolis, F., Provencher, M.D., et al. (2003). Group cognitive-behavioral therapy for generalized anxiety disorder: Treatment outcome and long-term follow-up. *Journal of Consulting & Clinical Psychology, 71*(4), 821–825.

   Dugas, M.J., Freeston, M.H., & Ladouceur, R. (1997). Intolerance of uncertainty and problem orientation in worry. *Cognitive Therapy and Research, 21,* 593–606.

2. Dugas, M.J., Gosselin, P., & Ladouceur, R. (2001). Intolerance of uncertainty and worry: Investigating specificity in a nonclinical sample. *Cognitive Therapy and Research, 25,* 551–558.

   Ladouceur, R., Gosselin, P., & Dugas, M.J. (2000). Experimental manipulation of intolerance of uncertainty: A study of a theoretical model of worry. *Behaviour Research and Therapy, 38,* 933–941.

3. Tallis, F., Davey, G.C., & Capuzzo, N. (1994). The Phenomenology of Non-pathological Worry: A Preliminary Investigation.

In G. Davey & F. Tallis (Eds.), *Worrying: Perspectives on Theory, Assessment and Treatment* (pp. 61–89). New York: Wiley.

4. Matthews, G., & Wells, A. (1999). The Cognitive Science of Attention and Emotion. In T. Dalgleish & M.J. Power (Eds.), *Handbook of Cognition and Emotion* (pp. 171–192). Brisbane, Australia: Wiley.

   Wells, A., & Papageorgiou, C. (1995). Worry and the incubation of in-trusive images following stress. *Behaviour Research and Therapy, 33*(5), 579–583.

   Borkovec, T.D., & Hu, S. (1990). The effect of worry on cardiovascular response to phobic imagery. *Behaviour Research and Therapy, 28,* 69–73.

   Borkovec, T.D., Alcaine, O.M., & Behar, E. (2004). Avoidance Theory of Worry and Generalized Anxiety Disorder. In R.G. Heimberg, C.L. Turk, & D.S. Mennin (Eds.), *Generalized Anxiety Disorder: Advances in Research and Practice.* New York: Guilford.

5. Mennin, D.S., Turk, C.L., Heimberg, R.G., & Carmin, C.N. (in press). Focusing on the Regulation of Emotion: A New Direction for Conceptualizing and Treating Generalized Anxiety Disorder. In M.A. Reinecke & D.A. Clark (Eds.), *Cognitive Therapy over the Lifespan: Theory, Research and Practice.* New York: Guilford.

6. Leahy, R.L. (2002). A model of emotional schemas. *Cognitive and Behavioral Practice, 9*(3), 177–190.

7. Carter W., Johnson, M., & Borkovec, T.D. (1986). Worry: An electrocortical analysis. *Advances in Behavioral Research and Therapy, 8,* 193–204.

8. Foa, E.B., & Kozak, M.J. (1986). Emotional processing of fear: Exposure to corrective information. *Psychological Bulletin, 99,* 20–35.

9. Kennedy-Moore, E., & Watson, J.C. (1999). *Expressing Emotions: Myths, Realities and Therapeutic Strategies.* New York: Guilford.

10. Grossarth-Maticek, R., Bastiaans, J., & Kanazir, D.T. (1985). Psychosocial factors as strong predictors of mortality from cancer, ischaemic heart disease and stroke: The Yugoslav prospective study. *Journal of Psychosomatic Research, 29,* 167–176.

Grossarth-Maticek, R., Kanazir, D.T., Schmidt, P., & Vetter, H. (1985). Psychosocial and organic variables as predictors of lung cancer, cardiac infarct and apoplexy: Some differential predictors. *Personality and Individual Differences, 6,* 313–321.

Schwartz, G.E. (1995). Psychobiology of Repression and Health: A Systems Approach. In J.L. Singer (Ed.), *Repression and Dissociation: Implications for Personality Theory, Psychopathology, and Health* (pp. 405–434). Chicago: University of Chicago Press.

11. Pennebaker, J.W., & Beall, S.K. (1986). Confronting a traumatic event: Toward an understanding of inhibition and disease. *Journal of Abnormal Psychology, 95,* 274–281.

Pennebaker, J.W., & Francis, M.E. (1996). Cognitive, emotional, and language processes in disclosure. *Cognition and Emotion, 10,* 601–626.

Pennebaker, J.W., Mayne, T.J., & Francis, M.E. (1997). Linguistic predictors of adaptive bereavement. *Journal of Personality and Social Psychology, 72,* 863–871.

12. Greenberg, L.S. (2002). *Emotion-focused Therapy: Coaching Clients to Work Through Their Feelings.* Washington, DC: American Psychological Association.

13. Leahy, R.L. (2002). A model of emotional schemas. *Cognitive and Behavioral Practice, 9*(3), 177–190.

14. Leahy, R.L. (2002). A model of emotional schemas. Paper presented at the annual meeting of the Association for the Advancement of Behavior Therapy, Reno, NV, November.

15. Greenberg, L.S., & Paivio, S. (1997). *Working with Emotions.* New York: Guilford.

Greenberg, L.S., & Safran, J.D. (1987). *Emotion in Psychotherapy: Affect, Cognition, and the Process of Change.* New York: Guilford.

Greenberg, L.S., Watson, J.C., & Goldman, R. (1998). Process-experiential Therapy of Depression. In L.S. Greenberg & J.C. Watson (Eds.), *Handbook of Experiential Psychotherapy* (pp. 227–248). New York: Guilford.

Safran, J.D. (1998). *Widening the Scope of Cognitive Therapy: The Therapeutic Relationship, Emotion and the Process of Change.* Northvale, NJ: Aronson.

16. Greenberg, L.S., & Paivio, S. (1997). *Working with Emotions*. New York: Guilford.

    Greenberg, L.S., & Safran, J.D. (1987). *Emotion in Psychotherapy: Affect, Cognition, and the Process of Change*. New York: Guilford.

    Greenberg, L.S., Watson, J.C., & Goldman, R. (1998). Process-Experiential Therapy of Depression. In L. S. Greenberg & J. C. Watson (Eds.), *Handbook of Experiential Psychotherapy* (pp. 227–248). New York: Guilford.

17. Neimeyer, R.A., & Mahoney, M.J. (Eds.). (1996). *Constructivism in Psychotherapy*. Washington, DC: American Psychological Association.

18. Elhers, A., & Clark, D.M. (2000). A cognitive model of post-traumatic stress disorder. *Behaviour Research and Therapy, 38,* 319–345.

    Hayes, S.C., Jacobson, N.S., & Follette, V.M. (Eds.). (1994). *Acceptance and Change: Content and Context in Psychotherapy*. Reno, NV: Context Press.

    Greenberg, L.S., & Paivio, S. (1997). *Working with Emotions*. New York: Guilford.

    Greenberg, L.S., & Safran, J.D. (1987). *Emotion in Psychotherapy: Affect, Cognition, and the Process of Change*. New York: Guilford.

19. Greenberg, L.S., & Paivio, S. (1997). *Working with Emotions*. New York: Guilford.

    Greenberg, L.S. (2002). *Emotion-focused Therapy: Coaching Clients to Work Through Their Feelings*. Washington, DC: American Psychological Association.

20. Greenberg, L.S. (2002). *Emotion-focused Therapy: Coaching Clients to Work Through Their Feelings*. Washington, DC: American Psychological Association.

21. Smucker, M.R., & Dancu, C.V. (1999). *Cognitive-Behavioral Treatment for Adult Survivors of Childhood Trauma: Imagery Rescripting and Reprocessing*. Northvale, NJ: Aronson.

22. Loevinger, J. (1976). *Ego Development*. San Francisco: Jossey-Bass.

Mayer, J.D., & Salovey, P. (1997). What Is Emotional Intelligence? In P. Salovey & D.J. Sluyter (Eds.), *Emotional Development and Emotional Intelligence: Educational Implications* (pp. 3–34). New York: Basic Books.

23. Kennedy-Moore, E., & Watson, J.C. (1999). *Expressing Emotions: Myths, Realities and Therapeutic Strategies*. New York: Guilford.

10: Step Seven: Take Control of Time

1. Riskind, J.H., & Williams, N.L. (1999). Cognitive case conceptualization and treatment of anxiety disorders: Implications of the looming vulnerability model. *Journal of Cognitive Psychotherapy, 13,* 295–315.

    Riskind, J.H. (1997). Looming vulnerability to threat: A cognitive paradigm for anxiety. *Behaviour Research & Therapy, 35*(8), 685–702.

2. Dugas, M.J., & Ladouceur, R. (1998). Analysis and Treatment of Generalized Anxiety Disorder. In V. E. Caballo (Ed.), *International Handbook of Cognitive Behavioural Treatments of Psychological Disorders* (pp. 197–225). Oxford: Pergamon Press.

3. Kabat-Zinn, J. (1990). *Full Catastrophe Living: The Program of the Stress Reduction Clinic at the University of Massachusetts Medical Center*. New York: Delta.

    Linehan, M.M. (1993). *Cognitive-Behavioral Treatment of Borderline Personality Disorder*. New York: Guilford.

    Kabat-Zinn, J., Lipworth, L., & Burney, R. (1985). The clinical use of mindfulness meditation for the self-regulation of chronic pain. *Journal of Behavioral Medicine, 8,* 163–190.

    Kabat-Zinn, J., Massion, A.O., Kristeller, J., Peterson, L.G., Fletcher, K.E., Pbert, L., Lenderking, W.R., & Santorelli, S.F. (1992). Effectiveness of a meditation-based stress reduction program in the treatment of anxiety disorders. *American Journal of Psychiatry, 149,* 936–943.

    Baer, R.A. (2003). Mindfulness training as a clinical intervention: A conceptual and empirical review. *Clinical Psychology: Science and Practice, 10,* 125–143.

4. Kabat-Zinn, J. (1990). *Full Catastrophe Living: The Program of the Stress Reduction Clinic at the University of Massachusetts Medical Center*. New York: Delta.

11: Social Worries: What if Nobody Likes Me?

1. Watson, D., & Friend, R. (1969). Measurement of social-evaluative anxiety. *Journal of Consulting & Clinical Psychology, 33*(4), 448–457.

2. DiBartolo, P.M., Frost, R.O., Dixon, A., & Almodovar, S. (2001). Can cognitive restructuring reduce the disruption associated with perfectionistic concerns? *Behavior Therapy, 32*(1), 167–184.

3. Kocovski, N.L., & Endler, N.S. (2000). Social anxiety, self-regulation, and fear of negative evaluation. *European Journal of Personality, 14*(4), 347–358.

4. Thompson, T., Foreman, P., & Martin, F. (2000). Imposter fears and perfectionistic concern over mistakes. *Personality & Individual Differences, 29*(4), 629–647.

5. Gergen, K.J. (1991). *The Saturated Self: Dilemmas of Identity in Contemporary Life*. New York: Basic Books.

6. Harter, S. (1999). *The Construction of the Self: A Developmental Perspective*. New York: Guilford Press.

7. Crittenden, P. (1988). Relationships at Risk. In J. Belsky & T. Nezworski (Eds.), *Clinical Implications of Attachment* (pp. 136–174). Mahwah, NJ: Erlbaum.

8. Harter, S. (1999). *The Construction of the Self: A Developmental Perspective*. New York: Guilford Press.

Pekrun, R. (1990). Social Support, Achievement Evaluations, and Self-concepts in Adolescence. In L. Oppenheimer (Ed.), *The Self-concept: European Perspectives on its Development, Aspects, and Applications* (pp. 107–119). Berlin, Heidelberg: Springer.

9. Harter, S., Whitesell, N.R., & Junkin, L.J. (1998). Similarities and differences in domain-specific and global self-evaluations of learning-disabled, behaviorally disordered, and normally achieving adolescents. *American Educational Research Journal, 35*(4), 653–680.

12: Relationship Worries: What if My Lover Leaves Me?

1. This is more of the uncertainty intolerance that Dugas and Ladouceur discussed above. As in most things, worriers believe that uncertainty means that things will not work out. Of course, you can also think that uncertainty is neutral. It's neither good nor bad.

2. Jacobson, N.S., Follette, W.C., Revenstorf, D., Baucom, D.H., Hahlweg, K., & Margolin, G. (1984). Variability in outcome and clinical significance of behavioral marital therapy: A reanalysis of outcome data. *Journal of Consulting and Clinical Psychology, 52,* 497–504.

    Epstein, N.B., & Baucom, D.H. (2002). *Enhanced Cognitive-Behavioral Therapy for Couples: A Contextual Approach*. Washington: American Psychological Association.

13: Health Worries: What if I Really Am Sick?

1. Salkovskis, P.M. (1996). The Cognitive Approach to Anxiety: Threat Beliefs, Safety-seeking Behavior, and the Special Case of Health Anxiety and Obsessions. In P.M. Salkovskis (Ed.), *Frontiers of Cognitive Therapy* (pp. 48–74). New York: Guilford.

    Starcevic, V., & Lipsitt, D.R. (Eds.). (2001). *Hypochondriasis: Modern Perspectives on an Ancient Malady*. New York: Oxford University Press.

2. Nease, D.E., Jr., Volk, R.J., & Cass, A.R. (1999). Does the severity of mood and anxiety symptoms predict health care utilization? *Journal of Family Practice, 48*(10), 769–777.

3. Conroy, R.M., Smyth, O., Siriwardena, R., & Fernandes, P. (1999). Health anxiety and characteristics of self-initiated general practitioner consultations. *Journal of Psychosomatic Research, 46*(1), 45–50.

4. Barsky, A.J., Wyshak, G., & Klerman, G.L. (1992). Psychiatric comorbidity in DSM-III-R hypochondriasis. *Archives of General Psychiatry, 49*(2), 101–108.

5. Barsky, A.J., Wool, C., Barnett, M.C., & Cleary, P.D. (1994). Histories of childhood trauma in adult hypochondriacal patients. *American Journal of Psychiatry, 151*(3), 397–401.

Mabe, P., Hobson, D.P., Jones, L., & Jarvis, R.G. (1988). Hypochondriacal traits in medical inpatients. *General Hospital Psychiatry, 10*(4), 236–244.

6. Salkovskis, P., & Wahl, K. (2004) Treating Obsessional Problems Using Cognitive-Behavioral Therapy. In M.A. Reinecke and D.M. Clark (Eds.), *Cognitive Therapy Across the Life-span: Evidence and Practice* (pp. 138–171). New York: Cambridge University Press.

7. Salkovskis, P.M. (1996). The Cognitive Approach to Anxiety: Threat Beliefs, Safety-seeking Behavior, and the Special Case of Health Anxiety and Obsessions. In P.M. Salkovskis (Ed.), *Frontiers of Cognitive Therapy* (pp. 48–74). New York: Guilford.

8. James, A., & Wells, A. (2002). Death beliefs, superstitious beliefs, and health anxiety. *British Journal of Clinical Psychology, 41,* 43–53.

14: Money Worries: What if I Start Losing Money?

1. Leahy, R.L. (2003) *Psychology and the Economic Mind: Cognitive Processes and Conceptualization.* New York: Springer.

Leahy, R.L. (2003). *Cognitive Therapy Techniques: A Practitioner's Guide.* New York: Guilford.

2. Veblen, T. (1899/1979). *Theory of the Leisure Class.* New York: Mentor.

3. Emmons, R.A., & McCullough, M.E. (2003). Counting blessings versus burdens: An experimental investigation of gratitude and subjective well-being in daily life. *Journal of Personality and Social Psychology, 84,* 377–389.

Seligman, M.E.P. (2003). *Authentic Happiness: Using the New Positive Psychology to Realize Your Potential for Lasting Fulfillment.* New York: Free Press.

4. Taleb, N.N. (2001). *Fooled by Randomness: The Hidden Role of Chance in the Markets and in Life.* New York: Texere.

5. Leahy, R.L. (2003) *Psychology and the Economic Mind: Cognitive Processes and Conceptualization.* New York: Springer.

6. Markowitz, H. (1952). Portfolio selection. *The Journal of Finance, 7,* 77–91.

Leahy, R.L. (2003). *Psychology and the Economic Mind: Cognitive Processes and Conceptualization*. New York: Springer.

15: Work Worries: What if I Really Mess Up?

1. Harvey, J.C., & Katz, C. (1985). *If I'm So Successful Why Do I Feel Like a Fake: The Imposter Phenomenon*. New York: St. Martin's.

2. Walster, E., Berscheid, E., & Walster, G.W. (1973). New directions in equity research. *Journal of Personality and Social Psychology, 25*(2), 151–176.

3. Frone, M.R. (2000). Work-family conflict and employee psychiatric disorders: The national comorbidity survey. *Journal of Applied Psychology, 85*(6), 888–895.

4. Maslach, C. (1982). *Burnout: The Cost of Caring*. Englewood Cliffs, NJ: Prentice Hall.

    Maslach, C. (1993). Burnout: A Multidimensional Perspective. In W.B. Schaufeli & C. Maslach (Eds.), *Professional Burnout: Recent Developments in Theory and Research* (pp. 19–32). London: Taylor & Francis.

5. Schaufeli, W., Maslach, C., & Marek, T. (Eds.). (1993). *Professional Burnout: Recent Developments in Theory and Research*. London: Taylor & Francis.

6. Schor, J.B. (1991). *The Overworked American: The Unexpected Decline of Leisure*. New York: Basic Books.

7. Putnam, R.D. (2000). *Bowling Alone: The Collapse and Revival of American Community*. New York: Simon & Schuster.

8. Kabat-Zinn, J. (1990). *Full Catastrophe Living: The Program of the Stress Reduction Clinic at the University of Massachusetts Medical Center*. New York: Delta.

9. Greenberg, L.S. (2002). *Emotion-focused Therapy: Coaching Clients to Work Through Their Feelings*. Washington, DC: American Psychological Association.

PERMISSIONS ACKNOWLEDGMENTS

PENN STATE WORRY QUESTIONNAIRE
© 1990 Elsevier Science. Items reprinted in Meyer, T.J., Miller, M.L., Metzger, R.L., & Borkovec, T.D. (1990). Development and validation of the Penn State Worry Questionnaire. *Behaviour Research and Therapy, 28,* 487–495. Reprinted with permission from Elsevier Science and T.D. Borkovec, Ph.D.

WORRY DOMAINS QUESTIONNAIRE
Items reprinted in Tallis, F., Eysenck, M., & Mathews, A. (1992). A ques-tionnaire for the measurement of nonpathological worry. *Personality and Individual Differences, 13,* 161–168. © Elsevier Science. Full measure reprinted in Tallis, F., Davey, G.C.L., & Bond, A. (1994). The Worry Domains Question-naire. In G.C.L. Davey & F. Talis (Eds.). *Worrying: Perspectives on Theory, Assessment, and Treatment* (pp. 287–292). New York: John Wiley and Sons, Ltd. Reprinted with permission of Elsevier Science, John Wiley & Sons, Ltd., and Frank Tallis, Ph.D.

METACOGNITIONS QUESTIONNAIRE
Item printed in Wells, A. (1997). *Cognitive Therapy of Anxiety Disorders: A Practice Manual and Conceptual Guide.* New York: John Wiley and Sons, Ltd. Reprinted with permission of John Wiley and Sons, Ltd.

INTOLERANCE OF UNCERTAINTY SCALE
© Mark H. Freeston, Michel Dugas, Hélène Letarte, Josée Rheaume, & Robert Ladouceur. Laboratoire de thérapies behaviorales, École de psychologie, Université Laval, Québec, 1993. Items reprinted in Freeston, M.H., Rheaume, J. Letarte, H., Dugas, M.J., & Ladouceur, R. (1994). Why do people worry? *Personality and Individual Differences, 17,* 791–802. Reprinted with permission from Elsevier Science and Mark H. Freeston, Ph.D.

PERSONAL BELIEFS QUESTIONNAIRE
© 2003 by Aaron T. Beck, M.D., and Judith S. Beck, Ph.D. Reprinted with permission of The Beck Institute.

COGNITIVE DISTORTIONS AND EXAMPLES
From Robert L. Leahy, *Cognitive Therapy: Basic Principles and Applications,* © 1996 Jason Aronson Publishing Co.

INDEX

Note: Page numbers in **bold** refer to diagrams. Page numbers in *italics* refer to information contained in tables.

ABOUT THE AUTHOR

DR ROBERT L. LEAHY is the president of the International Association of Cognitive Psychotherapy, the president-elect of the Academy of Cognitive Therapy, and the director of the American Institute for Cognitive Therapy, NYC. He lives in New York City. Visit him at www.cognitivetherapynyc.com.